www.wadsworth.com

www.wadsworth.com is the World Wide Web site for Thomson Wadsworth and is your direct source to dozens of online resources.

At *www.wadsworth.com* you can find out about supplements, demonstration software, and student resources. You can also send e-mail to many of our authors and preview new publications and exciting new technologies.

www.wadsworth.com
Changing the way the world learns®

The Mechanics of State Legislative Campaigns

The Mechanics of State Legislative Campaigns

JOHN S. KLEMANSKI
Oakland University

DAVID A. DULIO
Oakland University

THOMSON
WADSWORTH

Australia ▪ Brazil ▪ Canada ▪ Mexico ▪ Singapore
Spain ▪ United Kingdom ▪ United States

THOMSON
WADSWORTH

Publisher: *Clark Baxter*
Executive Editor: *David Tatom*
Assistant Editor: *Rebecca Green*
Associate Development Editor: *Rebecca Green*
Editorial Assistant: *Cheryl Lee*
Technology Project Manager: *Michelle Vardeman*
Marketing Manager: *Janise Fry*
Marketing Assistant: *Teresa Jessen*
Marketing Communications Manager: *Kelley McAllister*
Senior Project Manager, Editorial
  Production: *Kimberly Adams*
Creative Director: *Rob Hugel*

Executive Art Director: *Maria Epes*
Print Buyer: *Lisa Claudeanos*
Permissions Editor: *Stephanie Lee*
Production Service: *Interactive Composition Corporation*
Copy Editor: *Margaret Berson*
Illustrator: *Graphic World*
Cover Designer: *Bartay Studio*
Cover Image: *Digital Vision/Getty Images*
Cover Printer: *Thomson West*
Compositor: *Interactive Composition Corporation*
Printer: *Thomson West*

© 2006 Thomson Wadsworth, a part of The Thomson Corporation. Thomson, the Star logo, and Wadsworth are trademarks used herein under license.

ALL RIGHTS RESERVED. No part of this work covered by the copyright hereon may be reproduced or used in any form or by any means—graphic, electronic, or mechanical, including photocopying, recording, taping, web distribution, information storage and retrieval systems, or in any other manner—without the written permission of the publisher.

Printed in the United States of America
1 2 3 4 5 6 7 09 08 07 06 05

For more information about our products, contact us at:
Thomson Learning Academic Resource Center
1-800-423-0563

For permission to use material from this text or product, submit a request online at
http://www.thomsonrights.com.

Any additional questions about permissions can be submitted by e-mail to
thomsonrights@thomson.com.

Library of Congress Control Number: 2005926735

ISBN 0-495-09140-5

Thomson Higher Education
10 Davis Drive
Belmont, CA 94002-3098
USA

Asia
Thomson Learning
5 Shenton Way #01-01
UIC Building
Singapore 068808

Australia/New Zealand
Thomson Learning
102 Dodds Street
Southbank, Victoria 3006
Australia

Canada
Nelson
1120 Birchmount Road
Toronto, Ontario M1K 5G4
Canada

Europe/Middle East/Africa
Thomson Learning
High Holborn House
50/51 Bedford Row
London WC1R 4LR
United Kingdom

Latin America
Thomson Learning
Seneca, 53
Colonia Polanco
11560 Mexico
D.F. Mexico

Spain/Portugal
Paraninfo
Calle Magallanes, 25
28015 Madrid, Spain

For Samantha, Coby, and my wife, Sheryl
J. S. K.

For Jim Thurber and Candy Nelson
D. A. D.

Brief Contents

1 STATE LEGISLATIVE CAMPAIGNS AND ELECTIONS: AN OVERVIEW   01

2 THE MECHANICS OF A POLITICAL CAMPAIGN: THE CAMPAIGN PLAN   15

3 THE CAMPAIGN SIMULATION AND EXERCISES   27

4 MICHIGAN'S 10TH STATE SENATE DISTRICT   71

5 TEXAS'S 32ND STATE HOUSE DISTRICT   105

6 NORTH CAROLINA'S 115TH STATE HOUSE DISTRICT   133

7 LESSONS LEARNED   151

BIBLIOGRAPHY   159

INDEX   165

Contents

1 STATE LEGISLATIVE CAMPAIGNS AND ELECTIONS: AN OVERVIEW 01
Existing Knowledge on Campaigning and Electioneering 03
Comparing Elections 03
    National and Statewide Campaigns vs. State Legislative Campaigns 04
Next Steps 12

2 THE MECHANICS OF A POLITICAL CAMPAIGN: THE CAMPAIGN PLAN 15
Organizing a Campaign 16
Creating a Campaign Plan 17
    Detailing the Components of a Plan 19

3 THE CAMPAIGN SIMULATION AND EXERCISES 27
Campaign Roles and Responsibilities 28
Creating the Campaign Plan 29
    Section 1. District and Demographic Analyses 30
    Section 2. Electoral Research 35
    Section 3. Opposition and Candidate Research 40
    Section 4. Campaign Message 49
    Section 5. Budget and Fund-Raising Plan 52
    Section 6. Volunteer Recruitment and Use 54
    Section 7. Paid Media 56
    Section 8. Earned Media 62
    Section 9. Get-Out-The-Vote 64
    Section 10. The Campaign Calendar 64
Additional Exercises: Crisis Management and Campaign Ethics 65
    Crisis Management 65
    Campaign Ethics 67

4 MICHIGAN'S 10TH STATE SENATE DISTRICT 71

The Michigan Political Context 72
    Michigan Primary and General Elections 73
    Fund-Raising and Campaign Finance Law in Michigan 74
The Campaign 75
    The Candidates 76
Creating a Campaign Plan 78

5 TEXAS'S 32ND STATE HOUSE DISTRICT 105

The Texas Political Context 107
    Texas Primary and General Elections 109
    Fund-Raising and Campaign Finance Law in Texas 111
The Campaign 112
    The Candidates 113
Creating a Campaign Plan 115

6 NORTH CAROLINA'S 115TH STATE HOUSE DISTRICT 133

The North Carolina Political Context 134
    North Carolina Primary and General Elections 136
    Fund-Raising and Campaign Finance Law in North Carolina 137
The Campaign 139
    The Candidates 139
Creating a Campaign Plan 140

7 LESSONS LEARNED 151

Campaigns and Fingerprints 152
    The Campaign Context 153
    The Campaign 156

BIBLIOGRAPHY 159

INDEX 165

List of Tables, Figures and Boxes

LIST OF TABLES

Table 3.1   Vote History Example for a Hypothetical State House District   37

Table 4.1   Michigan's 10th State Senate District Voting History, 1994–2000   99

Table 5.1   Texas's 32nd State House District Voting History, 1994–2000   126

Table 6.1   Party Registration, North Carolina Voters (in percent)   135

Table 6.2   North Carolina's 115th State House District Voting History, 1994–2000   150

LIST OF FIGURE

Figure 3.1   Calculation and Estimation of Voter Turnout Votes Needed to Win in a Hypothetical District   38

LIST OF BOXES

Box 2.1   Hypothetical Campaign Organizational Chart   17

Box 2.2   Outline of a Campaign Message Box   22

Box 4.1   Michigan at a Glance   75

Box 5.1   Texas at a Glance   112

Box 6.1   North Carolina at a Glance   138

Preface

Since 1996, students at Oakland University in Rochester, Michigan have been able to take a course entitled simply "Political Campaigns." From the beginning, the philosophy of the course was to blend theory and academic scholarship related to campaigns with real-life, practical applications of campaigning. As such, students have been able to read the literature of political campaigns, but also listen to a wide variety of candidates, campaign professionals, campaign volunteers, political party leaders, journalists, and elected officials who have shared their experiences in our classroom.

Moreover, beginning in the year 2000, students in the course have had an opportunity to manage the campaigns of Michigan State House candidates after they successfully completed the course. An arrangement was made with both major parties in the state to hire our students once they completed the course and were deemed ready to manage a state house campaign. Both parties expressed a need for trained campaign managers and saw a talent pool being created at Oakland University in this course. The arrangement has been a winning formula for everyone involved—the students were offered paying jobs, the parties hired individuals with training to manage a campaign, and Oakland University found a unique way to offer opportunities to its students beyond the classroom learning experience.

Because of that experience, the Political Campaigns course began to focus on state legislative campaigns. Despite the fact that there are many more state legislative campaigns than statewide or national campaigns, the political science literature has tended to ignore these contests. This book aims to accomplish a series of goals by presenting three state legislative campaigns as cases in which readers can engage in a simulation of campaign activity (see Learning Objectives box). Broadly, these goals are to allow readers to engage in activities that are part of an actual campaign as if they are a member of the team contesting a race, and to understand the inner workings of a campaign. This kind of learning experience, in turn, we believe, benefits students in that they obtain a more

> **Learning Objectives**
>
> Learning objectives are measured by knowledge, skills, and values or attitudes. Students successfully completing this simulation will:
> 1) Understand all of the elements of a political campaign
> 2) Understand the differences between national-level political campaigns and state-level or local-level campaigns
> 3) Be able to create a campaign plan
> 4) Be able to work as part of a team
> 5) Have an ability to work under time pressure
> 6) Be prepared to manage and respond effectively to crises
> 7) Understand the importance of a campaign message
> 8) Understand voter targeting strategies and political behavior
> 9) Have an awareness of ethical issues in political campaigns
> 10) Have an understanding of campaigns and elections that will help them become more informed voters and citizens

complete understanding of campaigns and elections in the United States. By focusing on what the individuals on the inside of a campaign—candidates, campaign managers, political consultants, and volunteers—have to deal with during a race, readers will broaden their understanding of concepts such as campaign advertising, media coverage of campaigns, and voter turnout, to name only three.

This book is a natural outgrowth of the initial philosophy behind the first Political Campaigns course. Among the most rewarding segments of the course over the years have been the classroom exercises that present real-life scenarios to the students, who then must work in small teams to respond to or resolve them. These exercises have brought to life much of the academic literature on campaigns that students become familiar with in a more traditional course on the subject in a way that has enhanced students' understanding of political campaigns, campaign organizations, and political behavior.

The foundation of the Political Campaigns course and this book is a campaign plan. The plan is essential to effective campaigning, as it provides a reasoned and rational place for decision making during those chaotic weeks called the "campaign season." Without a campaign plan, a political campaign is likely to only react to events around them, spend money unwisely, and stay in a defensive mode throughout the campaign. In short, without a written plan, a campaign is doomed before it has even begun.

Conducting field research is an important part of creating a campaign plan. The research involves knowing the district and its voters, knowing something about the opposing candidate (as well as one's own candidate), and understanding the relevant environment of the campaign. Some of the information that would need to be collected by a campaigner in the races included here is provided for the reader; other information will have to be gathered.

In addition to the exercises designed to simulate campaigns in Michigan, Texas, and North Carolina, we have included exercises in both crisis management decision-making and campaign ethics. In the crisis management exercises, readers will confront challenging and time-sensitive scenarios that many campaigns face. These will help readers to learn to think on their feet. The exercises on campaign ethics will expose readers to the ethical dilemmas that many campaigners face. We hope these will teach readers to know that they can win campaigns and do the right thing at the same time. We have included an instructors' manual located on a companion Web site that we hope will help guide the conduct of the simulation. It includes outlines of how the simulation can be structured, as well as guidelines for evaluating answers to the exercises associated with the simulation.

In short, this book focuses on several components to increase and advance a reader's learning about campaigns and elections in the United States. Getting involved with "real-life" decisions that campaigners have to make on a daily basis, struggling with the interpretation of different data and information critical to those decisions, and having to go out and gather some of that information on one's own will give readers a more nuanced understanding of what happens in elections at all levels in the United States.

Acknowledgments

Many campaign professionals and candidates have visited the Political Campaigns course over the years. Some of them also kindly agreed to review drafts of this book. In particular, we would like to thank Alan Mann, the Director of Public Opinion Research for the Michigan House Republican Caucus; Ken Brock, a Democratic political strategist; Lee Dryden, a reporter with the *Oakland Press;* Rick Pluta, Program Director at Michigan Public Radio; David Doyle, Vice President at the Republican political consulting firm Marketing Resource Group; Mark Brewer, Executive Chairman of the Michigan Democratic Party; John F. Kelly, a former Michigan state senator, and Mark Hornbeck, a reporter at the *Detroit News,* for their help from the beginning. This book, and the Political Campaigns course, would not exist without their willingness to share their wealth of experiences.

We would also like to thank State Senator Michael Switalski from the Michigan 10th State Senate District, and State Representative Bruce Goforth from the North Carolina 115th House District, for allowing us to meet with them and conduct personal interviews regarding their campaigns. They provided helpful insights into their races and the campaign process in general.

A great deal of thanks also goes to Tim Neville, who collected much of the information that appears in this book for each of the three districts. His thorough and timely assistance was invaluable throughout the process of writing this book.

Oakland University has provided substantial support and encouragement, dating back to the initial creation of the Political Campaigns course in 1996. We would like to thank former department chair and current Associate Dean C. Michelle Piskulich, College of Arts and Sciences Dean David Downing, and Oakland University Provost Virinder Moudgil for their encouragement of this project.

We also would like to thank the students of Oakland University's Political Campaigns course over the years. We have jointly explored ways to improve the teaching and learning process of political campaigns, and their suggestions and input have greatly improved this effort. Three anonymous reviewers provided important feedback that helped us improve the quality of this book. David Tatom and Sheila Berger at Wadsworth Press were also great colleagues to work with and did a fine job of seeing this project through the publication process. Any errors that remain are our own.

About the Authors

John S. Klemanski is Professor and Chair of the Department of Political Science at Oakland University. Klemanski has served as an occasional campaign consultant for state legislative and judicial campaigns since 1994. He is the author or co-author of over 20 articles and books, mostly on urban economic development politics and policy. His books include *The Urban Politics Dictionary* (with John W. Smith, ABC Clio, 1990), and *Power and City Governance* (with Alan DiGaetano, University of Minnesota Press, 1999).

David A. Dulio is Assistant Professor of Political Science at Oakland University. He is the author of *For Better or Worse? How Political Consultants are Changing Elections in the United States* (State University of New York Press 2004) and *Vital Signs: Perspectives on the Health of American Campaigning* (with Candice J. Nelson, Brookings Institution Press 2005). Dulio is the editor of *Crowded Airwaves: Campaign Advertising in Elections* (with James A. Thurber and Candice J. Nelson, Brookings Institution Press 2000) and *Shades of Gray: Perspectives on Campaign Ethics* (with Candice J. Nelson and Stephen K. Medvic, Brookings Institution Press 2002) as well as many other articles and book chapters on campaigns and elections.

1

State Legislative Campaigns and Elections: An Overview

John F. Kelly is a veteran of many political campaigns, as he has run for offices from the state house and state senate to the U.S. Senate in the state of Michigan. Recently, he recounted his first foray into campaign politics. The lessons of his story are the reasons for this book.

> I first ran for office when I was 24 years old. My best friend and I were political science graduate students, and we wanted to change the world—or at least our little corner of it. I became a primary election candidate in a state representative race, running against an incumbent in a district that heavily favored our party, and my friend was my campaign manager. We knew enough then to know that if we won the primary, we'd win the general election easily.
>
> With all modesty, we were fairly smart and articulate people, and we certainly had youth, enthusiasm, and energy on our side. What we didn't have was an understanding of how to run a political campaign. We ran a clean campaign, and we ran an issue-based campaign. We didn't do any negative advertising, and we were able to energize other young people to become involved in the election. But in the end, we took only 34 percent of the vote—we got beat by a 2-to-1 margin. I don't think I had ever felt so bad. However, I am still proud of that campaign in many ways.
>
> While there were several positives, I reflect on that campaign now and realize that there were some powerful negatives as well. What I remember most about that campaign was the feeling that we were never prepared. For instance, we didn't have a clear and concise message at the start, we didn't know how we were going to raise money or how much we needed, and we had no volunteer recruitment plan. We were familiar with our district, but didn't even consider conducting a formal district analysis. Throughout the campaign, we reacted to events that happened to us, and did so in a haphazard, uncoordinated way. We had a few fund-raisers, but I don't ever remember talking about the timing of those fund-raisers to meet our needs for extra money to pay for a new literature piece or for more lawn

signs. We didn't target voters and we didn't have an effective communications plan.

In short, we simply didn't have any kind of overall campaign plan. Our opponent, a much more seasoned campaigner who had the skills and expertise needed to run a successful campaign, took the initiative and we were on the defensive during the entire campaign. Our activities weren't framed in a consistent campaign message—simply because we didn't have one. We actually were able to recruit a number of college students to serve as volunteers, but we weren't prepared to use them effectively, and they went home early a couple of times—never to return.

Two years later, armed with the experience and lessons of running a failed campaign, I ran in a five-person primary election for a state senate seat. I won the primary by a handful of votes, and went on to serve in the state senate for 16 years. The experience of that first campaign certainly helped me in the senate race, but I also had learned about the need for organization and planning. The lessons boil down to one simple piece of advice: If you don't have a plan as to how to be victorious, don't bother running at all. (Kelly 2004)[1]

Ultimately, John Kelly learned about campaign planning the hard way. This book examines how modern state legislative campaigns are waged; it can provide the reader with some of the basic tools necessary to create and execute an effective campaign plan. We have chosen to focus on state legislative races for three reasons. First, we hope to fill a gap in the information that is available on campaigns, as most literature (both academic and popular) tends to emphasize higher-profile federal races for offices such as president of the United States, the United States Senate, or the United States House of Representatives.

Second, some of the more recent scholarship investigating state politics has noted an increasing importance of state legislative politics. For example, some scholars have noted that most state legislatures wield considerable influence across national and state policy decisions (see Dye 2000). In part, this is because of policy devolution to the states that has occurred since the 1980s, giving additional jurisdiction to state governments. But the importance of state legislatures extends beyond policy decisions because of their role in state redistricting decisions that can go a long way toward shaping the makeup of legislative bodies in each state and in Washington, D.C.[2] The redistricting authority that most state legislatures hold is important because it can impact more substantive policy decisions at both the state and national levels in that redistricting can help create a majority for one party or the other in the state legislature or the U.S. House of Representatives. And, with majority party status comes considerable power both formally (through control of the chamber's schedule and committee chairmanships, for instance), and informally (for example, through control of the chamber's agenda)—because legislatures, for the most part, are majoritarian institutions. Therefore, creating and maintaining majorities is crucial for both major parties. The National Conference of State Legislatures has noted that although many redistricting decisions have created large numbers of "safe districts" (that is, districts where either the Democratic or the Republican candidate is almost assured victory in the general election because of the makeup of the district), the few competitive districts that remain often determine which party will retain or obtain majority party status (NCSL 2005). In several states, the majority party holds a razor-thin edge in seats. In the North Carolina State House, for example, two recent legislative sessions have seen the two parties almost evenly split among the 120 House members; the split has been so close that the two parties at times have agreed to a shared Speaker arrangement.³

The final reason we selected state legislative campaigns is a more pragmatic one: Seats in state legislatures constitute the vast majority of legislative seats in the United States compared to the U.S. Congress; there are over 7,000 state legislative seats, whereas there are only 535 seats in the U.S. House and Senate combined. Moreover, for simulation purposes, state legislative campaigns simply are more manageable than races for the U.S. House or U.S. Senate. The district populations in the three cases presented in later chapters are all manageable and range from approximately 67,000 in North Carolina's 115th State House District, to 139,000 in Texas's 32nd State House District, to 270,000 in Michigan's 10th State Senate District. These populations will be much easier to handle in terms of many of the concepts presented in this book than those in a typical U.S. House of Representatives district (which today totals about 650,000 individuals) or a statewide U.S. Senate seat (which in our case states ranges from 8 million to 20 million people).

EXISTING KNOWLEDGE ON CAMPAIGNING AND ELECTIONEERING

To say that the existing academic literature on elections and campaigns is extensive is an understatement. Much of what exists, however, has tended to focus on presidential campaigns or elections for the U.S. Congress. Moreover, rather than electioneering, these works have emphasized the processes and players involved in campaigns including discussions of campaigns as part of a larger treatment of voter turnout and party identification, the presidential nominating process, the Electoral College, or campaign finance, to name only a few. An extensive review of this literature is beyond the scope of this book, however.⁴

Relatively new to the scholarly literature, however, is a focus on how campaigns are run, and the professionals who run them. Robert Agranoff (1972) was an early voice noting a "new style" of political campaigning. Taking off on this general approach are works that have focused on the strategic component of professional consultants' services to candidates.⁵ Still others fall into a category that might be considered "how to" books that detail how a candidate for a (usually) lower-level race might organize and run a campaign. Among the books in this category are *Winning Elections* (1996) by Dick Simpson, *The Campaign Manager* (2000) by Catherine Shaw, *Running for Office* (2002) by Ron Faucheux, and *Winning Political Campaigns* (1998) by William Bike. In addition to what we believe we offer in this volume, a book that offers a good balance between theory and practice is *Campaign Craft* (2001) by Dan Shea and Michael John Burton. It provides true-to-life campaign sensibilities while reminding readers of the bigger-picture theories. Another positive feature of Shea and Burton's book is its emphasis on the planning needed to wage a successful campaign.

COMPARING ELECTIONS

What the average American knows about campaigns and the process of campaigning falls into a conventional wisdom that does not necessarily reflect reality in the lion's share of electoral contests in the United States. There are different kinds of campaigns in the United States—from president of the United States to sheriff (and even dogcatcher in some areas)—and each type of campaign has its own unique characteristics. However, many times, what we "know" about campaigns tends to involve only one kind of campaign—those at the highest levels for the highest offices in the land. This is for good reason. For instance, anything that the average American knows about campaigns is likely to be related to upper-level or national political campaigns simply because the media tends to cover them so much more, as evidenced by the seemingly 24-hour, 7-day-a-week coverage of the 2004 presidential race, than they do down-ballot contests. Also, higher-level campaigns are more likely to be able to afford to advertise on television and radio, so the electorate sees and hears these paid media efforts more often. Therefore, members of the electorate are more likely to see the images and hear the sounds of those races much more than lower-level races, which usually cannot afford to buy airtime for a radio or television commercial. But the information we have about more prominent campaigns does not necessarily provide much accurate information about what happens in lower-level elections.

What follows here is a brief discussion of some of the differences between those campaigns with which Americans are most familiar—campaigns that are national or statewide in scope—and those that are less studied, those that are covered less by the media, and therefore are less understood and familiar to the vast majority of the electorate.

National and Statewide Campaigns vs. State Legislative Campaigns

Our discussion of the differences between those campaigns that are waged for offices such as president, the U.S. Congress (both House and Senate), and governor, and those that are conducted for offices such as state house or state senate (or other down-ballot races such as mayor, county commissioner, or city council) is centered on some of the most important and most recognizable distinctions between these types of races. These differences include, but are not limited to, media attention, salience among the electorate, party involvement, candidate recruitment, advertising and campaign communication, outside influences such as interest groups, and campaign finance.

We do not claim that this is an exhaustive list of differences between national and local campaigns. Certainly, there are obvious differences in that state and local campaigns cover smaller geographic areas, and therefore have smaller electorates than federal races, and the offices sought after in lower-level races typically deal with a different set of issues than those linked to the highest offices in the land. The following sections illustrate more subtle differences that the reader may not realize exist, and give an indication of how most of the campaigns in the United States differ from those with which we are most familiar but are smaller in number. More importantly, for our purposes these differences greatly reflect how the campaigns for these offices are waged. The types of campaigns that one sees played out on television—in both media coverage and campaign advertising—are typically not like those that we detail through the case studies in the chapters that follow. However, one final point is important. The differences that we point out between high-level races and down-ballot campaigns are not either/or scenarios where one is black and the other white; rather, these differences should be viewed as gradations and matters of degrees. In other words, we do not view types of races as strict categories to which every race of each type nicely conforms. Rather, in the sections that immediately follow, we are describing tendencies. Some lower-level races do resemble federal and statewide campaigns, but for the most part, the differences we describe hold across types of races.

Media Attention Presidential elections are likely the most covered spectacles in American politics. Rarely do other events receive as much attention for such long periods of time. As noted earlier, the 2004 presidential race nicely illustrates this point. Candidates for this office garner immediate national attention when they announce that they intend to enter the race. Think back to only one example during the 2004 presidential campaign. When retired General Wesley Clark declared he would seek the Democratic Party's nomination, there was immediate news coverage of his decision, even to the point where television newscasts had reports of his standing in public opinion polls almost instantly.

Moreover, the national media cover the primary election campaign on a daily basis, sometimes for more than a full year before any primary or caucus is held. For instance, during the 2004 presidential primary season, the first debate among Democrats seeking their party's nomination was held, and received national media coverage, on May 3, 2003, a full 8 months before the first caucus or primary and 14 months before the nominating convention.

Similarly, although the coverage of the parties' conventions has decreased over time (Maisel 2002), the fact remains that this is significant exposure for both major party candidates. During the 2004 conventions, the major networks aired only one hour of coverage on three of the convention's four nights. They opted to show their regularly scheduled programs—"CSI: Crime Scene Investigation," "Amazing Race," and "Law and Order: Special Victims Unit," for example—rather than speakers at the convention, including Senators Edward Kennedy and John McCain at the Democratic and Republican conventions, respectively (Harper 2004; Lamb 2004). At their previous low point of coverage—the 2000 campaign—the major networks devoted eight and a half hours of airtime to each convention (Wayne 2004). Though small relative to past amounts of coverage, convention coverage is time and attention that no other candidate for any other office in the country can demand and receive. Furthermore, although coverage of federal campaigns has tended to be framed as a "horse race" (that is, who is ahead and who is behind) rather than about policy issues, the fact remains that this is still coverage of the campaign that is not available to all types of candidates in the same quantity.

Gubernatorial and congressional elections receive less media attention than do presidential campaigns, but they receive much more coverage than local and state campaigns. So-called earned media—which is defined as reports of a candidate's campaign that appear in newspapers or on television and radio—is important to any campaign because it represents exposure the campaign would not otherwise receive. Again, the coverage that is garnered in congressional and gubernatorial races is mostly focused on the "horse race" aspect of the campaign. However, one important difference is that campaigns for the U.S. House are much less likely to get coverage by television stations, compared to U.S. Senate and gubernatorial races. Television news media are still likely to cover

Senate campaigns, whereas newspapers are the place where House candidates look to attract earned media.

Although U.S. House candidates have difficulty attracting earned media attention from television sources, state legislative campaigns have trouble attracting any significant media attention from *any* media source. It is rare that a major newspaper in a large city will devote much coverage to the local-level races that are on the ballot. Many times, coverage of the kind of campaign we focus on in this book is found only in local papers in the communities that are affected by the race, many of which are published on a weekly basis. There is clearly a hierarchy of media coverage in campaigns with presidential races that receive a great deal of coverage from many sources at the top, and state legislative campaigns that get little coverage from only a few media outlets near the bottom.

Salience Salience, which measures attention paid to the campaign by the public, is closely tied to media attention. Because the media pay a great deal of attention to presidential and other high-profile races, the salience of those campaigns is very high. The fact that presidential candidates are very visible—often jetting from state to state, event to event, and fund-raiser to fund-raiser—plays a part in the high salience of these campaigns as well. Moreover, the issues that presidential (and some senatorial and gubernatorial campaigns) emphasize make potential voters stand up and take notice. The issues of the 2004 presidential campaign clearly bear this out; issues such as the war on terrorism, taxes and the economy, as well as the state of such fundamental government programs as Social Security and Medicare, are important to a great number of Americans. Therefore, many feel there is quite a bit at stake during campaigns for the highest office in the land.

Again, a different picture emerges when we consider state legislative campaigns. This is for at least two reasons. "First, potential voters are not stimulated by a highly visible presidential campaign to get them thinking about politics. Second, the candidates and issues are often not as important to the average voter as are the candidates and issues in presidential campaigns" (Maisel 2002, 111). For instance, although a presidential campaign may focus on the differences between the candidates in terms of how to fight the war on terror or how to solve problems with Social Security or Medicare, a state legislative campaign may be about local road conditions, the quality of the parks in the district, or other local issues. In addition, even when compared to campaigns for the U.S. House of Representatives, many potential voters do not know how the candidates stand on the issues that are central in down-ballot campaigns (Maisel 2002).

For these reasons, candidates and campaigns for lower-level offices do not register much on the voting population's radar, even as Election Day approaches. These offices simply are not considered that important to many voters. Consequently, when considering candidates for state legislative offices, many voters will use traditional decision-making shortcuts or heuristics, such as selecting a candidate with a name they may recognize (perhaps an incumbent, a candidate who is well known in the district, or someone with a certain ethnic-sounding name), selecting a female candidate (or specifically not), voting by party affiliation, or not voting at all. Therefore, party affiliation (of both voter and candidate) can be an important trigger in elections at this level. This does not necessarily mean that the state (or local) party organizations are active in these campaigns, or that candidates are able to rely on the party organization for assistance, but party can play a dominant role in determining the outcomes of state legislative races and other low-salience campaigns.

Role of Parties Political parties can serve many functions in campaigns, from recruiters of candidates to providers of electioneering services (Herrnson 1988, 2004). The role and impact of parties, at all levels of campaigns and with regard to electioneering, has changed substantially over time (Herrnson 1988; Aldrich 1995; Dulio 2004). Although some will argue that parties have surged in relevance in recent years, the fact remains that parties are much less involved in campaigns than they were at the height of their power (Herrnson 1988; 2004; see also Sorauf 1980; Kayden and Mahe 1985; Menefee-Libey 2000). Even today, parties engage in different activities with varying degrees of effort in different levels of campaigns.

Consider only three examples—party organization, candidate recruitment, and provision of services to candidates' campaigns—to see the differences in activities across different types of elections. One of the easiest differences to identify between the federal level and the local level is simple organization. Elements of the national parties today—the Republican National Committee, the Democratic National Committee, and their campaign committees focused on each chamber of Congress[6]—are very well organized, very well funded, and very active on a year-round basis. This is in contrast to the local and state level where there is great variation in how well organized the party apparatus is (Hershey 2005; Aldrich 2000). For instance, some state parties are more sophisticated than others; some have part-time staffs and others are staffed with full-time employees, some have large budgets and others do not, some are active year-round but others are operational only during the election season. At the local level, most counties in the United States have a party organization that has formal rules and a slate of officers, but how active they are and the size of their budget is another story.

For federal races, political campaigns are considered to be "candidate-centered" as opposed to "party-centered" (Salmore and Salmore 1985; Wattenberg 1990; Menefee-Libey 2000). This means that candidates at these higher levels tend to rely less on political party organizations for financial (and other) assistance, plus voters tend to orient themselves to individual candidate characteristics and issue positions, rather than party affiliation or party labels. Although there remains considerable debate about the exact influence and role of political parties in elections (through party identification and the role of party organizations), more voters appear to focus on campaign-specific matters (that is, candidate characteristics and issues) for higher-level campaigns than they do for lower-level races.

Campaigns for the state house and state senate generally are not considered to be as candidate-centered as upper-level campaigns. However, this does not necessarily mean that political party organizations fill the void. Even if a state political party organization is strong and active, it may only target between 10 and 15 legislative races (or even fewer) each year[7], with the hope of capturing open seats, defeating a vulnerable incumbent, and/or taking or retaining the majority of legislative seats. It is in those few races that the state and local party organizations tend to allocate their scarce financial and volunteer resources.

Although political parties used to be the sole selectors of the candidates that would run in the general election, the amount of candidate recruitment done by parties today is minimal. This is likely truest at the presidential level where every four years various candidates throw their proverbial hats into the ring. Sometimes, these candidates are not the individuals that the party might like to see run. For instance, originally in 2000, ten Republicans entered the race for their party's nomination. The GOP would likely have preferred it if individuals such as Alan Keyes, Gary Bauer, and Steve Forbes had stayed out of the race so as to make it easier for the party to unite behind the early front runner, George W. Bush. The same was true of the 2004 primary on the Democratic side, when individuals such as Dennis Kucinich and Al Sharpton entered the race. Rather than a crowded primary field that includes candidates with little chance of winning (for example, Keyes, Bauer, Kucinich, and Sharpton), the party would like to control the primaries and settle on a nominee early in the process, but this does not always occur. In 2004, the Democrats got their way, as John Kerry became the presumptive nominee five months before the party's convention in July.

Many candidates for the U.S. House and Senate are long-time party loyalists and have served the party as an elected official in some other capacity prior to running for federal office. Such candidates are sometimes recruited by their state, congressional district, or local party organization. In targeted races that appear to be competitive, even the party's national committee leadership may be active in identifying and contacting an individual to run for office, usually with the promise of party support. However, many other candidates self-select into their candidacy because they are wealthy and have the ability to spend the money necessary to run a campaign at this level, have high name recognition in the district, or believe they have some other advantage over their opponents.

The same is not necessarily true at the local and state levels, where the recruitment function remains an important part of the party organizations' role (Maisel 2002). In particular, this is the case in the "safe" districts we mentioned earlier. Because the candidate or party that holds the advantage in the district is likely to win by a sizeable margin, candidates of the disadvantaged party are not typically eager to step forward to be their party's sacrificial lamb. Especially at the local level, it is incumbent upon the party organization to fill the open slots in their area with quality candidates.

In the area of parties providing electioneering services to their candidates, important differences again appear between types of races. During the 1980s, the national party committees began to offer services to their candidates for the U.S. House and U.S. Senate, ranging from assistance with the production of television ads and direct mail pieces to polling data and fund-raising assistance (Herrnson 1988). The modern party organizations help candidates obtain the services that they demand and need, but they have chosen to hire outside professional political consultants to provide or perform the services rather than provide them in-house (Dulio 2004; Kolodny and Dulio 2003). This is done through the large budgets with which these organizations have to work. Again a much different picture emerges at the state and local levels, where campaigns remain a more labor-intensive effort. Because "local candidates cannot afford the cost of modern campaigning," including television or radio ads and survey research, the local party helps candidates by focusing on volunteers at the local precinct levels (Maisel 2002, 71).

Campaign Communication The differences between high-level campaigns such as those for president, U.S. Senate, and a state's governor's mansion, and down-ballot races for offices such as state house, state senate, and city council could not be clearer in the area of how candidates for each of these offices typically spread their campaign messages. Again, a presidential campaign is the most familiar example because this is the type of campaign to which Americans are most exposed. And most Americans see presidential campaign communications because many of them come over the airwaves in the form of television commercials. During the 2004 campaign, George W. Bush and John Kerry spent hundreds of millions of dollars delivering their message to voters on broadcast and cable television. In campaigns for governor and U.S. Senate, television is also a very important tool that many candidates employ. However, candidates in these high-level races also use direct mail to send very specific messages to potential voters, often based on the voter's personal characteristics. In addition, some campaigns have recently taken to using sophisticated telephone calling programs that send recorded messages to targeted members of the electorate, often featuring the voice of a famous individual or someone who would get the attention of the person being called. In short, a wide variety of techniques is used by candidates in high-level races to communicate the messages they want the voting public to hear.

Candidates in down-ballot races also use various approaches to reach potential voters. However, these techniques comprise a very different set of tactics. In lower-level races, direct mail is likely the most sophisticated electioneering communication tool that is employed. Candidates in most down-ballot races simply do not have the funding to utilize television or even radio. Moreover, campaigns in these types of races do not target voters with specific messages as higher-level races do. Rather, all potential voters receive the same message from the candidate.

Candidates in lower-level races also turn to less expensive methods of communication such as door-to-door canvassing and leafleting, literature drops, and speeches before groups of potential voters. In short, communication is taken just as seriously in down-ballot campaigns; it is simply done with less technically sophisticated means. The only exceptions tend to be targeted, competitive races where more funding is available and campaigns can afford to produce television commercials (and purchase commercial airtime).

Campaign Finance The ways in which campaigns are funded may be the largest and most significant difference between high-level and down-ballot races. The differences are stark, and they have important consequences for how the campaigns are run. Campaigns that are visible, that cover large geographic areas, and that must communicate to large numbers of potential voters are usually very well funded. Presidential campaigns are the best-funded campaigns in the United States. They need to be well-funded because they cover the most ground, and must communicate with the greatest number of people. As an example of the kind of funding present in modern presidential races, consider the 2004 contest between President George W. Bush and Senator John Kerry. Each candidate raised and spent roughly $200 million before the traditional start of the fall general election campaign, as they crisscrossed the country meeting potential voters and blanketed the airwaves with expensive television ads.[8] Both Kerry and Bush spent similar amounts after their party's nominating convention until Election Day because general election campaigns in the United States are publicly funded and each candidate receives a stipend from the federal government (in 2004, George W. Bush and John Kerry each received roughly $75 million in public funds). These funds go to purchase the tools and tactics of the modern campaign—television advertising, public opinion polling, direct mail campaigns, and high-profile fund-raising events.

The funds necessary to run a viable campaign for the U.S. House of Representatives, the U.S. Senate, or other statewide campaigns like a governor's race, are not as staggeringly high, but they can be very substantial. Campaigns for the U.S. House commonly cost upwards of $1 million in the modern reality of electioneering because many of the same technologies that are used by presidential candidates are now demanded and employed by many candidates for Congress. And in some cases, it can cost $5 million to wage an effective campaign for the U.S. House of Representatives. The funds spent in U.S. Senate campaigns are even higher, again because these candidates employ modern campaign technologies (television, sophisticated direct mail campaigns, and so on), and because they are communicating to a large number of potential voters. Some U.S. Senate campaigns may cost $2 to $3 million, but others can even exceed $10 million. One Senate candidate, Jon Corzine, who is now the senior Senator from New Jersey, spent over $64 million *of his own money* during his campaign in 2000. Others, such as Michael Huffington, spent about $30 million and lost his U.S. Senate race in California.

Potentially more significant are other sources of funding in these visible campaigns. Political parties and interest groups (in the form of political action committees) are very active (see Herrnson [2004] for a detailed description). During the late 1990s, political parties became very active in races for the presidency and in U.S. House and Senate campaigns thanks to some creative interpretations of campaign finance law and court rulings on the topic. The most important area where parties wielded power in spending money is that of so-called soft money; these are funds that parties raised and spent in unlimited and unregulated amounts. In the 2000 presidential campaign, the Republican and Democratic parties together raised and spent roughly $500 million in soft money on activities to assist their presidential candidates. The parties' congressional campaign committees were also very active in spending soft money in both House and Senate races. In the mid-term elections of 2002, Republican and Democratic party committees each raised roughly $250 million in soft money (FEC 2002).

The role of money in federal campaigns was fundamentally changed in 2002 when Congress passed and President Bush signed the Bipartisan Campaign Reform Act (BCRA). Under the terms of this law, the national parties are forbidden to raise and spend soft money; however, state parties may raise and spend these types of funds in limited amounts and for some very specific purposes (see Herrnson 2004; Malbin 2003; Barber 2003 for interpretations of the consequences of the law). Political action committees (PACs) are also very active in high-level campaigns. Many candidates (especially incumbents in the U.S. House and Senate) rely on contributions from PACs during their campaign to raise the requisite funds to run their campaigns (Jacobson 2004; Herrnson 2004). Although PACs can become very active in campaigns for the U.S. Congress, they are much less active in down-ballot races for the state legislature. When they do get involved, state-level PACs tend to adopt one of two strategies when supporting state legislative candidates: (1) corporate and labor-based PACs have tended to give more money to incumbents and other likely eventual winners because they have adopted a strategy that seeks to ensure access to lawmakers; and (2) those PACs considered to be "ideological" (for example, Right to Life or Planned Parenthood) have tended to support challengers more than the corporate and labor PACs because they are seeking to change the balance of power in legislatures in favor of their issue or issues (Klemanski 1989).

A clear trend in presidential and congressional campaigns is that they have gotten more expensive over time (Maisel 2002). A similar trend in campaign costs is present at the state and local levels. One estimate tracks spending in state and local elections as having increased from $465 million in 1980 (all races) to over $1 billion in the 1996 elections (see Maisel 2002, Chapter 11). Of course, there is significant variation across states, which is driven by the political and legal context (campaign finance laws, for example) in the particular state, which makes direct comparisons difficult. However, it is clear that state and local campaigns are also seeing a great increase in the role and presence of money.

Outside Influences In addition to making contributions to parties and candidates' campaigns, interest groups, labor unions, and other outside influences are heavily felt in high-level races, as they often get involved in communicating messages about the candidates during the campaign (Magleby 2000; Magleby and Monson 2004). This activity is so pervasive in some races that a candidate's campaign can find it hard to communicate its own message in the midst of the clutter outside groups can create in terms of campaign communication (Thurber 2001). Outside groups may also become involved in high-level campaigns by providing certain services for candidates. One of the most important, and most visible, of these activities falls in the category of voter mobilization, or get-out-the-vote (GOTV) efforts near Election Day. In the 2004 presidential race, America Coming Together, an outside group formed solely to undertake voter mobilization for Democrats, raised and spent tens of millions of dollars on this activity. In addition, labor unions continue to be a major player for Democratic candidates in this area.

Although most of the discussion thus far has illustrated areas where campaigns that are the most visible and for the highest offices in the land differ from those campaigns that are more local in nature, outside group influence is one area where the two can be similar. Even though outside groups such as labor unions and interest groups are not likely to enter the fray of a state house campaign by buying airtime for a television commercial, they may do a piece of literature to try to communicate to potential voters who will decide the outcome of the election. Many groups, such as labor unions, also get involved in GOTV activities close to Election Day.

General Electioneering Principles The differences between races for the presidency, governorships, and seats in the U.S. Congress, and those for offices that are more local in nature should be clear. High-level races are characterized by large amounts of money, a good deal of media coverage, and sophisticated communication techniques. In short, they have fully adapted to the "new style" of campaigning Agranoff (1972) noticed three decades ago. Public opinion polling, television advertising, massive fund-raising appeals, and the presence of professional political consultants who can provide all the services a campaign demands are all staples in these high-level races. David M. Farrell (1996) labels these kinds of campaigns "capital-intensive" campaigns, and contrasts these campaigns with those that are "labor intensive." Modern campaigns for down-ballot races such as those for state legislature, city council, mayor, county commissioner, and others tend to be more like the latter. In the vast majority of cases they simply do not see the same kind of technology, fund-raising, and media attention that high-level races do. These local campaigns are normally characterized by shoe leather rather than television commercials, and volunteers rather than professional consultants. In many cases, these campaigns consist of little more than the candidate himself and a couple of volunteers; it is up to these individuals to make sure they do not run into the same difficulties that John Kelly and his volunteer campaign manager found themselves having to deal with. Indeed, part of the lesson of campaign planning is that it is most important for those campaigns with just a few volunteers to have a solid campaign plan in place before the campaign begins. Only with such a plan in place is an efficient use of scarce resources possible—an important feature when only three or four people are running a political campaign by themselves.

NEXT STEPS

In the chapters that follow, we guide the reader through information that describes, and exercises that illustrate, the kinds of decisions that a candidate (or her campaign manager) running in a state legislative race has to make, and activities that must be completed when formulating a plan on how to win the election in which the candidate is competing. As readers move through the rest of this book, they will confront the same choices and assessments that actual candidates in three actual campaigns had to make.

We have chosen three cases (one each from Michigan, North Carolina, and Texas) based on a series of factors that vary across the three districts. These variables include: the type of race—state senate or state house; different regions of the country; legislatures that are full-time and part-time; states that have term limits versus those without term limits; campaign finance regulations; length of the general election period; and districts that are a mixture of urban, suburban, and rural populations. In short, we selected the cases so that the reader would be presented with a wide variety of different types of races and contexts in which to take on the tasks we include in the simulation activities. An additional benefit to employing districts that vary in important ways is that by comparing the different political contexts and climates of the races, the reader will see that campaigning is as much an art as it is a science. In other words, what "works" in one district may not work in another. In short, there is not a formula *per se* for campaigning that can be transferred from campaign to campaign.

However, one constant across each of the three races is that they are all competitive. We were careful to select races that were in competitive districts because one or two wrong decisions in these campaigns could make the difference on Election Day. Also, it is simply not as much fun to simulate a campaign where the outcome, for one reason or another, is all but assured. More importantly, the races we have selected for this simulation have the potential to have a huge impact in determining the direction of public policy for each of their respective states. They are truly the important "battleground" districts in their respective states.

In each of the chapters that offer material on specific state legislative races, we present some general background information on the states and districts so the readers can become familiar with the context in which they would be working if they were actually participating in the race. We also provide information that the candidate (or his campaign manager) would likely collect in his efforts to put together a plan to run the race. The material we present in each of the case chapters is all public information available to the average person. It is also boilerplate material to which any campaign would want access. However, we do not provide everything. The reader must do some of the work on her own. As will become clear, sometimes half the battle of planning how to win a race is doing the research that is necessary to find all the relevant information.

Before we introduce the reader to the case chapters that contain the information for the simulation, in Chapter 2 we illustrate some of the principles needed to develop a campaign plan that can lead to victory on Election Day. In Chapter 3, we present the reader with a guide to the simulation and a series of exercises that simulate what a candidate or campaign manager would undertake during the development of a campaign plan as well as the execution of that plan. These exercises are designed to present real-life challenges that a candidate or campaign manager faces in an actual campaign. The reader will have to take the information provided in the case chapters that follow and analyze it while keeping in mind the political implications of that information. The reader will also be asked to perform some tasks that require some creative thinking. Through the simulation exercises, the reader will find the truth in the statement that campaigning is both an art and a science.

NOTES

1. This excerpt is taken from a personal interview of John F. Kelly with the authors on May 20, 2004, and is reprinted with Mr. Kelly's permission.

2. In most states the redistricting process—the redrawing of district borders for state house, state senate, and the U.S. House of Representatives that usually takes place after each decennial census—is a political process. Usually the state legislature draws up a plan that must pass both houses and then be signed by the state's governor (an exception is the nonpartisan commission employed in Iowa). Because partisan officeholders usually try to help their fellow partisans, gerrymandering (that is, drawing district lines for partisan purposes) can occur. This can have important effects on who serves in the particular body. Take, for example, the outcome of the redistricting process in the state of Michigan after the 2000 census. Both the state house and state senate were controlled by the GOP, as was the governorship. The U.S. House delegation before redistricting favored Democrats by a count of 9 to 7. After the redistricting process, the delegation that was elected in 2002 favored the GOP 9 to 6. (Michigan lost one House seat in the reapportionment that took place after the census.)

3. The Speaker of the House (either in the U.S. House or state house chambers) is typically the leader of the majority party. However, in this circumstance when the party balance was so close, the two parties decided to share the power that came along with the speakership. This type of arrangement, it should be noted, is rare, even in instances when party control is so closely divided.

4. See, for example, Troy (1991), Jackson and Crotty (2001), Mayer (2000, 2004), Polsby and Wildavsky (2003), Pomper (1997, 2001), Wayne (2003), Campbell (2000), Holbrook (1996), or Miller and Gronbeck (1994) for presidential elections, and Herrnson (2004, 1988), Jacobson (2004), Campbell (1993), Kahn and Kenney (1999), or Kazee (1994) for

congressional campaigns. See also Dolan and Ezra (2002) and Bell (2005) for books on congressional legislative simulations.

5. See Thurber and Nelson (1995, 2000, 2004), Johnson (2000, 2001), Dulio (2004), Medvic (2001), and Perlmutter (1999), for example.

6. These are: the Democratic Congressional Campaign Committee, the National Republican Congressional Committee, the Democratic Senatorial Campaign Committee, and the National Republican Senatorial Committee.

7. We should note that this limited number of races on which parties focus is a function of the large number of "safe" seats that exist in each state, which are mainly a product of the redistricting process noted earlier.

8. Of course, each candidate focused only on the "battleground" states (that is, those states that were deemed to be the most competitive in the November voting), which means that some Americans rarely, if ever, saw one of the candidate's ads, or had the candidate visit their state.

2

The Mechanics of a Political Campaign: The Campaign Plan

This book is ultimately about how campaigns are waged in that we take the reader through several activities that candidates and their campaigns must carry out in order to have a chance to win on Election Day. However, before any of these activities can begin, the candidate must make a fundamental decision—whether or not to run. This is the the most important decision a prospective candidate will make regarding the race. Making the decision to run for political office can be very difficult, and should be taken seriously. Political campaigns are grueling, demanding, and often frustrating. They require a commitment of time that many first-time candidates do not realize.

Many potential candidates make this decision, in part, by having a series of conversations with trusted confidants. This process often resembles a progression through a series of concentric circles. In the innermost circle (and the first to be consulted) are the prospective candidate's most trusted friends and family members. Of course, any would-be candidate first needs to determine if his spouse and children are willing to accept the personal and domestic upheaval that will inevitably occur. After family, many candidates consult close friends and extended family members. Support from this group, both financial and in executing the campaign, is key to being successful. The next set of individuals in this series of concentric circles likely includes the potential candidate's professional and personal network, with similar questions about support being posed.

Prospective candidates also must consider a number of factors beyond family matters when deciding whether or not they should run for office. In addition to their own personal circumstances, they should consider other dynamics over which they have little or no control, such as the social, economic, and partisan nature of the area where the campaign will be waged, as well as other factors, such as state or national political and economic forces that may impact the campaign.

In terms of the nature of the district in which a candidate is looking to run, a major question that must be answered centers on the partisan makeup of the district. For example, if the majority of the people in the district in which a candidate is considering a run for office are Democrats, and the potential candidate is a Republican, how likely is it that the Republican candidate will be able to overcome this built-in disadvantage? More importantly, a prospective candidate must consider and evaluate whether the current officeholder is going to seek re-election. Incumbents have many advantages that can tip the election in their favor, such as high name recognition, campaign experience, a sound fund-raising base and operation, and an established track record (although this may be a liability as well, depending on how the incumbent has performed in office).[1] The potential candidate must ask herself whether she could successfully challenge the incumbent in a primary election if they are of the same party, or beat him in a general election (this latter scenario, of course, assumes that the potential candidate is able to win her own primary).

In terms of broader forces that may be at work, would-be candidates also should consider the state and national economy. Economic conditions might be a help or hindrance to the campaign. If the incumbent officeholder is running again and has represented the district well and overseen strong economic times, it might not be the right time to challenge the incumbent. On the other hand, if economic conditions in the district are not good, it might be time to strike while the iron is hot. In addition, scandals or negative media stories about the potential candidate's party, some of his fellow party members, or even the potential candidate could impact the decision.

Two examples illustrate the profound effects the larger political landscape can have on the outcomes of campaigns. After the Watergate crisis in 1973, Republicans in Congress were dealt a serious blow as dozens of new Democratic members were elected to the U.S. House of Representatives. This was a good time for Democrats to run for office. Not only were Americans disappointed with Republicans in the wake of the scandal, but many quality Republican candidates decided not to test the waters in such a volatile political climate. Another example of a national trend affecting decisions of potential candidates to run was evident in 1994. After two years of disappointments and failures by the Clinton administration and Democrats in Congress, most notably the Clinton health care initiative, Republicans scored one of their biggest political victories. The nation was frustrated with the Democrats in Washington, D.C., and this created an opening for the GOP. Republicans took advantage of the anti-incumbent feeling in the nation, and ran many strong candidates, while many Democrats decided not to run because of the difficulties the Clinton White House and Democrats on Capitol Hill experienced. The political context affected the decisions of many potential candidates, which paved the way for dozens of new Republicans to get elected to Congress, allowing the GOP to gain control of Congress for the first time in 40 years.

Each of the factors noted so far (and others not mentioned) can impact a candidate's success or failure, even before the candidate publicly declares her intention to seek public office. This decision is a serious one and should be treated as such.

ORGANIZING A CAMPAIGN

Smart and successful candidates are able to bring together committed and skilled individuals to help with their campaign. In many cases, a state legislative campaign organization may be able to recruit only a few people who will be

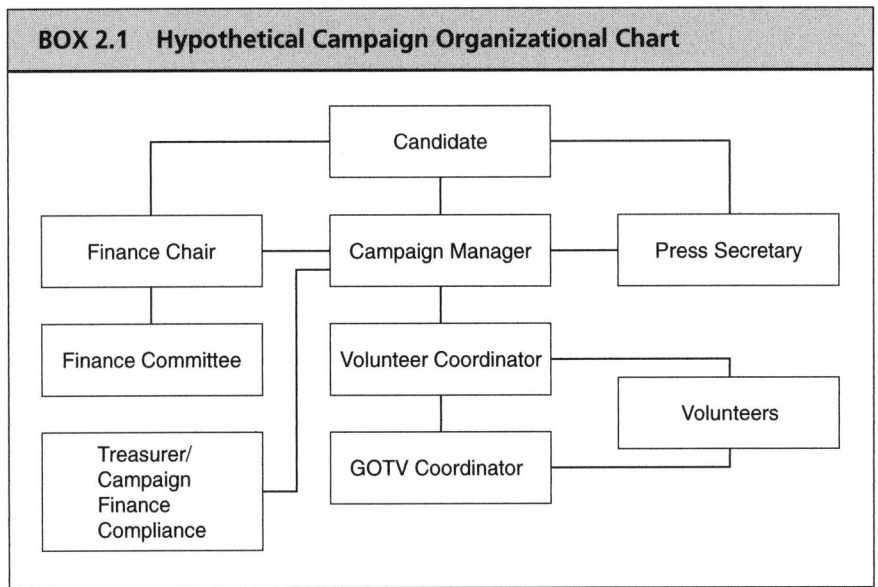

BOX 2.1 Hypothetical Campaign Organizational Chart

considered part of the core team. Sometimes a campaign with limited resources is able to staff only the campaign manager's position, and perhaps find another person who is willing to serve as a volunteer coordinator. Whether the campaign organization has 3 or 10 core members, a single individual will likely perform a number of different functions during the campaign.

There are many ways to organize a political campaign. The chart in Box 2.1 illustrates one example of a campaign organization based on different duties that must be undertaken. Of course, some campaigns will have a core team of only two or three individuals, and therefore will need to divide the many different campaign responsibilities among only a few people. Other campaigns will be able to staff the organization with an office manager, a scheduler, an event coordinator, and chairs of outreach committees, which would spread the tasks around and take some of the burden off the candidate and campaign manager. In larger campaigns, many candidates are involved directly only in fund-raising, as media spokesperson for the campaign, and in making voter contacts. The rest of the work of the campaign then falls to the campaign manager and whoever else has a major role in the campaign organization.

CREATING A CAMPAIGN PLAN

As we noted in Chapter 1, creating a campaign plan is critical to running a successful campaign. Prior planning is key to developing an overall strategy and being able to execute that strategy. In fact, to have a chance of being successful in a campaign—and this holds for campaigns for school board president to president of the United States—a plan of attack must be created. This plan puts down on paper every aspect of the coming campaign and how it should ideally be carried out. This even includes a campaign announcement speech. Therefore, the best plans are in place even before a candidate files papers with the state to enter the race. In one sense, a campaign plan is like a game plan a coach develops for a football game. For the coach, a game plan is a plan of attack that will lead his team to victory. However, any decent coach does not wait to develop the game plan until the second quarter or halftime. Instead, the game plan is developed before the game and is implemented in practices leading up to the game so that by kickoff the team is ready to begin executing the plan.

The purpose of the campaign plan is no different. Every aspect of what will confront the candidate in the coming campaign must be anticipated and dealt with. Moreover, every aspect of the plan should be consistent and complementary, from scheduling and organizing events to making contacts with voters, and from debating the opponent to communicating the campaign message. As one campaign expert has noted:

> [W]riting a comprehensive plan forces campaign managers and strategists to think through their options. It imposes a sense of order on a process that otherwise can be chaotic and totally inefficient. A political campaign should not be merely a series of events and activities haphazardly sequenced and arbitrarily timed. It should be rolled out with clear purpose as part of a logical plan. (Faucheux 2004, 26)

Although such planning requires time and effort prior to the beginning of the campaign, it ultimately saves time and helps avoid duplicated or wasted efforts once the campaign begins. In addition to planning for activities that are expected—fund-raisers, debates, literature drops, and so on—the plan should also help the candidate and her team anticipate potential roadblocks and bigger-picture occurrences. For instance, a campaign plan might include different budget figures—a high and a low budget—to be used depending on how successful the candidate was with fund-raising. If the candidate accomplished the fund-raising goal, the campaign might operate under the high budget figure, but if the candidate was not able to meet the fund-raising goal (a real possibility in many campaigns), the campaign might operate under the low budget figure. In other words, the plan even includes contingencies, and tries to plan for events that may or may not occur.

In short, a campaign plan defines what is to be done, when it should be done, who should be doing it, and what resources will be needed to complete the job (see Beaudry and Schaeffer 1986, especially pp. 43–44). A solid campaign plan lays out the contextual information of the district, voter information, campaign strategy and tactics, and staffing and resource requirements. Therefore, the major elements of a campaign plan[2] include the following:

- A *district analysis* includes geographic, social, economic, and demographic information on the district, and a breakdown of the political implications of that information.

- *Electoral research* focuses on the district's voting history, voter turnout, recent redistricting outcomes, and other voting trends in the district. Electoral research also helps a campaign estimate the ultimate question in a campaign: "How many votes do I need to win?"

- *Candidate and opposition profiles* focus on the major personal, political, and policy characteristics associated with all candidates in the race (including the candidate himself).

- In the *campaign message* a candidate answers the question, "Why am I running?" Also, the campaign message provides reasons to support a candidate. For instance, if a supporter is asked in a line at the grocery store, "I see you are wearing a John Doe button. Why are you supporting him for the state legislature?", the supporter's response is the campaign message: "I'm voting for John Doe rather than Joe Public because...."

- *Budget and fund-raising plans* are separate, but related, activities. Creating a budget informs the campaign about how much money it needs to raise and how it will be spent (for example, for paid media, fund-raisers, postage for mailings, and so on). The fund-raising plan tells the campaign how the funds specified in the budget will be raised; it projects not only an amount that will be raised and the sources from which it will likely be raised, but more importantly the specific strategies the campaign will use to raise the money.

- A *volunteer recruitment and volunteer use plan* focuses on how to identify and recruit volunteers, how to use them most efficiently and effectively when they show up, and how to keep them happy and coming back to volunteer again.

- A *paid media plan* centers on the strategic decisions that involve all paid communications or advertisements (for example, direct mail literature, newspaper, TV, or radio ads, and billboards) and all campaign collateral materials (for example, lawn signs, campaign buttons, bumper stickers, and GOTV literature). The paid media plan also will include information on the planned timing of ads, when literature will be mailed, and so on.

- An *earned media plan* designs activities geared toward generating enough media interest in the campaign so the campaign's events are covered as a news story. The earned media plan needs to be specific and cover activities such as interviews with journalists, and speeches the candidate will give, and candidate forums or debates that are likely to be covered by the news media.

- A *get-out-the-vote (GOTV) plan* informs the campaign on how voters who have been identified as supporters will be mobilized on Election Day.

- The *campaign calendar* brings all the different elements of the plan together in chronological order. Since all campaigns work with the same time constraints—there are only a certain number of days until Election Day—proper planning through the use of a campaign calendar helps ensure that time-consuming activities are completed at the appropriate time by detailing the dates by which all campaign activities must be performed.

Detailing the Components of a Plan

In this section we add some detail to the plan components introduced in the preceding section. Contextual information about an area a candidate is seeking to represent can be key to the success of a campaign because it gives the candidate a sense of what the people in the district are like and what kind of district it is generally. This information is obtained by conducting a *district analysis* that details information on the district's geography, economy, infrastructure, and transportation networks. The ideal candidate also knows his district intimately, including the little details of the district that can be used to his advantage during the campaign. For example, the candidate might want to know where the well-kept neighborhoods are, details about the local schools (including their sports teams and mascots), where the potholes in the roads are, where the dangerous traffic intersections are located, and so on. Candidates who do not already know these details must learn them. Early in their campaign, a candidate and campaign staff member may drive around the district identifying and noting the important characteristics of the district by conducting a so-called windshield survey. The district analysis also includes a demographic analysis of the district, focusing on voter characteristics such as partisanship, race, gender, age, and so on.

The key in a district analysis is the analysis. It is not enough to collect the information about the district; one must be able to pull out the important political information from the data collected as part of the district analysis so that it is useful to the campaign. Many times savvy campaigners can uncover issues important to the district in this information and make them central parts of the campaign in which they are working.

Part of the voting data to be collected is the electoral history of the district; that is, the prior voting patterns in terms of turnout and candidate/party preferences. This information can inform the candidate and her campaign team about the kind of district in which they will be campaigning. Is it a Democratic or Republican district, or is it a swing district where neither party holds an historical electoral advantage? This *electoral research* and voter analysis can also help the campaign identify more precise information vital to the campaign. For instance, a few numbers can tell a candidate where the high turnout precincts are, where the candidate's base of support is located, where the opponent's base of support is located, and which precincts have high numbers of swing voters. All of these data are important because campaigns at the state legislative level usually work with very scarce resources, and knowing what voting characteristics different areas show can help decide how resources should be allocated.

Research makes up a large portion of the campaign plan, only part of which is the district and demographic analyses and electoral history. The plan is nearly useless unless *opposition research,* which seeks to compile information about the candidate's opponent(s) that might be used for the candidate's own advantage, is conducted. This type of research, however, goes beyond the opponent(s). Any sound campaign will also include similar detailed research on its own candidate so as to be ready for what the opponent(s) will be gathering. Opposition research typically uses public sources of information (as opposed to gossip or private information) and is campaign-relevant (Shea and Burton 2001, 58).

Opposition research can be tricky, however, because what is relevant to the campaign is a subjective question. Many voters consider delving into a candidate's background and using it in one's own campaign to be "negative campaigning," and generally unfair or mean-spirited. If a campaign uses information it has collected that the public deems inappropriate, it can backfire on the campaign and create a backlash that can damage the candidate's chances. Not all opposition research is unseemly, however. An example of relevant personal information to a campaign would be a scenario where the opponent is running as a candidate touting her fiscal responsibility, but has filed for personal or business bankruptcy in the past. The candidate's campaign might use this information to counter the opponent's claims of fiscal competency or trustworthiness. Moreover, recall that we noted earlier that campaigns are about providing potential voters with a choice. Pointing out differences between two candidates (and therefore creating a contrast) cannot be done without knowing what the opponent has done or said in the past. Typical opposition research investigates a candidate's past political life (if he has held or run for office in the past) through his roll-call voting record—what policy solutions has he supported (or failed to support) in the past—and public statements about public policy and solutions to problems.

One of the first questions people will ask a candidate when she tells them she wants to run for office is "Why are you running?" This single question is the central piece to any candidacy. It is a question for which every candidate must have a clear and concise answer. Many people a candidate meets going door-to-door, in small group meetings, or in media interviews also want to know. The best example of the importance of this is a candidate who could not answer the question satisfactorily—and succinctly. During his 1980 bid for the Democratic Party's presidential nomination, Senator Edward Kennedy (MA) was asked in a "60 Minutes" interview why he was running for president. After several minutes of going on about a number of things, it was clear that Kennedy did not have a good answer for the seemingly simple question. After the televised debacle, Kennedy's campaign was all but over.

The answer to the simple question, "Why are you running?" is called the *campaign message*. The message is the foundation for much of what the candidate will communicate to voters throughout the campaign. The most effective campaigns reinforce the same message in every one of their speeches and door-to-door conversations, in all of their campaign literature, and in interviews and debates. Only through continual repetition will the candidate's rationale for running and the reasons potential voters should choose the candidate over his opponent sink in with the electorate. In other words, the message should reverberate through every portion of the campaign and campaign plan.

Because the message often provides information about both candidates and issues, it is important to know enough about the district (through district and demographic analyses) and each candidate (by conducting candidate and opposition research) to be able to create comparisons that will be beneficial. Remember, campaigns are about giving voters a choice, and it is the campaign's purpose to show voters why their candidate should be the preferred choice. Along with opposition and candidate research, some campaigns conduct a SWOT (Strengths, Weaknesses, Opportunities, Threats) analysis of the candidates, the context, and the issues. Identifying positives and negatives about each candidate continues to help the people running the campaign identify potential comparisons that may be useful to the candidate throughout the campaign.

A related device commonly used when developing a campaign message and identifying contrasts between candidates is a message box. Similar to a SWOT analysis, a message box identifies strengths and weaknesses of each candidate. However, it goes a step further and helps campaign personnel identify contrasts that will give their candidate an advantage with voters. In the message box, a candidate tries to define herself, define her opponent(s), and define the issues in the campaign by dividing strengths and weaknesses into the quadrants of the box. This helps the campaign to identify what each candidate is likely to try to say during the campaign (see Box 2.2). In this way, a campaign can be positioned relative to its opponent(s), and be better able to offer voters choices that favor the candidate.

What messages work the best? There is no blueprint or standard message that will appeal to all voters in all districts across time. However, some general messages have been used consistently in campaigns at all levels for many years. For example, in a state legislative general election in a district where the Republican Party is clearly dominant (this would be clear from the electoral research conducted), the best message may simply be "I'm the Republican candidate running for the state legislature." In nearly all campaigns, though, the

BOX 2.2	Outline of a Campaign Message Box
Us on Us What we want to say about our candidate and our campaign	**Us on Them** What we want to say about the opponent and the campaign
Them on Us What our campaign anticipates the opponent will say about our candidate and our campaign	**Them on Them** What our campaign anticipates the opponent will say about himself candidate and his campaign

campaign team will find it necessary to define a message that reflects the nature of their particular district and race.

Closely related to the campaign message is the campaign theme. The theme differs from the message in that the *theme* is what the campaign is about, whereas the *message* tells potential voters why the candidate is the best choice rather than the opponent. Incumbents running for re-election may employ a theme that encourages voters to "stay the course" or maintain the status quo. Many themes are used again and again, and have been utilized in campaigns over many years. For instance, in his 1864 re-election campaign, President Abraham Lincoln said, "Don't change horses in the middle of the stream"; many incumbent candidates use this same theme today, including George W. Bush in his 2004 re-election bid. In contrast, challenger candidates may use a theme centering on "change" for their campaign to try to urge potential voters to fire the incumbent. Messages stem from the theme, and are usually more specific statements that are tied to issues in the campaign.

Before moving any further, we should note that we do not mean to convey that a campaign message begins and ends with research into the district, the electorate, or the opponent. Rather, a campaign message begins with what the candidate wants to do once he is elected to office. A candidate's campaign is about his vision for the future and his policy ideas. To be successful, a candidate must have an idea of where he wants to go once elected and what he wants to do for his constituents. The research that is conducted helps refine those ideas and create contrasts between the candidate and the opponent(s), illustrating the choices voters have between the candidates.

A *campaign budget* is one of the most important elements of a campaign plan—and of course, the campaign itself. Readers will likely not be surprised to learn that campaigns at all levels continue to be more costly, so much so that it may cost $100,000 or more to run an effective campaign for a competitive state house seat. However, successful campaigns can be run on a small budget too. For purposes of this simulation, we have limited the amount of money available to each campaign so that readers are forced to make strategic choices that are typical of the majority of state legislative campaigns operating with relatively small budgets. A campaign's budget serves the same purpose as any household budget—it identifies how much money a campaign has to work with and how much it needs to operate. The budget will also detail how much money is coming in (see the fund-raising section that follows) and how much money is going out. This kind of cash flow information is important because the campaign will need certain amounts of money at certain points in the campaign; for example, yard signs will have to be ordered and paid for, postage will have to be paid for mailers that are sent out, and so on. If the campaign does not have an idea of what kind of funds it needs and when it needs them, it will be flying blind throughout the campaign.

Generally, a *fund-raising plan* is created in conjunction with the budget in order to detail how the campaign will raise the money needed to execute the strategy outlined in the campaign plan. Knowing how much the campaign needs to spend (based on other strategic decisions outlined in the plan) will determine how much it will need to raise. The reverse is true as well. Having a realistic understanding of how much money the campaign will likely raise can provide a realistic idea of how much money the campaign will likely have available to spend.

Lower-level races often rely solely on volunteers for much of the day-to-day business of the campaign—stuffing envelopes, making phone calls, walking door-to-door with campaign literature, putting up yard signs, and working polling places on Election Day, to name only a few. Campaigns need to know how to identify individuals who are willing to help in the campaign, as well as have activities prepared for volunteers on any given day. A well-organized campaign with a *volunteer recruitment and volunteer use plan* can produce substantial benefits during the campaign and on Election Day. Without such a plan, a campaign is likely to experience the same kind of disappointing volunteer activity that John Kelly's first campaign experienced, with eager individuals showing up only to find little or nothing to do. Volunteers are a great resource for any campaign; good campaign developers know how to use them and plan for their arrival.

Should the candidate try to talk to every resident in the district? Of course not. First, we know that not every resident votes because not every person in the district is of voting age. Second, not every person of voting age is registered to vote. And third, not every registered voter makes it to the polls on Election Day, especially in lower-level races. In fact, it is quite likely that those who turn out on a consistent basis in state legislative races might be closer to one-third (or less) of a district's registered voters. Finding those registered voters who will participate on Election Day is key to any campaign strategy. This is partly accomplished through the kind of electoral research noted previously. However, beyond identifying potential supporters and what the candidate will say to them (that is, the campaign message), the campaign personnel must devise a strategy to communicate that message to those potential supporters.

To accomplish this, an overall communication plan is critical to the campaign plan. After all, what good is the choice between two candidates that a campaign offers to voters if it does not reach those voters? A communication plan includes what the campaign will say, in the form of the message, and the means through which that message will be delivered (for example, TV, radio, newspapers, direct mail, door-to-door literature, and so on). There are two basic elements to a general communication plan: paid media and earned media.

Make no mistake; although the type of paid media advertising employed will likely be different in different types of races, a sound *paid media plan* is just as important for lower-level races as it is for federal campaigns. A paid media plan incorporates research conducted on the media outlets that cover the candidate's district to determine the best outlets and strategy for communicating the campaign's message. One key decision that must be made centers on the type(s) of paid media that will be employed during the campaign. To help make this decision, information about all television (network affiliate and cable) and radio stations (including audience demographic information as well as advertising rates), as well as information on local—both daily and weekly—newspapers (including circulation and coverage) is needed. Again, largely due to cost, campaigns at the state legislative level likely will not use network-affiliate TV advertising unless the district is in a minor media market and airtime is inexpensive. Cable television is becoming an option in some state legislative districts, but that viewership can be low in many cases. More often than not, the medium used in state legislative campaigns is direct mail. Mass mailings to targeted individuals in the district (that is, individuals in the electorate who have been identified as having some meaningful characteristic—either as part of a demographic group that the candidate may want to communicate to, or an attitude or opinion that the candidate believes she can connect with) offer campaigns the ability to communicate a specific message to specialized groups of potential voters. (For example, "security moms" and "NASCAR dads" are two groups of voters with identifiable characteristics who were targeted in the 2004 presidential election.)

Earned media is considered to be any campaign story covered as a news item. It is sometimes called "free media" because the campaign does not directly pay for the advertising as it would with a paid communication. But as any campaign expert will note, free media is far from free. Campaign personnel expend time and effort in attempting to gain the attention of a newspaper reporter, a TV or radio station, or other media source so they will cover the campaign as a news story. Getting a return on the investment of time and effort can be difficult, however, because, as we noted earlier, lower-level political campaigns do not receive much earned media from newspapers, and they receive even less from television or radio stations.

Therefore, a carefully crafted *earned media plan* is vital to the larger campaign plan. Unless potential voters know that the candidate held a rally, made a speech, or attended a meeting with citizens, it might as well not have happened. To this end, campaign developers need to have an idea of what strategies they are going to employ to try to attract media attention from local journalists. Knowing who the local political reporters are and cultivating a relationship with them can be a large advantage to any campaign. Beyond this, campaign developers must know how they are going to communicate information about the candidate's activities so as to make them newsworthy and to attract media attention.

In many campaigns (especially those with few resources) a lot of time and effort is spent seeking to attract earned media attention, but a word of caution is appropriate because therein lies a trade-off between cost and control. Just because a journalist covers a campaign's event does not mean that there is a guarantee that the resulting story will be favorable to the candidate. Any kind of interview, speech, or other event covered by the media is subject to interpretation or editing by the reporter. For example, during the first debate in the 2000 presidential campaign between then-Vice President Al Gore and then-Governor George W. Bush, the Gore campaign lost a battle with the media over control of the message that came out of the event. After the debate, the press covering the campaign focused great attention on Gore's appearance and body language during the debate. "In various reports, Mr. Gore was called annoying, optimistic, condescending, civil, dull, likable and presidential, among other things. He interrupted, smirked, bragged, asserted, sighed and chuckled. . . . Mr. Gore caught flak for his makeup, [too]. Some thought he wore too much for comfort" (Harper 2000, A10). Indeed, for some this was more of a story than the exchange of ideas between the two candidates. The Gore campaign certainly would have preferred that the substance of the arguments made by the Vice President be the story rather than his appearance, but they could not control what reporters said on television or wrote in the newspaper. The story out of this campaign event was so prominent that NBC's "Saturday Night Live" picked up on it and satirized the candidates in a skit that millions of potential voters saw (many of whom, it is likely, did not see the actual debate, which meant that this was the only information they received about the event). In an interesting twist of fate, it was George W. Bush, who, in his 2004 re-election bid, found himself in a similar position, as his facial expressions and reactions to his opponent were the story coming out of his first debate with Senator Kerry (Milbank 2004, A10). Even though there is always potential for an earned media opportunity to backfire or not convey the right message, any campaign with hopes of success must plan for ways to attract positive media attention from the local press.

Everything that a candidate and his campaign team have accomplished over the course of a campaign will be meaningless if the candidate's supporters do not show up at the polls on Election Day. Therefore, a *GOTV plan* is absolutely crucial to the success of the campaign, as it focuses on creating the most efficient and effective use of campaign resources leading up to and including Election Day. Typically, campaigns have identified likely supporters through previous contacts in the weeks and months of the campaign. In the days leading up to Election Day, volunteers can make another contact with known supporters to remind them to vote. Because campaigns for lower-level offices tend to be low-information races, such reminders are even more important for state legislative elections.

Finally, a good campaign plan will include a *campaign calendar*. Earlier, we emphasized the importance of time, and noted the time constraints all campaigns work under, as there is an ever-decreasing number of days until Election Day. However, time is also one of the resources a campaign has at its disposal, even if it is the most scarce. (Candidates can always try to raise more money, but they cannot add hours to the day or extend the campaign beyond Election Day.) Campaign planners with hopes of winning must have a handle on what is going to happen and when it needs to happen. For instance, when does the candidate begin her door-to-door walking? When do the direct mail pieces go out? When are the fund-raisers scheduled? When can lawn signs be put up (as many communities have restrictions on this)? Timing is crucial in terms of the campaign budget, as raising and spending money allows all the other activities in the campaign to go on. More importantly, campaigners need to know at what points during the campaign they will need certain amounts of cash—to send direct mail, order lawn signs, or hold another fund-raiser—and how that money is going to be made available. These and many other issues must be addressed. One method employed by veteran campaigners is to plan backward in time—starting from Election Day and working back toward the candidate's announcement. The campaign calendar is filled out to form a flow chart of sorts which, when implemented correctly, can get all the parts of the campaign moving in a coordinated fashion. The campaign calendar pulls all of the sections of the plan together into a useful document.

When put all together, the campaign plan can be used throughout the entire campaign. When the unexpected happens (which can be something the campaigners do by mistake, something the opponent does that requires a response, or something completely outside of the race itself), the plan ideally informs the campaign about the best approach to take. In other words, even when facing the unexpected, a good plan can help decide whether it is worth it to do something that is not part of the plan, to respond within the context of the plan, or to simply continue to follow the plan.

The importance of the campaign plan cannot be overstated. Without a written plan of attack, the campaign cannot be successful. Although it takes time, effort, and resources to create a campaign plan, it gives a candidate the best chance to win on Election Day. It may seem easier to run a campaign without going through the effort to create a plan, but the time spent preparing will result in time saved when the campaign is in full swing. Better to take the time at the beginning to develop and design a strategy to win than be left wondering what went wrong on Election Night.

NOTES

1. For more details on the incumbency advantage in Congress, see Mayhew (1974), Fiorina (1978), or Fenno (1978), to name only a few. Of course, not all potential candidates have to worry about incumbents. Open seat races where there is no incumbent running (either because of the retirement of the incumbent or term limits in states that impose them) often represent the best opportunity for a new candidate to have success.

2. There are many ways to divide the sections of a campaign plan. In the pages that follow we have divided the plan into 10 sections. Others may have different divisions of tasks and divide the plan into more or fewer sections. The important point should not be the number of sections a plan has, but the information contained therein.

3

The Campaign Simulation and Exercises

This chapter contains a guide to the campaign simulation based on a series of exercises that allow the reader to experience some of the activities and decisions a campaigner would carry out in a state legislative campaign. In Chapter 2, we introduced the concept of a campaign plan, its components, and its importance to any campaign. The guide in this chapter continues the discussion of the different elements of a plan and describes how to complete different tasks associated with each of those elements. The heart of the simulation is the series of exercises that correspond to each aspect of the plan.

As we have already noted, running a political campaign is both a science and an art. The data collected through the research that makes up a significant portion of the campaign plan is part of the "science" aspect of the process. Crafting the message and knowing how to allocate resources, to name only two, are examples of the "art" of campaigning. Developing a sound campaign plan can prepare the reader for much, but not all, of what will occur during a campaign; however, as there are several other judgments that are also part of the art of electioneering that a campaigner may be forced to make in response to events that cannot be predicted. For example, crises occur all of the time in campaigns, and no campaign goes as smoothly as the candidate would like. When something goes wrong in the campaign, there is often more than one way to deal with the problems that arise.[1] These dilemmas, or situations where there may be more than one possible response to a set of circumstances, can be very challenging and can even affect the outcome of the campaign.

Moreover, there may be times in a campaign when an individual campaigner's morals and ethics are challenged by a situation. Because there is no rulebook for how campaigns are waged (save for public laws that govern how money is raised and spent) and the First Amendment to the Constitution broadly protects political speech, questions of ethics often arise in campaigns. Those watching a campaign may not see these ethical questions at first glance, or at all, because they most likely occur behind the closed doors of the campaign. However, rest assured they do occur. Questions of what to do in a certain scenario when the "right" answer is not abundantly clear and decisions about how to handle a crucial situation likely come up in every campaign. Most of the time, these scenarios also come in the form of dilemmas because there is no obvious right or wrong answer. To tap into the type of decisions that present themselves during crises and challenging ethical circumstances, we have included a series of crisis management scenarios and ethical dilemmas. These types of decisions are equally important to understanding what happens in a real political campaign, and also represent the art of campaigning, which at times is more challenging than the science of campaigning.

Within any campaign there are several tasks and responsibilities that fall to a number of different actors in the process. Candidates and campaign team members have many important responsibilities, but so do actors outside of the campaign. For instance, journalists play a large role in any modern campaign in that they report on the campaign, and thus convey a good deal of information to the electorate. For this reason, along with exercises associated with the campaign plan, in some of the following sections we have included exercises meant to simulate activities performed by journalists covering a campaign. This is done to introduce the importance of the campaign–press relationship that exists during an election season. Citizens also have duties as well, including gathering information so as to be informed about candidates and issues, and participating on Election Day.

All the exercises in this chapter are typical of decisions that must be made and tasks that must be completed in any campaign. We have designed these exercises to roughly reflect the different parts of a campaign plan that a candidate or campaign manager would create before waging a campaign. As we noted in the last chapter, the plan template that we suggest is only one version of how to organize the different elements of a campaign plan; if one were to ask a number of campaign managers or political consultants how they would construct a campaign plan, one would likely receive a variety of answers and interpretations. However, the definition of what belongs in a campaign plan should not be the focal point here. Rather, our aim is for the reader to examine and participate in the kinds of activities that go on during a competitive campaign so the reader gets a feel of what kinds of decisions those involved in a campaign must make.

All in all, the following tasks, exercises, and scenarios present the reader with a selection of decisions that have to be made and responsibilities that have to be accounted for in the modern campaign. The reader will be able to create answers that likely will differ substantially from the way another reader would approach the same task or question. This is extremely beneficial; it can be instructive to see how someone else approached the same question, data, or scenario.

CAMPAIGN ROLES AND RESPONSIBILITIES

There are several different roles that are part of any political campaign. Candidates, political advisors, volunteers, the media, and voters all play crucial roles in campaigns. In addition, different roles suit different skills and personalities. For example, because the candidate is always at the forefront of the campaign, giving speeches, engaging in debates, and meeting voters, an individual who is outgoing and has strong verbal and interpersonal skills is well suited for this role. The campaign manager should have strong organizational skills, in order to orchestrate all of the different activities that are occurring at the same time. In addition, the manager must make sure that all tasks are completed on time. The press secretary must have good people skills, be able to interact with different people, and be able to think on her feet because she may be asked to deal with several individuals or respond to several inquiries pertinent to the campaign at the same time. Volunteers usually like research and other tasks that will mainly require them to work behind the scenes as part of a team. Reporters and journalists have strong writing and observational skills.

Of course, the role of the candidate is the most obvious one in a political campaign. After all, the campaign is the candidate's, as it is his name on the ballot and in the end he is responsible for what the campaign does, and the success or failure thereof. In addition, the candidate's activities are most easily seen from outside the campaign. In some down-ballot campaigns, the candidate does virtually everything; she may execute every phase of the campaign and be responsible for making sure every task is complete.

In other campaigns, the candidate has help. He is assisted by his spouse, his friends, volunteers, and in some cases, paid staff. In these instances the duties of the campaign are divided among all the participants. In Chapter 2 we presented a hypothetical organizational chart of a campaign that included the candidate, the campaign manager, the finance chair, the press secretary, the volunteer coordinator, and others. This represents one way to organize a campaign, and does so in a way that is based on the different tasks in the campaign. One might find in a campaign that the division of labor does not fall neatly along these suggested lines. In fact, we will venture to say that few campaigns at the local and state level will divide the responsibilities along strict lines of any type. Although some campaigns at this level have even begun to hire professional political consultants to provide specific technical services—such as survey research, micro-targeting of voters, and media production—these instances are rare. Rather, in most campaigns of this type, anyone with a free hand pitches in to help the cause. In other words, although someone might be the campaign's volunteer coordinator, they might also help to prepare a paid media advertisement; similarly, the campaign manager might find that he is doing much of the opposition and candidate research in addition to his managerial duties. In short, in small campaign organizations like the ones in many state legislative races, there are no strict job descriptions.

CREATING THE CAMPAIGN PLAN

In Chapter 2 we discussed the purpose and importance of the campaign plan to operating a successful campaign. In the remainder of this chapter, we detail how selected pieces of each component of the plan are actually created. We have divided the plan into 10 different components, with the exercises associated with each section following directly. The sections of the campaign plan are generally chronological in order. However, this does not always hold because some tasks must be done simultaneously and others will have to be done throughout the campaign. For instance, we have placed the budgeting and fund-raising sections near the middle of our discussion. However, fund-raising is something that should be done continually; it should start early and run throughout the campaign. Additionally, we should stress again that the campaign plan should be complete before the campaign begins. In the sections that follow, we will discuss certain activities that would take place during the course of the campaign. We want to be clear in making a distinction between the campaign *plan* (which, again, needs to be complete before the campaign begins) and campaign *activities* (which are carried out to execute the campaign plan).

Section 1. District and Demographic Analyses

The district analysis provides important background information on the district's geography, economy, and demographics. A full understanding of the district will help a campaign team form a message—the backbone of any successful campaign—and help the candidate speak knowledgeably about the district, as well as demonstrate to potential voters that the candidate understands the district's needs. The information culled from the district analysis will help form a message because it can be used to help identify what the district's population looks like, as well as, and very likely more importantly, what issues may be important to district voters.

Geography: The district analysis provides the most basic of information—for example, what exactly are the district's boundaries? This information tells the campaigner who the potential voters are. This is important because these individuals, and these individuals only, are the target audience for the campaign. For example, when it comes time to send out a direct mail piece, the campaign does not want to mail to individuals who are unable to vote for the candidate because these individuals do not live within the district's boundaries. In addition, a good geographic analysis will tell the savvy campaigner some important information about the district; is the district a rural, suburban, or urban district, or is it some combination of the three? Each type of district is very different from the others and lends itself to different issues being of major import. For instance, in an urban district, public transportation could very well be an important issue; in a rural district, road construction could be at the top of the list. Moreover, it can help decide tactics the campaign will employ—how realistic is it for the candidate or volunteers to walk the entire district door-to-door given the geographic nature of the area? The sources of information about one's district can be easy to identify and access in many cases. A detailed map of the district can be provided by the state or county elections bureau. We have provided basic district maps for each of the districts included in this simulation, but more detailed maps may be obtained with a little resourceful research.

Economy: Many counties or communities—often through their planning and/or economic development departments—provide relatively up-to-date information on the local economy.[2] The target audience for these reports is usually businesses seeking information about the area with the prospect of locating or relocating in that community. The economic information usually is fairly comprehensive, often published as a "Community Profile," which is typically available on the county's Web site. The data available can include information on the area's labor market statistics (such as labor costs and availability, unemployment rates, and so on); transportation; hospitals (and other health care data); government and public services that are available; crime rates; utilities; local tax rates (as well as any tax incentives that are available); and so on.

A campaign might be able to identify potential issues from the data provided in these publications. For instance, an increasing or high unemployment rate could be a possible campaign issue, as could high taxes or crime rates. If the communities in the district in which the campaign is being waged offer a lot of tax incentives to businesses, that could mean that the local economy is in decline, or that property tax rates are high. This can send a signal to the savvy campaigner about an issue that may be important for the coming campaign.

Demographics: Demographic information such as race, gender, age, educational attainment, income, and so on, may be available through the community profile sources noted earlier, but it is also a good idea to consult the U.S. Census Bureau Web site, as it is an excellent source of critical information. To obtain information on a specific community, once at the main site (www.census.gov), navigate the following links:

- Your Gateway to Census 2000
- Census 2000 Databases
- Demographic Profiles
- Demographic Profile Data Search
- At this point, select the state and type in the name of the county or community for which information is being sought.[3]

We have included summaries for the county and/or communities in the districts that are part of the simulation, but additional information on the districts can be found through more thorough research.

As we have noted, the critical aspect of a district or demographic analysis is the analytic component. Simply collecting statistics and information on the area in which one is campaigning will provide little strategic value. The trick is to use this information as a tool to help the candidate create a comparative advantage over the opposition. We have provided a few examples of how the information in a district analysis can yield potential campaign issues in this section. However, our examples will not hold in every district, and they should not be seen as an exhaustive list of potential issues. Each district analysis will produce information and issues that are specific to the race being contested.

District Analysis Exercises

1. Create a district analysis for your district by pulling out the most important pieces of political information from the data that you gather. Use this information to identify possible issues for the campaign to focus on. For example, what kinds of employment, housing, and population trends are seen in the district? What are the major employers in the district? What other kinds of organizations are in the community that might tell you about the district (and play a role in the campaign)? For example, are organizations such as Veterans of Foreign Wars, the Chamber of Commerce, and labor unions present in the district? The important question to

consider after gathering this information is: What will these data mean for the campaign?

2. Conduct a demographic analysis of your district. What are the people like who live in the district? Characteristics such as race, gender, age, ethnicity, poverty rate, and income should be included in your analysis, but feel free to go beyond these. For instance, what kind of educational levels do the district's residents have? Much of this information can be obtained from the data provided, but a more complete picture can be found by looking to other data found on the U.S. Census Bureau Web site or other sources specific to the district in which one is working. Again, the important question here is: How do these demographic characteristics of the district impact your campaign strategy (for instance, who are your likely supporters, and what issues might be important in this district)?

DISTRICT ANALYSIS WORKSHEET

What are the main boundary lines of your district? _____

_____

_____

_____

What are the main geographic features of your district, and are there any defining characteristics of the district such as major lakes, rivers, mountains, and so on?

_____

_____

_____

Is your district located in an urban, rural, or suburban area, or is it a mixture of two or more types of areas?

_____

_____

_____

What are the major economic conditions of the district—unemployment rate, poverty rate, housing costs, home ownership rate, crime rate, and so on?

_____

_____

_____

What are the major employers in the district? What industries or services are represented? _____

_____

_____

_____

What does this information mean? What kinds of issues might be important in this district given what you have found about the area? This is the important part of this analysis. _____

_____

_____

_____

DEMOGRAPHIC ANALYSIS WORKSHEET

What is the racial makeup of your district? What percent of the population is African American, Hispanic American, Asian American, and so on?

___

Are there any large blocks of specific ethnicities (Italians, Germans, Hungarians, and so on) in your district? ___

___

What is the average age of the people in your district? What is the breakdown of different age categories—18 and under, 19–25, 26–35, 36–45, 46–55, 56–65, and 65 and over?

___

What is the gender breakdown of your district? ___

___

How much money do people make in your district? Is it a wealthy area, a poor area, a middle class area, or is it mixed, with some areas of each type? If so, what are those different areas?

___

How educated are the people of your district? How many have high school diplomas, college degrees, graduate degrees, and so on? What kind of elementary and secondary schools are there in the district—are they known as good schools or poorly performing schools? Are there a lot of private schools in the district? ___

___

What does this information mean? What kinds of issues might be important in this district given what you have found about the area? This is the important part of this analysis. ___

___

Section 2. Electoral Research

Understanding the district includes understanding its voters. Note that we use voters here rather than citizens or residents. This is not an oversight, but done specifically to make a point in this section. When push comes to shove, on Election Day what matters is which candidate has more voters mark his name on the ballot. Knowing about past voting trends is critical to understanding what has to be done during the present campaign to help a candidate get to the ultimate goal—winning the election.

The importance of electoral research cannot be overstated, and, like the district analysis, it should be conducted and completed well before the campaign begins. For instance, in some cases, an analysis of a district's voting history might convince a candidate that winning the election is not very likely, because the voters have historically supported candidates of another party. This may even impact a potential candidate's decision to run. However, if the candidate definitely has decided to run for office, research on the district's past voting patterns will go into the set of information that helps the candidate and her campaign team decide how best to approach the rest of the campaign.

There are a great many areas where electoral research can help a campaign. In this simulation, we will focus on two. First, the research conducted will help the campaign team estimate the answer to the critical question "How many votes do we need to win?" We also encourage campaign teams in the simulation to ask (and try to answer) another important question early on—where are the supporters likely to be within the district (that is, where are they located in the district geographically)? In answering these questions, a campaign team will begin to focus on both a strategy and a set of tactics that will become part of the campaign plan's framework. Second, electoral research will inform the campaign about what kind of district it is facing—is it a strongly Democratic district, a strongly Republican district, or is it a swing district where neither party has an historical advantage?

Campaigns for president of the United States and other high-level races tend to have resources to identify and track (through survey research) levels of voter support and what a candidate's "favorability" ratings are with voters. In down-ballot races such as those we are focusing on, sometimes only basic voter information is accessible and affordable. However, some important information can be obtained for little or no money by accessing results from previous races similar to that in which one is competing, and determining vote totals for party candidates in the district.

Voting Statistics: Despite the fact that increasing numbers of voters in high-level campaigns make their vote choices based on candidate characteristics or issues—and not party affiliation—campaigns in lower-level races, such as those for state legislative seats, will probably find party affiliation the most important predictor of a person's vote. State legislative races have been called "low-information" races because voters tend to know little about the candidates or the issues, and the lack of media attention they tend to receive. Consequently, when voters do not have much information about a race, they tend to adopt one of several different decision rules, each of which can be classified as a heuristic or decision-making shortcut: (1) they simply do not vote for that office; (2) they vote for a candidate based on the candidate's ethnicity; (3) they vote for a candidate based on gender; or (4) they vote for the candidate of their favorite political party.

Because of the role that partisanship plays in these races, a central component of electoral research is identifying the "base party vote" in a given precinct or district. This calculation can give a campaigners an idea of how many party loyalists will support the candidate and how many will support the opponent. Once those figures are calculated, the remaining voters in the district can be considered "swing" voters (or "persuadable" voters).

The base party vote calculation is simple. In reviewing the district's voting history (results from past elections are obtainable from the county or city clerk or the state's chief election official), look for the candidate from each party who received the *lowest* percentage of votes in the district in any of the previous elections for which data have been collected (we provide the last three) (also, the lowest percentage can be for a candidate running for any office being contested). This estimates the absolute worst that a candidate of that party will do in an election. The idea is as if one is saying, "If that many people in this district will vote for that candidate, that is the absolute worst we could do." In other words, the percentage of the vote garnered by a party's worst performing candidate estimates the party's base vote.

For instance, in the example of a hypothetical state house district and its voting history presented in Table 3.1, there were a few poorly performing Democrats since 1994—the U.S. House candidate in 1998 received just over 32 percent of the vote; and the state house candidate in 1994 totaled just shy of 36 percent. However, the worst-performing Democrat was the gubernatorial candidate in 1998 at 29.9 percent of the vote. Democrats in this district can assume that roughly 30 percent of the voters in this district will vote for their party's candidate, no matter who the candidate is. Again, the logic is that if this number of people voted for a Democratic candidate who performed that poorly, at least that many will vote for *any* Democrat who is running. In the same kind of examination of Republican performances, we find that the worst-performing candidate was a state senate candidate in 1998 who garnered 40.5 percent of the vote. Therefore, the base vote for Democrats and Republicans in this hypothetical district is 30 percent and 40 percent, respectively, and the remaining 30 percent of the district can be characterized as swing voters. This is one indication that the district leans toward the GOP.

One factor in this calculation that cannot be conveyed in this kind of example is the "feel" that may be needed for the calculation. Although it is a simple calculation, this kind of research also has an art to it in that seasoned campaigners may know something about a specific campaign or candidate that might make the numbers misleading. For instance, an individual might have been a strong candidate, but a scandal hit the campaign at the last minute, causing large numbers of voters to support the opposition, thus skewing the figures for the base vote calculation. Or, it may have been that a certain year was just a bad year for one party because of some national or statewide trends in politics and voter turnout. For instance, 1998 may have been affected by the Clinton–Lewinsky scandal. The 1994 elections, which we noted in Chapter 2, would also potentially qualify as an outlier because of the banner year Republicans had nationally. Without this kind of knowledge of the district, one could not factor this into the calculation. Examining old newspaper reports or talking to seasoned politicos in the district are only two strategies for finding this kind of information.

As for estimating how many votes a candidate needs to win, it is again a simple calculation. The purpose of this is to approximate the number of votes that

TABLE 3.1 Vote History Example for a Hypothetical State House District

	1994		1996		1998		2000	
Registered voters	64,007		63,989		64,112		64,004	
Turnout	34,823		45,173		33,002		45,532	
Turnout percent	54.4%		70.6%		51.5%		71.1%	
Election Results								
	Votes	Percent	Votes	Percent	Votes	Percent	Votes	Percent
President								
Republican			19,876	44.7%			21,960	48.2%
Democrat			23,941	53.9%			22,779	50.0%
Other			602	1.4%			793	1.8%
			44,419				45,532	
Governor								
Republican	18,466	56.4%			22,842	70.1%		
Democrat	14,269	43.6%			9,755	29.9%		
	32,735				32,597			
Atty. General								
Republican	17,536	53.4%			17,241	52.4%		
Democrat	15,298	46.6%			15,665	47.6%		
	32,834				32,906			
U.S. Senate								
Republican	17,756	51.2%					22,474	50.9%
Democrat	16,921	48.8%					21,622	49.1%
	34,677						44,096	
U.S. House								
Republican	18,943	59.7%	23,616	54.2%	21,739	67.7%	25,020	59.0%
Democrat	12,796	40.3%	19,917	45.8%	10,374	32.3%	17,404	41.0%
	31,739		43,533		32,113		42,424	
State Senate								
Republican	17,652	55.5%			12,756	40.5%		
Democrat	14,170	44.5%			18,737	59.5%		
	31,822				31,493			
State House								
Republican	20,747	64.2%	24,624	57.7%	20,375	63.9%	22,326	51.1%
Democrat	11,578	35.8%	18,063	42.3%	11,505	36.1%	21,362	48.9%
	32,325		42,687		31,880		43,688	

The number of registered voters in this district for this election is: 65,154.

the candidate will have to garner on Election Day to win. The first step in calculating the number of votes needed to win is to go back to the two (or more) previous elections in the same type of campaign (that is, if it is a presidential year, use previous presidential elections; if it is a mid-term election year, use previous mid-term election results) and identify the voter turnout for the same type of race (that is, a state house race, a state senate race, or a race that is similar in form). Once the past voter turnout percentages have been determined, simply take the average of the turnout percentages from those campaigns. This figure represents an estimate of the turnout percentage for the current election.[4] To identify the number of votes needed to win, simply take the estimated

1994 Turnout
1994 turnout in the state house race: 32,325
Total registered voters in the district: 64,007
Turnout percentage for 1994: 32,325 / 64,007 = **50.5%**

1998 Turnout
1998 turnout in the state house race: 31,880
Total registered voters in the district: 64,112
Turnout percentage for 1998: 31,880 / 64,112 = **49.7%**

Estimated Turnout for Current Election
50.5% + 49.7% / 2 = **50.1%**

Predicted Voter Turnout for Current Election
Total registered voters in district for this election: 65,154
Estimated turnout percent: 50.1%
Estimated turnout: 50.1% x 65,154 = 32,642.1, or **32,643**

Estimated Number of Votes Needed to Win
(32,643 / 2) +1 = **16,322.5 or 16,323**

FIGURE 3.1 Calculation and Estimation of Voter Turnout Votes Needed to Win in a Hypothetical District

turnout percentage, multiply it by the number of registered voters for the current election cycle, divide by two, and add one (1). This figure is 50 percent plus one vote of the estimated voter turnout in a similar race in the district—the lowest number a candidate needs to win the race.[5] Many seasoned campaigners will use this figure as a low estimate and shoot for a higher vote total on Election Day—better to try to achieve more votes than necessary and have a safe margin of victory than shoot too low and achieve that vote total only to lose because the estimate was inaccurate.

In the hypothetical district shown in Table 3.1, the estimated number of votes needed to win would be 16,323. This figure is determined by going back to the two previous similar campaign cycles—1994 and 1998—and looking at the number of individuals who voted in the type of race (state house) in which we are interested. From this we see that in 1994, 32,325 people cast a ballot for state house; in 1996, that number was 31,880. To calculate the voter turnout percentage in these races, find the total number of registered voters and simply divide the number going to the polls by the number of registered voters; here, in 1994 that would be 32,325/64,007 = 50.5%, and in 1998 the calculation would be 31,880/64,112 = 49.7% (see Figure 3.1). The average turnout percentage over these two cycles is 50.5% + 49.7%/2 = 50.1%. Once the turnout percent—50.1%—has been estimated, one can figure the number of votes needed to win by applying that estimated turnout percent to the number of registered voters for the current campaign (65,154 in this example; this can be obtained from the local or county elections office); 50.1% multiplied by 65,154 = 32,642.1. In order to be safe, one always rounds these numbers up. This process yields a predicted turnout figure of 32,643, which represents the estimated number of individuals who will show up at the polls on Election Day in the current election. The number needed to win is simply 50% of this estimate plus one vote. In this example, half of the expected turnout is 16,321.5, or 16,322 (again, always rounding up);

adding one to this figure reveals the estimated number of votes needed to win (16,323).

As we noted earlier, the types of voter statistics we described are available through a county clerk's office in most cases, or potentially a city clerk (if the city is large enough and district boundaries do not extend beyond a single city), or even the state board of elections or secretary of state's office. With the "motor voter" registration reforms of the mid-1990s, many state elections bureau offices maintain centralized qualified voter file records, which track which voters are registered, as well as their addresses, and (in some states) whether they have registered with a political party.

Estimates of the district's base party vote and the number of votes needed to win will drive the campaign's strategy and the tactics used to execute that strategy. Although the number of votes needed to win is the Election Day goal of the campaign, there are also important strategic and tactical components of the information that must be considered. A campaign for state house might approach its race one way if it estimates that it needs 20,000 votes on Election Day, but a state senate campaign would likely approach things much differently strategically and tactically if it found that it needed 200,000 votes to win. In addition, the base party vote can inform the campaign about some of the steps it needs to take to reach its vote goal. For instance, if one finds that a district has a Democratic base vote of 39 percent and a Republican base vote of 27 percent, both candidates know that all their work and effort can be focused on attracting those voters who are part of their party's base votes and the swing vote; they do not have to worry about attracting voters from the opponent's base (which can be the case in many districts).

Though not a part of this simulation, there are some sources of information available to campaigns that can identify specific voters' history of participation. For instance, campaigns can identify those individuals who are regular and frequent voters in all general elections, those who tend to vote only in presidential elections, those who vote regularly in primary elections, and so on. This information (usually offered as a service from private vendors) can be very valuable to a campaign, especially in a primary election, where perhaps only a small percentage of the district's registered voters go to the polls. Knowing who the habitual voters are will help a campaign spend its resources wisely and target its communications carefully.

Again, though it is not part of this simulation, knowing *where* each candidate's base voters are as well as *where* the swing voters tend to be located is central to a campaign plan (and specifically the communication and/or voter contact strategy). In many state legislative races, knowing exactly which voters are supporters and which voters are not may only come from door-to-door or other personal contacts (for example, by telephone). However, some aggregate voter statistics can also be helpful in identifying where certain voters are located. For instance, which precincts tend to be high-turnout precincts? Which are low? For readers interested in a more sophisticated analysis, the figures outlined in the preceding example can also be calculated for each precinct in the district in addition to the district as a whole. This can yield very important information such as the areas that rank high in base voters, areas that rank low in base voters, and areas that are high turnout areas as well as low turnout areas. This information can also be used to target the campaign's communication and voter contact efforts, and at a minimum, should help inform the campaign which polling places must be covered on Election Day as part of a GOTV plan. Voter statistics like those noted here tend to be fairly stable over time (unless the district or precinct boundaries have changed because of a recent redistricting) and one will likely discover that voting turnout patterns are fairly consistent; for example, the same precincts tend to be high turnout (or low turnout) over several elections.

Electoral Research Exercises

1. Based on the data provided about your district, estimate the base vote for each party by using the example in Table 3.1 as a guide. What does this tell you about the district? Is the district friendly territory for candidates of your party or is it hostile? How might this affect your strategy later in the campaign?

2. While others in the campaign are compiling a district and demographic analysis, work must begin on the electoral research analysis. Using information on the electoral history of the district, determine the estimated number of votes you will need to win the election. Use the example in the preceding section as a guide. Remember to account for any important contextual issues that may affect the current campaign, such as whether higher-level races (such as president of the United States or governor) will increase turnout. Also, go back to other elections (not included here) to incorporate more election results if the turnout in the races varies dramatically. The estimate of the number of voters needed to win is one way to set a vote-total goal for the campaign will attempt to reach and answers the question "How many votes do we need to win?" In addition, what other factors should be considered and accounted for in this calculation?

Section 3. Opposition and Candidate Research

As noted in Chapter 2, the ideal campaign message is a combination of issues and candidate characteristics that provide the best advantage to the candidate and is consistently communicated to voters throughout the campaign. Although we will describe the basic process for creating an effective message in the next section, any sound message begins with research into the strengths and weaknesses of the candidate and her opponent. The best way to do this is to conduct an issue and personal inventory of each candidate in the race. Part of the research needed for the message will be obtained from the district and demographic analyses, as it may help identify issues that might be important during the campaign. The rest is conducted through research focused on both candidates in the race in the form of candidate and opposition profiles.

Opposition research is a process through which a campaign examines its opponent's public past in search of information that can be used to highlight reasons why that candidate should not be elected to office. "Opposition research taps into the process of retrospective evaluation. It is an attempt to convey the perils of selecting the opponent by pointing out the shortcomings of past behavior" (Shea and Burton 2001, 60). In addition to knowing as much as possible about the opposition, all campaigns should practice one strategic principle: Know thyself. No campaign should be unprepared for what the opposition will say about its own candidate based on something that the candidate has done in the past. "The only way to be prepared for negative attacks is to know what the opposition might have" (Shea and Burton 2001, 60).

Opposition and candidate research is a way for those involved in the campaign to get to know the candidates and to identify those areas where their candidate has a comparative advantage over the opponent and vice versa.

The research on one's own candidate might appear to be simple at first glance. However, this activity requires a frank discussion between the campaign manager (usually) and the candidate, including detailed descriptions of any candidate weaknesses that might be relevant to the campaign; in other words, the candidate must face, and be prepared to deal with, any skeletons in her closet. This can be a difficult subject for team members to raise with candidates because some of the material may be uncomfortable to discuss.

True opposition research focuses on aspects of a candidate's public record (activities that the individual has engaged in while serving in public office, for example), or elements of his life that could affect his ability to serve in office. There are several sound ideas of how to conduct opposition research and what kinds of information needs to be collected (see Shea and Burton 2001), but here we will limit the discussion to the two basic types of information just noted that will allow a campaign to identify strengths and weaknesses about both candidates: personal and public information. The candidates' public record can be broken down into the following categories:

- *Roll-call voting record:* If the candidate (remember that research of this nature holds for both the campaign's opponent and its own candidate) has held elected office in the past, how has he voted on key issues relating to the district or issues that are important to the district's voters?

- *Public statements:* If the candidate has previously served as a public official or has run for office before, what has she said to the public and the press about public policy problems? If the candidate is a first-time candidate, this may be a bit more difficult, but even first-time candidates may have made public statements as part of some other activities.

- *Declared bankruptcy:* Has the candidate filed for personal or business bankruptcy? This may be relevant in a campaign where economic issues are important or if the candidate is running on a platform of "fiscal responsibility."

- *Arrests and Lawsuits:* Have the courts found the candidate to be liable for any civil or criminal infraction? If so, what were the allegations and penalties? Has the candidate been a party to a lawsuit? If so, how recent are the lawsuits and what were the circumstances?

- *Residency:* How long has the candidate lived in the district? Would the candidate be considered a political opportunist or "carpetbagger" (that is, moving into a district just to run for office)?[6] Beyond simple residency, it is often useful to inquire as to whether the candidate is an active member of civic or community organizations.

- *Voting record as a citizen:* Has the candidate voted regularly in all elections at all levels? If not, such information might be used to suggest the candidate does not take his citizenship responsibilities seriously.

Information about each candidate's personal characteristics is generally divided into some of the following categories:

- *Education:* Does the candidate have an educational background that makes her qualified to be an elected public official (for example, a Master's of Business Administration [MBA] or Master's of Public Administration [MPA] degree, or an Accounting or Finance degree)? In addition, if education is an issue in the campaign, it may be useful to find out whether the candidate went to public or private school (and if she has children, where they go to school). If a candidate is making public education a centerpiece of the campaign but attended private school and sends her children to private school, she will have to deal with this contradiction.

- *Occupational history and experience:* What has the candidate been doing prior to seeking elective office? Again, are there any special features that either make him more or less qualified? Does he have prior experience as an elected official? (Remember, this kind of experience can be an advantage or disadvantage, depending on the context.)
- *Military background:* Did the candidate serve in the U.S. armed forces? If so, did he distinguish himself? Did he serve in a combat area or during a war?

Research into one's own candidate should also include aspects that may not seem particularly relevant at first. For instance, a good candidate is someone who likes people, who enjoys talking to people, and who is a good listener. Many, if not most, candidates in state legislative races will likely include walking door-to-door as a part of their voter contact plan. If a candidate does not like to "walk and talk," she will not personally meet as many voters as she probably should. This kind of information will also obviously affect the campaign's strategy and tactics.

Other personal characteristics that have been used in campaigns in the past such as a candidate's religion, marital status, or sexual orientation are considered by many to be out of bounds. It is up to each campaign to decide if characteristics such as these are appropriate for the campaign they are waging.[7]

A well-run campaign will also check to make sure everything on its opponent's (and its candidate's) résumé and all other claims are accurate and truthful. Did the candidate actually earn a degree, or did she just take a few classes toward it? Did he actually serve in the military? If not, the candidate has a lot of explaining to do and may be in big trouble. It is always better to find out about these facts earlier rather than later.

Many campaigners find it useful to organize the information they gather into a summary document called a SWOT analysis, where SWOT stands for Strengths, Weaknesses, Opportunities, and Threats. For instance, strengths are factors that can be counted as assets by the campaign, including certain attributes of the candidate (for example, incumbency, expertise in a certain issue area, or high name recognition among the electorate), support from major voting blocks in the electorate (for example, African Americans, union members, or voters from one part of the district), and financial resources (Powell and Cowart 2003). Weaknesses include negative information from the candidate's public record (for example, votes they have taken while in office, questionable business practices, or failing to pay one's taxes), or an inability to raise money and attract significant support (Powell and Cowart 2003). Opportunities include factors outside of the campaign that *might* prove to be beneficial to the campaign including the state of the economy, prior voting trends in the electorate, a mood among the electorate, or a potential campaign issue that favors the candidate (Powell and Cowart 2003). Threats are the opposite of opportunities; they are external factors that *might* be detrimental to the campaign, and include a weak economy or the departure of an important industry from the district if the candidate is an incumbent. Threats can also include anything that might be used against the candidate, including a possible scandal involving an elected official from the same party (Powell and Cowart 2003). The presence of higher-level races (for example, presidential, U.S. Senate, U.S. House, or gubernatorial campaigns) can be either threats or opportunities, depending on the context of the election cycle.

Opposition and Candidate Research Exercises

1. It is crucial to the campaign that you know as much about the political backgrounds of the opponent against whom you will be competing, as well as your own candidate, as possible. Write an opposition research report, and a candidate research report, on each candidate in the race (for simulation purposes, these are the two candidates in the general election). What kinds of information will you look for? Also, consider what kinds of information are out of bounds for this exercise. Begin with the Candidate Profile Worksheet included in this chapter. Then, expand your research to include other important information that might be relevant to the district and the race in particular.

2. Based on the research you have conducted—the demographic and district analyses, the opposition and candidate research, and the electoral history analysis—what are the strengths and weaknesses of your candidate? What are the strengths and weaknesses of your opponent? Additionally, what are the opportunities for and threats to each candidate? Conduct a SWOT analysis of the two candidates.

CANDIDATE PROFILE WORKSHEET

Candidate Name: _____

What is the candidate's prior career/occupational experience?
_____
_____

If the candidate has held elective office in the past, how did he or she vote on important issues to the district? What were the issues that were voted on and what was the vote that was best for the district? If the candidate did not vote in the best interest of the district, what is his or her explanation?
_____
_____
_____

What issues does the candidate care deeply about and what is his or her position on the issues? What does your candidate want to do once elected?
_____
_____
_____
_____

If the candidate has held elective office and/or run for office before, what kinds of public statements has he or she made to the press or at public rallies about his or her ideas for public policy solutions? If the candidate has not held elective office before, what has he or she said so far in this campaign, or in the past (for example, in op-eds to the newspaper)?
_____
_____
_____
_____
_____

What is the candidate's level of educational attainment and where did he or she attend school?
_____
_____

How long has the candidate been a resident of the district? _____

What kind of voting record does the candidate have as a resident of the district? Has the candidate been active in the democratic process?
_____

What is the candidate's marital and family status? Are issues related to family values going to be important in the campaign? _____

(continued)

CANDIDATE PROFILE WORKSHEET (*continued*)

Does the candidate have any declared bankruptcies or lawsuits, or other legal trouble?

What other personal characteristics, traits, or "skeletons in the closet" does the candidate have that the campaign team should be aware of that could affect the campaign?

Why is this information important? What does it tell you about the candidate? What does it tell you about what your opponent might say about your candidate? Are there any things that you want to avoid in the campaign because of the information you have discovered? In contrast, what kinds of things do you want to stress?

OPPOSITION RESEARCH WORKSHEET

Candidate Name: _____

What is the opponent's prior career/occupational experience? _____

If the opponent has held elective office in the past, how did he or she vote on important issues to the district? What were the issues that were voted on and what was the vote that was best for the district? If the opponent did not vote in the best interest of the district, what is his or her explanation?
_____
_____
_____

What issues does the opponent care deeply about, and what is his or her position on these issues?
_____
_____
_____

If the opponent has held elective office and/or run for office before, what kinds of public statements has he/she made to the press or at public rallies about his/her ideas for public policy solutions? If the opponent has not held elective office before, what has the candidate said so far in this campaign, or in the past (that is, in op-eds to the newspaper)?
_____
_____
_____

What is the opponent's level of educational attainment and where did he or she attend school? _____

How long has the opponent been a resident of the district? _____

What kind of voting record does the opponent have as a resident of the district? Has the opponent been active in the democratic process? _____

What is the opponent's marital and family status? Are issues related to family values going to be important in the campaign? _____

Does the opponent have any declared bankruptcies or lawsuits, or other legal trouble? _____

What other personal characteristics, traits, or "skeletons in the closet" does the opponent have that the campaign team should be aware of that could affect the campaign? _____
_____
_____

(continued)

OPPOSITION RESEARCH WORKSHEET (*continued*)

Why is this information important? What does it tell you about the opponent? What does it tell you about what you might say about as part of your message? Are there any things that you want to avoid in the campaign because of the information you have discovered? In contrast, what kinds of things do you want to stress?

_____
_____
_____
_____
_____

SWOT ANALYSIS WORKSHEET

Candidate
Strengths: _____

Weaknesses: _____

Opportunities: _____

Threats: _____

Opponent
Strengths: _____

Weaknesses: _____

Opportunities: _____

Threats: _____

Section 4. Campaign Message

As previously noted, the campaign's message summarizes the central reason why a candidate should be elected over the opponent. There is no single best way to create a message. However, one tool used by many campaigners is the message box. As we noted in Chapter 2, the message box helps a candidate detail what he would like to say about himself as well as his opponent, and anticipate what the opponent may try to say about herself and the candidate.

The "what we want to say about our candidate" section of the box likely includes strengths, accomplishments, opportunities, and other positive candidate characteristics, as well as issue positions the candidate holds that the campaign will focus on. In the "what we want to say about the opponent" section, the opponent's weaknesses, problems, threats, characteristics, and issues positions the campaign wants to highlight are included. This is the foundation of the comparisons the campaign wants to make between its candidate and its opponent. This is the material that will give voters a choice between the two candidates. The remaining sections of the box are used to try to anticipate what the opponent will say and the kinds of contrasts that she will make during the campaign based on perceived strengths and weaknesses of both candidates, and other opportunities and threats from the opponent's perspective. Notice how the research done on the district and the candidates creates the quadrants of the message box. The SWOT analysis done for each candidate can help make this even clearer.

There are multiple purposes served by creating a message box. Some campaigners use it to organize their thoughts and simply list different items in each part of the box, whereas others begin to develop the actual message by writing a short statement about the items in each quadrant of the box. The final message is then crafted by taking the different segments of the box into account so that one ends up with a strong (but relatively brief) statement that offers a comparison between the two candidates, and tells voters why they should vote for the candidate rather than her opponent.

We have provided enough campaign context and candidate profile information in each case chapter for readers to construct a message box and campaign message without consulting other sources of information. However, readers are encouraged to expand on the information provided, by collecting more elaborate information about the district, campaign issues, and candidate characteristics through research via the World Wide Web, newspaper article searches, and/or phone calls to government agencies holding public documents that would be useful to the campaign.

Message Box and Campaign Message Exercises

1. This campaign is about communicating to the electorate why your candidate should be elected to the state legislature rather than your opponent. However, any campaign needs to know what the candidate should say about him- or herself and what he or she should say about the opponent. Using the research and SWOT analysis your campaign has done, construct a message box for your campaign. Include at least three items in each quadrant of the box. What are the most important and advantageous contrasts to draw between your candidate and the opponent?

2. Take the information from the message box and craft a message for your candidate. This can be derived in part from what issues or characteristics you have identified as your opponent's strengths and weaknesses, but do not forget to reflect on your own candidate's strengths and weaknesses. Usually, the biggest challenge in creating a complete message box is anticipating what the opponent will say about your candidate in his message. Therefore, try to anticipate what your opponent will say and create a message that the opponent's campaign might use.

Message Box Worksheet

Us on Us
What we want to say about
our candidate and our campaign

Us on Them
What we want to say about
the opponent and her campaign

Them on Us
What our campaign anticipates
the opponent will say about our
candidate and our campaign

Them on Them
What our campaign anticipates
the opponent's organization will say about
their candidate and her campaign

Section 5. Budget and Fund-Raising Plan

Budgeting and fund-raising are separate, but related, activities. Creating a budget informs the campaign personnel about how much money they need to raise and how it will be spent; everything done in a campaign will cost money in one way or another. For instance, the advertisements created will have to be printed by a print shop, and if they are going to be mailed, postage will have to be paid; if a radio ad is created for the campaign, it will have to be produced and time will have to be purchased from the radio station(s) on which it will air; the volunteers who work hard for the campaign must be fed; and all the materials needed for research as well as crafting the message (for example, paper and other office supplies) must be purchased. The fund-raising and budget plans outline how the campaign money is going to be raised and spent. The fund-raising plan projects not only an amount, but also the specific strategies the campaign will use to raise the money.

Sources of Campaign Funds There are several ways to ask for money in a campaign. However, the most successful is a direct solicitation by the candidate either in person (ideally) or over the telephone. In addition, solicitations can be done through the mail with a fund-raising letter that is sent to supporters who are potential donors. In some campaigns, political action committees (PACs) and political party organizations will make direct contributions. Candidates and campaigns also hold events—dinners, coffees, dessert receptions, house parties, and so on. Sometimes a fee is required for these events, but in other cases, campaigners hope that invited guests pledge a contribution or make a donation on the spot to the campaign.

In sum, the basic sources of campaign funds are:

- *The candidate:* Candidates for state legislature often contribute (or loan) a good deal of money to their own campaigns.
- *Family and friends:* If a candidate cannot count on his closest allies for monetary support, he may as well not run.
- *Other individuals* (for example, acquaintances from church, co-workers, neighbors, fellow members of community organizations): Potential donors are everywhere.
- *Political party organizations:* Parties are not typically the best sources of money; they may be limited by state law, or just not able to contribute because they have other targeted races on which to focus. However, it never hurts to ask.
- *Political Action Committees (PACs):* PACs are similar to parties in that they may be limited in the amount that they can contribute, or they may simply decide to stay out of the race. However, some ideological, or "single issue," PACs may get involved (even potentially in a primary).

Fund-Raising Techniques In turn, the strategies or techniques used to raise political campaign money are fairly standard as well, but they should be in step with the campaign plan, the candidate, and the campaign message.[8] They include:

- *Personal solicitations* are requests made directly by the candidate. This is best done in person and should probably be restricted to the candidate, and not other members of the campaign team. This can be done at meetings specifically scheduled for this purpose, or can be accomplished at coffees, house parties, and other events where supporters and potential contributors are present. The main point to remember about fund-raising is that people will not give to a campaign unless they are asked. When raising money in this way, a candidate should always try to make the potential donors feel needed and that their contribution will be doing something that is vital to the campaign. For this reason, the appeal should be tied to some specific campaign-related event or cost that the money will be used for. For instance, a candidate may tell a potential donor, "I'm trying to raise $5,000 so we can put a radio spot on the air in two weeks as a final push toward Election Day." An important issue to remember about this kind of fund-raising is that the candidate needs to convey a sense of urgency and purpose with the appeal for a contribution.

- *Direct mail* is a technique that can be used for fund-raising as well as voter contact (see the Paid Media section). Used as a fund-raising technique, direct mail is a written solicitation mailed to targeted households. It is similar to an in-person appeal in that it must convey a sense of urgency to the recipient of the mail piece. However, it is often more difficult to obtain a significant return when appealing to potential donors with a direct mail solicitation for two reasons. First, it costs more than a personal solicitation by the candidate over the phone or in person—it costs money to send out hundreds or thousands of mail pieces—therefore, the net receipts are smaller. Second, it is much easier for the recipients to say "no"—they can simply throw the piece of mail away rather than say "no" to the candidate's face. For this reason, when employing a direct mail approach for fund-raising, the appeal must be even more urgent and purposeful. Because of the uncertainty of raising money with direct mail, many campaigns will use this technique only with individuals who have already demonstrated support for the campaign and a propensity to contribute.

Many campaigns that do use direct mail fund-raising, in addition to including a specific campaign-related purpose for the contribution, also use very emotional and attention-getting language that is targeted to a specific group of potential donors. For instance, a fund-raising appeal targeted at single women under 35 may include language such as: "If you don't send a contribution today, a woman's right to choose will be in jeopardy. Help me fight to protect a woman's right to choose!"

- *Ticketed events* include dinners, golf outings, theater or musical events, and the like. These events have the potential to raise a good deal of money if a large number of tickets are sold at the right price, or they could be a bust. One needs to remember that events such as these can cost a good deal of money to organize and put on, reducing the net revenue from the event, which is the real measure of success in fund-raising.

- *Telemarketing* is an appeal to potential donors by telephone. Some experts emphasize the importance of a "good prospect" list, rather than "cold calling." A known set of potential donors who may have donated to a candidate of the same party in the past is much more likely to produce a return than is a list of individuals who have no history of contributing (Shea and Burton, 2001). Some campaigns also use "peer-to-peer" calling, where campaign supporters volunteer to call their own friends and network of associates asking for contributions on behalf of their candidate.

- *Other techniques* Some campaigns have solicited small ($5–$10) contributions initially, which put contributors on an "Insiders" mailing list. Campaign updates and other special attention is given to these contributors, and larger contributions are solicited later. Some high-level campaigns (for example, for president of the United States, U.S. Senate, or governor) have had success in raising contributions via the Internet. These Web solicitations require very little overhead, but are less successful for lower-level races simply because the number of likely donors is so much smaller.

Earlier in this section we noted that a campaign's fund-raising plan should be consistent with its campaign message. It may seem like the fund-raising plan and the overall campaign plan would not conflict because in fund-raising the campaign is only raising money. In fact, the ways in which a campaign raises funds can easily conflict with the campaign's message. For instance, if a candidate is campaigning as a friend to organized labor, he should not hold a $500-per-plate dinner with heads of local industries. One final very important note needs to be conveyed: Regardless of the fund-raising strategy, remember that contribution limits established by the state's campaign finance laws (which vary from state to state) must be followed. For instance, do not have a $1,000-per-plate dinner if the legal limit on individual contributions is $750.

Budgeting and Fund-Raising Exercises

1. At the end of each case chapter is a budget figure that will serve as a contextual guide for the activities your campaign will engage in. This budget number is specific to the district in which you will be working. Although we have given you a budget for the campaign, you still have to be able to raise that amount of money. Develop a fund-raising plan that outlines how that money will be raised. From what sources are you going to solicit funds? How are you going to solicit funds? Are you going to use direct mail, personal solicitations, events, or a combination of tactics? Be sure to figure the *net* revenue from each fund-raising activity that you plan—remember, it takes money to make money! Most importantly, be sure to operate within the campaign finance regulations set out in state law. (These are covered in each case chapter.)

2. You have just finalized the last ad the campaign will mail out to swing voters (see the Paid Media section). The campaign needs to pay the printer and the post office in three weeks. Write a fund-raising letter for your campaign to send out on behalf of the candidate. Use the information given earlier in this section as a guide. Remember the importance of conveying urgency and emotion in fund-raising appeals. What issues will you talk about in the letter, or will you not discuss issues? How are you going to turn *potential* donors into donors? What else should you include in the letter?

Section 6. Volunteer Recruitment and Use

For many state legislative campaigns, much of what a campaign organization needs to accomplish will be done using volunteers. Many times, there are no paid staff members at all, and in other cases there is only one paid staff member—possibly the campaign manager. Any campaign that is able to recruit and retain volunteers will likely be more successful than one with few or no volunteers. In a large number of campaigns where only a few individuals are part of the "core team," the organization might include only the candidate, campaign manager, and a volunteer coordinator.

As one component of the overall campaign plan, a sound volunteer recruitment and use plan should be developed early on. The volunteer plan includes specific volunteer activities and tasks, and a calendar of when these activities will be performed.

Among the campaign tasks that could be assigned to volunteers:

- Dropping literature door-to-door
- Walking door-to-door with the candidate
- Making telephone calls (for example, for voter contact, GOTV, or other purposes)
- Working at campaign headquarters (for example, working with computer lists, sending press releases, and so on)
- Stuffing envelopes and putting address labels on envelopes
- Putting up yard signs
- Recruiting more volunteers
- Helping organize and participating in campaign events
- Selling tickets to fund-raiser events

A comprehensive volunteer plan is important because the campaign personnel need to be prepared to deal with any number of volunteers at any given time. A campaign might not see very many volunteers for weeks at a time, and then on one weekend day, 20 volunteers could show up. If there is nothing for them to do, they will likely become bored and leave (and probably never return). In many cases, campaign organizations have volunteer interest cards printed, on which contact information for a volunteer can be provided, and other information such as specific skills (for example, computer software knowledge) or interests (for example, telephone calling or walking the district) can be indicated. In this way, a volunteer's individual strengths can be tailored to the campaign's needs. The volunteers will also be happier about their campaign experience and more likely to return if they are doing something they enjoy. It is also a good idea to estimate how long each activity will take, as many volunteers become tired or bored after two or three hours; and a task only partially completed is not much use to the campaign. Proper planning in terms of the time needed to complete each task will help ensure a positive volunteer experience.

What are the primary sources of a campaign's volunteer base? Volunteers can come from anywhere. They can wander in off the street, be signed up during a door-to-door walk through the district, recruited at a community event, and so on; however, four mainstays include: family and friends, loyal party activists, issue activists, and students from local high schools and universities.

- Family and friends are the individuals who will likely be the core of a volunteer force because they have the closest ties to the candidate and probably the most emotional involvement in the campaign outside of the candidate.

- Political party activists are a good source of volunteers because they have likely been involved in campaigns in the area in the past and have some knowledge about what needs to happen in a campaign. They can be fairly easy to find because the party headquarters in the area may keep a list of names of potential volunteers.

- "Issue activists" friendly to the candidate's position on specific issues are another good source. These individuals will likely work very hard for the candidate simply because of their agreement on one issue. Potential groups to target could include pro-life or pro-choice groups, gun control activists or Second Amendment advocates, Chamber of Commerce members, veterans groups, or any number of other groups in the community. The difficult part here is identifying the groups that might be willing to help the candidate and getting commitments from their members to join the campaign team.
- University and high school students, especially those who have internship or community service requirements to fulfill, are also prime targets for a volunteer recruitment drive.

Volunteer Use Exercises

1. You are in the midst of a voter identification drive and you will be asking volunteers to go door-to-door to talk to potential supporters. However, you want them to be prepared and able to articulate the campaign's message at the first door they walk up to. Create a "walking script" for your campaign volunteers who will be canvassing door-to-door. Make sure the script is short and understandable. The script might start out with "Hello, my name is . . . and I am working for Joe Public who is running for state representative in this district." What other information should you include? Which (and how many) issues do you include? What must you say after you provide information about the candidate and campaign?

2. For the campaign you are working on, indicate where the most likely sources of volunteers will be, and explain your rationale. For example, does your candidate have certain qualities or characteristics that would encourage young people, church-goers, teachers, or other groups and individuals to volunteer? Be specific in your reasoning. How many volunteers do you expect to recruit? What will you have them do, and when will you have them do it? How will you ensure a positive experience so the volunteers will return?

Section 7: Paid Media

Once a candidate has decided on his campaign's message, the campaign needs to decide how the message will be delivered. Typically, candidates communicate to voters directly (that is, in person) or in a mediated way (that is, with radio, TV, or newspaper advertisements or direct mail). Direct voter contact comes through door-to-door canvassing, meetings with voters' or homeowners' groups, and small group gatherings of voters with the candidate (for example, fund-raisers, coffees, house parties, or meet-the-candidate events).

Although voters have a greater opportunity to meet personally with a state legislative candidate than they do a candidate for Congress or president of the United States, most voters still probably learn about candidates through paid or earned media. Paid media in lower-level races tends to take the form of direct mail and literature pieces left on doors during "lit drops." Some radio and television (cable or network affiliate) ads may be run in highly competitive—and expensive—state legislative campaigns. But, as we have noted previously, these instances are rare. Paid media also includes lawn signs, campaign buttons, bumper stickers, and GOTV literature.

Campaigns need to identify professional printers (for literature), photographers (to take still photos that will be used in literature), and companies that specialize in campaign lawn signs, buttons, billboards, and other printed advertising. A media specialist should have information on all newspapers, radio stations, and cable and network affiliate stations serving the district, as well as the advertising rates. Usually, TV and radio station representatives will tell the campaign about their viewership or listenership and the audience's demographics, which can help the campaign target its message to the right audience for maximum effectiveness (important because of the market segmentation taking place in radio and television). This, along with cost, is why targeted direct mail is often the most widely used paid media vehicle in lower-level races. As we noted in Chapter 2, specific messages can be sent to specific individuals who have certain characteristics. Ideally, a campaign sends mail only to likely voters, without wasting resources on those who will not be voting (or who may not even live in the voting district). We have included here some examples of paid media print advertisements so the reader can see what kind of materials are typically created.

LEADERSHIP INTEGRITY FAMILY

Addison Brandon Groveland Holly Lake Orion Oxford Rose

Small Business Owner: Opposes all tax increases and service charges.

Family: Watchdog on education; married, two children; Ortonville Methodist Church parishioner.

Education: B.A. Criminal Justice, Columbia College; Graduate of Oxford High School.

Service to Country: U.S. Navy 1986-1994.

Political: Oakland County Executive Board, Precinct Delegate, 2000 and 2004 Bush/Cheney Oakland County Co-Chair, Grass Roots Republican.

Affiliations: GOP, MI GOP, OCRP, NORC, American Legion, IOPP (Vice President, Detroit Chapter), Columbia College Alumni Association, Pontiac Chamber of Commerce, Clarkston Chamber of Commerce, North Oakland Headwaters Land Conservancy, Cycle Conservation Club of Michigan.

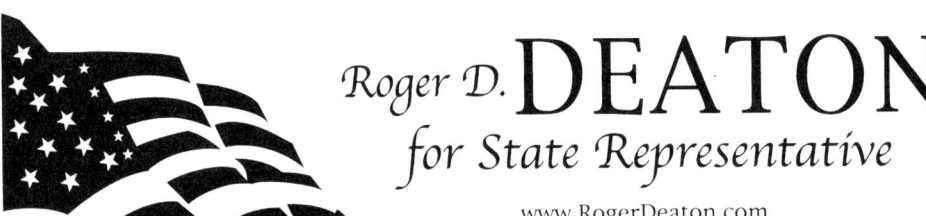

www.RogerDeaton.com

Yes, I would like to support Roger D. Deaton to be State Representative!

- ☐ Endorse Roger, may use name(s) for print and communication purposes
- ☐ Volunteer for Roger's campaign
- ☐ Would like to make a contribution to Roger's campaign

Name(s): _____

Address: _____

City: _____ MI Zip: _____

E-mail: _____ Phone: _____

Please make checks payable to *Friends of Roger D. Deaton* in any amount not to exceed $500. Mail all correspondence to 3175 Oakhill Place, Clarkston, Michigan 48348.

Paid for by Friends of Roger D. Deaton

Reprinted with permission from Roger D. Deaton.

Elect   *Elect*

Roger D.
DEATON

Republican for State Representative District 46

Vote August 3rd

Thank You for Your Support!
www.rogerdeaton.com
Paid for by Friends of Roger D. Deaton

Reprinted with permission from Roger D. Deaton.

Reprinted with permission from Sean Carlson.

SEAN CARLSON for State Senate
15TH DISTRICT
COMMITTED LEADERSHIP YOU CAN TRUST!

SEAN CARLSON for State Senate

Dear Citizens:

It is time to send a Senator to Lansing who will be committed to preserving the quality of life for all of Michigan's families and citizens. President Lincoln said, "government of the people, by the people, for the people." This principled statement reflects the importance of representation for all and is why I am running for State Senator in District 15.

We need leadership in Lansing that will bring a no-nonsense approach to resolving the issues that challenge Michigan today. I believe we need a Senator who will fight to ensure that tax dollars sent to Lansing are being spent wisely and effectively. This means focusing on practical solutions to real problems.

Citizens' confidence has been shattered by ineffective legislation and partisan politics. I believe that trust is the cornerstone of effective leadership. I will work hard everyday to earn your trust by working with both Democrats and Republicans to bring meaningful change and effective leadership.

I would like to ask for your vote. Join me in our fight to bring committed and trustworthy leadership to Lansing. Thank you for your time and consideration!

Sincerely,

Sean L. Carlson

P.O. Box 618
(248) 366-7121

Milford, MI 48381
www.carlsonforsenate.com

What others say about Sean Carlson...

"...You took the challenge seriously and performed admirably...Your success in helping the families of the victims in this accident is due to a team effort—one possible only through professionals like yourself who unselfishly did what ever it took when called upon. Again, I thank you for your hard work and concern for the families."

Sheila E. Widnall
Secretary of the Air Force

"Problem solver who gets positive results. His understanding of complex contracting problems and creative common sense approach has resulted in a savings to the Government totaling $2 million plus for 1994 alone."

Gary L. Delaney
Colonel US Air Force

"Sean's innovative ideas and leadership were key reasons why we were among one of the most profitable Market Units in Pepsi Bottling Group during 2001."

Greg Moore
General Manager, Pepsi Bottling Group

"When I retired and my pension was not coming in I made one phone call to Sean and he made sure that the matter was handled quickly. This is the kind of constituent service we need in Lansing."

Lenzie Waggoner
Retiree and 30 Year Employee,
Pepsi Bottling Group

SEAN CARLSON
for State Senate

Why Sean Carlson...

Qualified Business Background
- Manager at a Fortune 500 Company
- Promoter of fair paying jobs and equal pay for equal work
- Problem solver devoted to win-win solutions
- Bachelors in Business Administration, MSU
- Masters in Labor Relations & HR, MSU
- Juris Doctorate in Law, MSU-DCL

Dedicated To Country & Community
- At 17, enlisted in the Michigan Army National Guard.
- Commissioned as an Officer in 1992 and served on active duty at Andrews AFB, Maryland
- Currently a Captain in the US Air Force Reserves
- Mentored inner city school children
- Coached youth sports
- Teaches Sunday School
- Volunteer for Council Against Domestic Abuse, Teen Suicide Prevention and the American Cancer Society

Committed To Fighting For Michigan Taxpayers
- Track record for fighting against wasteful government spending
- Recipient of the Joint Services Medal of Honor for saving millions of hard earned taxpayers' dollars
- Committed to investigating and eliminating wasteful spending in Lansing

Trusted To Get The Job Done
- Committed to restoring your trust in elected officials
- Dedicated to placing Michigan families and citizens above petty politics

Why 2002...
TIME FOR BOLD NEW LEADERSHIP

Michigan families and businesses need a Senator who will go to LANSING and:

Protect family savings and income
- Attack double digit insurance premiums
- Sponsor affordable prescription drug programs
- Fight for affordable higher education
- Institute tax credits for families caring for senior family members

Promote legislation to strengthen the Michigan economy
- Reform property tax assessment so seniors are not pushed out of their homes and communities
- SBT deductions for employers that provide healthcare to their employees

Bring a no-nonsense business approach to government
- Cut wasteful government spending
- Advocate fiscal responsibility
- Sponsor campaign finance reform

Focus on improving public education
- Provide 21st Century Curriculum
- Ensure that more school funding $$ are reaching students in the classroom
- Reduce class size in grades K-4

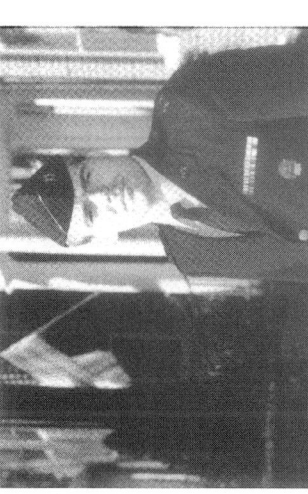

Committed Leadership
...You Can Trust!

Paid for by Sean Carlson for State Senate • Tony Zambelli, Treasurer
P.O. Box 618 • Milford, MI 48381 • (248) 366-7121

Paid Media Exercises

1. Prepare a literature piece for your campaign that could be used for a direct mailing, or as a "lit drop" piece. (Note: These are usually similar in form; only the delivery mechanism is different.) Refer to the examples included in this text to help you determine the general "look" of a typical literature piece (however, do not feel that you must adhere to these examples—use your creativity to create an eye-catching piece that connects and resonates with voters). Remember to focus on your campaign message and the information you created as part of your SWOT analysis and the development of the message box. Distribute the literature piece to voters (and be prepared to answer questions from reporters regarding its fairness and accuracy).

Press Exercise Related to Paid Media Exercise 1

1a. As a journalist, you have just seen the advertisements prepared by the campaigns. Write a critique of the ads for your newspaper. Did the advertisements contain relevant information? Did they contain attacks? Did they use truthful information? This exercise, when conducted by actual reporters, is called an "ad watch." For more information about these kinds of stories, conduct research on ad watches and look for news stories from television networks or newspapers.

2. Sometimes a campaign needs to try to move a large number of voters in its direction at the end of a campaign. This could be for several reasons—the campaign's message has not resonated with the voters thus far, the voters have not been paying attention to the campaign, or the opponent has simply waged a good campaign. Relying on the research the campaign has conducted and the message that has been crafted, create an advertisement for the campaign featuring the candidate that will come out one week before Election Day. This can be a print ad for the newspaper, or a radio spot that will be played on one or more of the stations serving the district. Remember this is an ad that is designed to come near the end of the campaign. Given the late timing of the ad, will you use different types of information? Will you focus on different issues? Be creative.

Section 8. Earned Media

Earned media includes any aspect of the campaign covered as a news story. This could include a short story on the evening news about a campaign event, but it could also include any interviews, speeches, and debates that are covered by the media. Campaigns (through the press secretary or media relations staff member) may also send regular press releases to all news outlets regarding campaign events or other campaign activities. As we noted in Chapter 1, attracting earned media in down-ballot races can be challenging. Sometimes the local media may only report on the campaign when the candidate first announces her candidacy, summarize all of the candidates running for office just prior to Election Day, and report the results after Election Day. The challenge to the campaign is to attract beneficial coverage of as many events as possible.

As part of an earned media plan, a campaign should identify all the ways in which they can attract coverage of the candidate by the local media. This can include press releases, media events, candidate forums and debates, or simple interviews with reporters. The candidate may also consider writing an op-ed piece for the local paper's editorial page.

As part of this work, a campaign should have information about all media outlets serving the district. (Remember, there will likely be some news organizations that are located outside of the district, but serve residents of the district.) Names of reporters, their phone and fax numbers as well as email addresses, and the names and phone numbers of editors should be obtained before the campaign begins.

Earned Media Exercises

1. You are part of the team working with the candidate to kick off the campaign with a bang. The candidate wants to hold a rally after filing paperwork with the state. Write a campaign announcement speech for the candidate. What should the candidate say to the electorate? What issues will be important to talk about in this speech? Remember, these are the first words that some potential voters will hear from your candidate. What might you have the candidate talk about so as to garner media attention?

2. Earned media is an important part of any campaign. Sometimes, however, it is difficult to get journalists to notice campaigns for offices such as state legislature. Write a press release in conjunction with the announcement speech event that will attract media attention for your candidate. What material about the candidate should you include? What kind of material and language should you include so as to attract media attention? Remember, unless the press covers it and people read or hear about it, the event may as well not have happened.

Press Exercise Related to Earned Media Exercises 1 and 2

2a. Both candidates have announced they will declare their candidacies in speeches tomorrow and have sent you press releases about the speeches. Write a news story covering the speech and the reaction to the speech. What did the candidates say that was important for the district? What did they fail to say? What was the reaction from potential voters?

3. Your candidate has agreed to debate the opponent before the upcoming election. It is incumbent on your team to prepare the candidate for the upcoming debate. Using the research you have done, prepare a briefing for the candidate, getting him or her ready for the debate with the opponent. Be sure to include questions that you think will be posed by both the moderator and the opponent during the debate. Also, work with the candidate to prepare answers to the questions you anticipate. Finally, try to anticipate what the opponent will say in answers to questions so you can have rebuttal responses ready.

Press Exercise Related to Earned Media Exercise 3

3a. The candidates have just held a spirited debate. Write a news story that reports on the debate and how the candidates handled themselves. Did they talk about issues? Which ones? Were they issues that were important to the district? (Note: To be a good reporter in this exercise, you must also know a good deal about the district. Therefore, performing similar district and demographic analyses to those described earlier will be beneficial.) Did the candidates attack each other? Did they answer the questions sufficiently? Did each candidate ask good questions of the other candidate?

Section 9. Get-Out-The-Vote

Near the end of the campaign, especially in the week or so before Election Day, campaigns put most of their energy toward "get-out-the-vote" (GOTV) efforts. By this time, the campaign will have identified likely supporters—and the campaign will want to make sure that these supporters vote! This also includes any activities related to GOTV efforts associated with absentee voters (that is, those voters who, for one reason or another, are not able to make it to their polling place on Election Day, and cast their ballot by mail), which usually begin in the month prior to the election (when absentee ballots are sent to voters—check with local election officials to find out exactly when).

GOTV activities can take a number of forms, in some combination of those listed here (or using all of these techniques). Volunteers sometimes place reminder "door hanger" literature the night before Election Day on doorknobs or handles of front doors encouraging people to vote. These would be placed *only* on known supporters' doors. Reminder telephone calls to identified supporters also may be made the evening before Election Day. Sometimes, in the week prior to the election, campaign volunteers will also send "friend-to-friend" postcards as a reminder to vote—and to support the candidate. Ideally, campaign volunteers will be able to staff each of the district's polling places throughout the day and hand out literature. However, depending on the size of the district, the number of polling places, and the number of volunteers the campaign has, the campaign may not be able to staff all of the precincts for the entire day. When such a situation arises, a good strategy is to prioritize the polling places by past turnout results (as identified through the electoral research) and to focus on high-turnout precincts and high turnout times of the day.

A GOTV strategy also needs to be mindful of where the candidate will be throughout Election Day. Usually the candidate votes early, then visits high-turnout polling places. Of course, the campaign's strategy will place the candidate at strategic polling places during peak voting times (in the morning before work, around lunchtime, and in the late afternoon and early evening after work).

Get-Out-The-Vote Exercise

1. The campaign is in the final push for votes, as the election is going to be close. Every last vote will be crucial to whether you win or lose. Devise a get-out-the-vote plan for the campaign for the final weekend before Election Day. Where should your candidate spend her time? What other kinds of efforts and activities should you focus on? What will you have volunteers do during this time?

Section 10. The Campaign Calendar

All campaigns work with the same time constraints. Proper planning helps ensure that time-consuming activities (door-to-door canvassing, for example) can be completed prior to Election Day. Specific dates for certain activities (for example, when lawn signs may go up, and when mailings go out) must also be identified. The campaign calendar details the dates by which all campaign activities need to be performed. To accomplish this, some campaigns may work backward from Election Day when planning to make sure all tasks have been accounted for by the proper date. In addition, the timing of fund-raisers must relate to when funds must be spent. The calendar is interwoven throughout the entire campaign plan, because timing plays a key role in all activities. For example, a direct mail piece cannot be purchased if the necessary funds have not been raised to pay for producing and mailing the piece. Additionally, the candidate will not finish walking door-to-door in the important precincts in the district if the time it will take to walk each precinct has been miscalculated. The timing of volunteer activities, the purchasing of necessary materials (for example, literature, yard signs, flyers, and so on), and when each is needed must all be coordinated. Fund-raising events must be planned weeks, if not months, in advance to secure a facility, order food and beverages, solicit door prizes, and sell tickets. An organized campaign always will have an advantage over a campaign that has not planned its calendar carefully because there is less chance of inefficient activity or wasted resources.

Campaign Calendar Exercise

1. Being in the right places during a campaign is important. It is likely that there are certain events that happen in the district that are "musts" for the candidate to attend throughout the course of the campaign. (Many of these events are related to the community and can be discovered by consulting the local Chamber of Commerce or the local board of tourism.) Create a calendar of events for the candidate over the course of the month preceding Election Day. What kinds of activities should the candidate be engaged in? How do you balance the other responsibilities of the candidate (work, family, and so on) with those of the campaign? Also, think about specific dates and deadlines. For example, when it is legally allowable for lawn signs to go up? When do you have to file your campaign finance reports? Fill in the calendar with as much detail as possible.

ADDITIONAL EXERCISES: CRISIS MANAGEMENT AND CAMPAIGN ETHICS[9]

In real-life campaigns, there are often crises and ethical dilemmas that arise unexpectedly. In many cases, campaigns must respond and react in a fairly short period of time. Oftentimes, the campaign's response must come in the form of a public statement to the media.

Crisis Management[10]

The exercises outlined in this section may be introduced at various points during the campaign simulation (or discussed independently), and are designed to stimulate thinking about how different, and sometimes competing, interests must be handled.

1. State election law requires that all campaign material and mailings have a disclaimer printed somewhere on the literature that indicates the name of the committee that paid for that literature (for example, "Paid for by the Committee to Elect John Doe"). A direct mail piece that you ordered (in a quantity of 10,000) comes back from the printer with no disclaimer on it. You are scheduled to mail it in two days, but your volunteers are arriving in six hours to stuff it into envelopes and prepare it for mailing. What do you do? Explain your decision.

2. Your candidate comes into campaign headquarters very angry after hearing an opponent's attack ad on the radio. The information in the ad is documented, but it is misleading and taken out of context. How do you handle the immediate problem with your candidate? Do you recommend responding to the ad? If so, how and why? Explain.

3. A local reporter claims to have discovered information that reveals your candidate smoked marijuana "on at least several occasions" while in college 20 years ago. Your candidate cannot be reached. As campaign manager, the reporter calls you and asks for an immediate response, as the reporter's deadline is two hours away. You sense that the reporter is writing a very negative article. How do you handle the initial phone call? What do you do in the next two hours?

4. A husband and wife each have made a $250 contribution to your candidate's campaign. This morning, they called campaign headquarters after hearing a negative ad on the radio that your campaign put out recently against your opponent. They feel they cannot support you any longer because they do not like the tone or approach of the campaign. They are seeking to have their contributions returned to them. What do you do? Explain.

5. After an early morning breakfast meeting, you walk into your campaign headquarters at 10 a.m. on Monday and are given the following three phone messages:

   a. The most-watched local TV news station has called for a reaction to a public opinion poll they commissioned, which has your opponent leading your candidate 50% to 35%, with 15% undecided. They will air the story on the noon news program and on the evening news.

   b. Your lawn sign captain called in to say that most of your campaign signs in Precincts 1, 2, and 7 have been taken down, or, in many cases, have been moved to unauthorized houses. Many residents have called campaign headquarters, and some have contacted the media, to complain.

   c. Your volunteer coordinator has been trying to reach you. There are 10 unhappy volunteers waiting in the office, ready to mutiny, because they are tired of dropping literature every day they go out. You were planning to have them drop literature again beginning at 10:30 a.m.

   How do you spend your time between 10 a.m. and 12 p.m.? Explain.

6. You and your candidate have just had a full day of campaigning. You are at an early dinner and need to schedule the remainder of the day. You have gotten a number of requests for the candidate's time for this evening. Knowing that the candidate cannot accept each of the invitations, establish a schedule from 6 p.m. until 10 p.m. based upon where you think the candidate should be. You have four hours left in the day, but have received numerous requests for the candidate's time. Which events do you go to and why?

a. Tomorrow morning at 9 a.m. your candidate has a TV debate with the opponent. She needs about 30 minutes of quiet time to prepare.

b. Your campaign organization's weekly meeting is tonight at the headquarters. The group usually meets from about 7 p.m. to 9 p.m.

c. Your candidate is drastically behind on her door-to-door schedule in some important precincts in the district. (This time of year, it stays light until about 9:00 p.m.)

d. Your finance chair wants the candidate to meet for 15 minutes with a potential large contributor. The contributor is available tonight from 5:00 p.m. to 7:00 p.m. at his residence (but it is on the other side of the district from where you are now).

e. The local Chamber of Commerce would like your candidate to speak to 200 members for about 15 minutes. The reception starts at 7:30 p.m., the meeting begins promptly at 8 p.m., and they would like the candidate to speak starting at 8:15 p.m.

f. One of the very active neighborhood associations is hosting a "Meet the Candidate" reception tonight from 7:30 p.m. to 9:00 p.m. and they would like the candidate to be there. The association expects 30 to 40 residents to attend and a few reporters to stop by.

g. The candidate's son has his first high school basketball game tonight. The game begins at 7:30 p.m. and ends about 10:00 p.m.

h. The president of a local labor union would like your candidate to debate the opponent on labor issues at tonight's meeting. About 300 members will be attending. The meeting and debate will begin at 8:00 p.m. and last about one hour.

Campaign Ethics[11]

The following exercises are a series of ethical dilemmas where the best course of action does not always immediately present itself. When thinking about each of these dilemmas, consider the different facets of each scenario as well as the actors and issues involved. Included here are considerations of who is involved, but also how it affects (in both the short- and long-term) the campaign in which you are involved.

1. You are sitting in a restaurant when you realize that the people in the booth behind you are campaign staffers from your opponent's campaign. They are discussing important strategic information about their campaign, which you overhear. Specifically, they are discussing the content for their next direct mailing that is to go out next week. The content will be very critical of your candidate on the issue of education, a central piece of your campaign agenda and message. Do you use this information in your own strategic planning? Why or why not?

2. You are having a drink in a bar near the university that is in the community where the candidate you are working for resides when you see your candidate's 19-year-old daughter enter, show an ID, and order a beer. When she sees you, she laughs and says, "Remember, you never saw me here." Not only is she under age, but her parents disapprove of drinking on religious grounds and are very strict. What do you do?

3. A member of your candidate's "kitchen cabinet" hands you an envelope containing $400 in cash and explains that a group of the candidate's friends, who wish, for reasons of privacy, to remain anonymous, took up a collection of $50 each and would like to contribute it to the campaign. What should you do?

4. As the campaign manager, you are concerned about your candidate's performance in a crucial upcoming debate. Returning from lunch, you find on your desk a list of questions. A note signed "a friend" suggests that you drill your candidate on these questions. Should you use this information? If so, do you tell the candidate how you obtained the information?

5. Your opponent is campaigning as an experienced businessman. Research into documents and information that are in the public record has revealed that several years ago he ran into financial trouble (he failed to pay his property taxes) in another state and lost his home, his two cars, and his boat. Should you use this information? Is the answer different if your opponent has been using the issue of fiscal responsibility as a centerpiece of his campaign?

6. A college student who supports your candidate has offered to pose as a volunteer for the opponent's campaign in order to get information. She has never been into your campaign headquarters and is not connected with the campaign, so you can easily deny knowing anything about it if she is caught. Will you accept her offer?

7. You have discovered in your opposition and candidate research that your own candidate has an inaccuracy on his resume, which gives a better impression of his military service than the reality. (He claims to have been promoted to captain, but he never received the promotion.) It will probably not be noticed, so can you just ignore it? Is your answer different if the inaccuracy is that your candidate claims to have been awarded a Purple Heart? If so, why?

NOTES

1. For more on crises in campaigns, see Garrett (2005).
2. In addition, regional or metropolitan-wide research organizations may also collect and report community profile data in certain areas.
3. The reader should note that this was the procedure for finding this information as of February 2005. The Census Bureau may change the search mechanism at some point.
4. This is only one way to estimate turnout; there are other calculations that can be done. See, for instance, Shea and Burton (2001) for other types of calculations.
5. This is obviously for a two-person contest. Races where three or more candidates are running present a much more complex picture; see Shea and Burton (2001) for a discussion of these issues.
6. Hilary Clinton's opponents tried to tag her with this label when she ran for the United States Senate seat in New York in 2000 after moving there only months before the election. Because of good candidate research, her campaign was able to handle this attack.
7. See Shea and Burton (2001) for a detailed discussion of ethics in conducting opposition research.
8. Several books have been published that outline these tactics and techniques more specifically than we do here. For more information on the specifics of campaign

fundraising, see, for instance, Shea and Burton (2001), Faucheux (2002), or Shaw (2000).

9. Note: These additional exercises are not tied to any specific case chapter that follows. The scenarios presented could happen in any race around the nation. Many of them are based on events that took place at one time or another.

10. Some of these exercises were taken from or are adjusted versions of those created by Alan Mann, Director of Public Opinion Research, of the Michigan House Republican Caucus. Our thanks to Mr. Mann for allowing us to use and revise some of these for purposes of this simulation.

11. The exercises in this section have been reprinted from or draw heavily on those exercises that appear in a curriculum guide prepared by the Center for Congressional and Presidential Studies at American University. We are grateful to the Center's director, James A. Thurber, for permission to reprint these exercises, and Carol Whitney, the original developer of the curriculum.

4

Michigan's 10th State Senate District

The 10th State Senate District in Michigan consists of the Macomb County communities of Sterling Heights, Clinton Township, Roseville, and Utica. Macomb County has been the subject of considerable political interest over the years, as it has been somewhat of a bellwether for the rest of the nation in that it has reflected some of the key political and social changes that have occurred over the past 40 years in the United States. For instance, it typifies the migration of individuals from the city to the suburbs that many urban areas have experienced. In southeast Michigan during the 1960s and 1970s, families began moving from the city of Detroit to their new homes in Macomb's suburban communities, located northeast of Detroit.

In the 1980s, many Macomb voters were part of the "Reagan revolution," in which large numbers of traditional Democratic voters, including many blue-collar labor union members, voted for the Republican presidential candidate and became "Reagan Democrats." The Michigan Democratic Party was so worried about this phenomenon that they hired Stanley Greenberg (who later became Bill Clinton's pollster in his 1992 presidential campaign) to conduct research in the area and find out what caused this apparent shift in voting patterns. Greenberg's investigation is chronicled in *Middle Class Dreams* (1995), which provides an important insight into the transformations that occurred in Macomb County voters, as well as the overall electorate in the United States, during that time.

During the first half of the twentieth century, Michigan was known as the automobile manufacturing capital of the United States, if not the entire world. In fact, by the mid-1950s, about half of all U.S. workers employed in automobile manufacturing worked in the state of Michigan (Browne and VerBurg 1995). The state's reliance on the automobile industry deeply affected Michigan's economy, which became subject to the cyclical forces inherent in automobile manufacturing. The industry created considerable wealth over time, but those economic highs were tempered periodically by downturns in the economy, and temporary (or in some cases permanent) layoffs. In fact, the state suffered recessions in the early 1970s (as part of the energy crisis aftermath), during the 1979–1981 "automobile recession," in the early 1990s, and in the first few years of the twenty-first century.

In addition to the automobile companies, after World War II, the automobile manufacturing labor union—the United Auto Workers (UAW)—became influential in the state as well. The union has been a powerful force in negotiating wages and working conditions for its members, but it also has been an important lobbying voice in Lansing (Michigan's state capital, located roughly one hour northwest of the 10th district). In addition to using its economic power to improve economic standards for its members, for many years the UAW has also advocated for progressive social policies in the state.

Although the automobile industry decentralized in the period after the 1973 energy crisis, and union membership declined (because jobs were eliminated or exported to other countries), the union remains a potent political force in the state capital. Other lobbying interests with a history of influence in Michigan politics include teachers (the Michigan Education Association), the real estate industry, trial lawyers, and the Chamber of Commerce (Browne and VerBurg 1995).

Michigan politicians and policy-makers must face regular challenges created by the long-term decline of the automobile industry and the short-term business cycle fluctuations mentioned previously. The auto industry also has revamped its production processes, so production workers can no longer rely only on a high school (or less) education. The consequences of these changes for Michigan have been a high level of unemployment compared to the rest of the nation, and a portion of the labor force population that does not qualify for jobs in the "new economy" (that is, high technology jobs). Moreover, because the state's economy relied so heavily on high-wage and high-benefit automobile-related industrial jobs, the 1994 North American Free Trade Agreement (NAFTA) created considerable concern among some elected officials over the impact of "free trade" on the state's unemployment rate. Labor unions—and many Democratic politicians—fought against NAFTA while it was being debated in the U.S. House and Senate. The NAFTA debate became an important issue in many Michigan political campaigns beginning in the 1990s, including both state legislative and congressional elections, and the policy continues to be hotly debated today.

THE MICHIGAN POLITICAL CONTEXT

With a reputation for progressive politics in the period after World War II, the state's balance of power has shifted since the late 1970s, as the state's politics have become more conservative. For instance, taxpayers in Michigan approved the Headlee Amendment to Michigan's constitution in 1978, which limits state and local taxes to specified levels, unless voters authorize a waiver. In 1992, voters in Michigan approved another constitutional amendment: term limits for state legislators—three terms for state house members (they can serve for a total of six years) and two terms (a total of eight years) for state senators. These are lifetime bans for a particular office, and one consequence of this has been term-limited office holders running for other offices once their last term has expired (that is, a state senator who is term-limited may run for state house). In 2004, the state approved yet another constitutional amendment, this one banning gay marriage and other similar unions.

A further indication of the increasingly conservative state politics is that Republicans generally have had substantial success in Michigan state-level elections over the past 20 years. Republican John Engler served three terms as governor (1991–2003), and the open-seat campaign to fill the governor's chair was hotly contested between eventual winner Jennifer Granholm (D) and then-Lieutenant Governor Dick Posthumus (R). Even though Granholm won with 51.4% of the vote, Republicans took the other major statewide offices that were on the ballot in 2002—secretary of state and attorney general—and the party has held majorities in both houses of the legislature since the early 1990s (although they briefly shared power with the Democrats in the house in the mid-1990s). Moreover, while the Democrats still maintain control over the state's two U.S. Senate seats, the GOP, thanks in part to recent redistricting plans (see Chapter 1), holds a 9-6 advantage in the U.S. House delegation.

Candidates for Michigan State House seats run every two years, while those for State Senate seats run every four years. Although term limits have opened up opportunities for more individuals to become candidates for the state legislature, it also remains true that redistricting decisions continue to create a large majority of safe districts at the state level, and only a few marginal or competitive districts. As we noted in Chapter 1, redistricting decisions can produce a context in which an incumbent running for re-election faces no opposition

By law, Michigan's legislative districts are considered "single member districts," or districts in which voters elect only one representative from a geographic area (this is opposed to multimember districts used in many European nations). There are no overlapping geographic boundaries for these districts. The electoral rules are also such that the candidate in the general election who garners a plurality of votes represents the entire district—these electoral rules are also called "winner take all" and are very similar to those used around the U.S. at all levels. Although this usually does not generate much controversy when only two candidates run in a general election (because, by definition, a winner must have at least one more vote than 50 percent of the votes cast), it can create some interesting dynamics when there are three candidates in the race. A winning candidate in a three-way race might garner only 40 percent of the overall vote, but would still represent the entire district because he or she received the most votes.

Michigan Primary and General Elections

Typical of the election process in the United States, candidates running for state legislative office in Michigan participate in both a primary and general election. A primary election determines which candidate will represent their party in a given district during the general election held in November.

The amount of time between when candidates must file for office and the primary election, and the time available between primary and general elections, is very important. First, it tends to be the only campaign resource that competing campaign organizations have in common. How a campaign uses that time can be the difference between winning and losing. Strategies regarding paid media advertising, door-to-door campaigning, and fund-raising are affected by when the primary and general elections are held and how much time exists in between them. For example, Michigan has a mid-May deadline to officially file papers declaring one's candidacy for office. With an early August primary election, the primary season is approximately 90 days long.[1] The general election season begins immediately after the primary, and runs approximately 90 days also—until early November. Therefore, the candidate who wins the primary must be ready to start the general election immediately. She must be ready to communicate a message to potential voters and have the funds available to do so.

All state senate seats are up in the same election cycle as the governorship—in presidential mid-term years; that is, in between presidential elections. Like the short general election timeframe, the presence or absence of higher-level races impacts several campaign-related matters, including voter turnout and ability to raise campaign funds. Michigan's State House races are held every two years in even-numbered years, which means that they are held both during presidential election years as well as during the off-years in which State Senate seats are contested and gubernatorial elections take place. These state legislative general elections take place on the same date prescribed for federal elections—the first Tuesday after the first Monday in November in even-numbered years.

Fund-Raising and Campaign Finance Law in Michigan

Michigan campaign finance regulations in the modern era were first codified under Public Act 388 of 1976. This act provides rules for campaign finance activities such as raising, spending, and borrowing campaign-related money, and the reporting of such activities. Gubernatorial races in Michigan are governed by public financing rules, and are similar to presidential elections in that each candidate receives an infusion of cash from the state government for their general election campaign. However, many recent gubernatorial candidates have opted out of the public funding mechanism so they can bypass the spending limits that accompany the acceptance of public funds; this is also a recent trend among presidential candidates in primary campaigns. There are no public funding provisions for state legislative campaigns in Michigan, so all candidates are left to raise the money for their campaigns through their own fund-raising efforts.

To accomplish this, some state legislative candidates in Michigan, as well as nationally, make fairly substantial contributions or loans to their own campaigns, especially those running for the first time. As is the case in U.S. congressional elections, incumbent candidates raise campaign funds more easily than their challenger opponents in state legislative races. Also consistent with federal races is the fact that some challengers have such a difficult time raising money they have a hard time seriously challenging an incumbent.

Under the rules set forth in Michigan law, candidates for state senate seats may accept contributions from individual citizens in amounts up to $1,000 in both the primary and general election (individuals may give only $500 to candidates for the state house in each election). Political action committees (PACs) are limited to $3,400 per candidate per election (that is, the primary and

BOX 4.1 Michigan at a Glance		
2000 population	9,938,444	
U.S. Congressional districts	15	
State Senate districts	38	
State House districts	110	
State Senate district population (avg.)	270,000	
State House district population (avg.)	90,000	
Full-time legislature	Yes	
Term limits	3 terms (6 years) in the state House; 2 terms (8 years) in the state Senate	
Voter registration by party	No	
Campaign finance contribution limits (per candidate per election)	*House*	*Senate*
Source:		
Individual	$500	$1,000
PAC	$3,400	$3,400
Party	$34,000	$34,000

general) for state legislative campaigns, whereas political parties can contribute up to $34,000 to a candidate. Although parties may contribute this much, they rarely do—even in competitive races like this one—and most candidates for state legislature in Michigan must raise campaign funds without much political party support. This, again, puts the onus on the candidate's campaign to raise the requisite funds to run the campaign.

Campaign finance compliance can be a complicated matter. Making sure reports are filed correctly, and on time, is often a challenge for a campaign staffer who might have several other duties. In Michigan, a statement of organization must first be filed, then preprimary, postprimary, pregeneral, and postgeneral election reports must be submitted. The pre-election reports are due roughly one week before the election and the postelection reports are due about one month after each election. A single annual report is also required for years in which an election is not being held, should a candidate operate her campaign committee between election cycles. All reports for statewide and state legislative seats are filed with the Elections Bureau of the Michigan Secretary of State's office in Lansing.

THE CAMPAIGN

In the election being contested in this simulation, the campaign for the Michigan 10th State Senate District seat is an open seat contest. The district was redrawn after the last census and redistricting process, and is considered to be almost evenly divided between Republican and Democratic voters. This split is found throughout the district, as two of the district's communities—Roseville and Utica—generally lean Democratic, but the larger communities of Sterling Heights and Clinton Township tend to lean Republican. The general election features State Representative Michael Switalski (D), from

Roseville, and Sterling Heights City Council member Stephen Rice (R). In the primary election, Switalski defeated former State Representative Sharon Gire, and Roger Maceroni, a Sterling Heights attorney whose name was familiar to voters because he was related to two Macomb County judges. Rice ran unopposed in the Republican primary.

Part of the context of this campaign are a gubernatorial race and a U.S. Senate seat that long-time incumbent Carl Levin is seeking against nominal and under-funded opposition. Both state political party organizations have targeted the 10th State Senate District because it is an open seat and because the partisan split is so evenly divided. Some extra party money will likely be spent because of this, but the vast majority of political party attention will center on efforts to capture the governor's mansion.

The Candidates

Michael Switalski (D) Michael "Mickey" Switalski, a 47-year-old Roseville resident, has been on a roll as a political candidate. Beginning with his campaign for Roseville City Council in 1989, Switalski has run for political office six times and won each one. After his City Council service, he was elected to the Macomb County Commission (1993-98), and was then elected to serve as a state representative for the 27th Michigan State House District; he first won with 70 percent of the vote in 1998, and was then re-elected with 73 percent of the vote in 2000.

During his tenure as a state representative, Switalski became known for his bipartisan nature and ability to work with Republicans on important issues. He became an expert on the state budget and had not voted for any tax increases while serving as a state representative. This "no tax increases" position was extremely popular with Macomb County voters and Switalski prided himself on being a fiscally responsible elected official (Switalski 2003). Switalski also has maintained a strong position in his party. In the Michigan State House session prior to this election, he had been elected by his peers to serve as the Chair of the House Democratic Caucus, and served as a member of the powerful House Appropriations Committee.

Mickey earned his Bachelor's and Master's degrees from Louisiana State University, and then continued his education in Scotland where he received an M.Litt. degree from the University of Aberdeen. Before throwing his hat into the ring as a candidate for office, Switalski worked as a newspaper reporter and editor, and as head of Labor Relations at the Detroit Arsenal Tank Plant in Warren, Michigan.

An important part of his service to constituents as a state representative was a newsletter, "The Insider," that he wrote and produced himself. In addition, he and several volunteers hand-delivered (rather than sending through the mail) the newsletters on a monthly basis to all households in his district. The newsletter often dealt with issues related to the district, and contained some political and governmental news, but just as often, it contained articles unrelated to politics. For example, he received a good deal of positive feedback from readers after he wrote a deeply emotional and personal piece about his father's death. Although Switalski knew that not everyone in the district voted, he firmly believed that all residents of his district should receive the newsletter, whether they were regular voters or not.

As noted earlier, in the state house, Switalski prided himself on being a problem-solver who was able to work with Republicans, but who would also take a principled position on an issue even if he stood alone. He has supported affordable health care policies, especially subsidies for prescription drug purchases for seniors. Switalski's newsletters often went to great lengths to explain the complexities of certain issues, and to defend his positions or votes. For example, one issue he has had to deal with is his pro-choice stance on abortion. In addition, Switalski has had to explain his votes supporting the "Detroit equity package," which is state funding for cultural organizations and activities operated by the city of Detroit and extra police protection for large-scale events such as the July 4th fireworks and the summer weekend ethnic festivals, both held on Detroit's riverfront. Critics have said Switalski cares more about Detroit than his own district.

His newsletter writing style is informal, witty, and engaging. It is unclear how much impact his newsletters have had on his electoral success, but it would be easy to believe that many voters have developed a connection of sorts to Switalski, both on a personal level and in understanding and respecting the choices he has made in Lansing, even if they disagreed with some of those choices.

Stephen Rice (R) Stephen Rice is a 44-year-old Sterling Heights resident and a long-time member of the Sterling Heights City Council. Upon entering the race for the 10th State Senate District seat, Rice had served on the council from 1985 to 1993, was defeated in his 1993 re-election bid, and then returned to the council in 1995. Rice also had served as mayor of Sterling Heights for two years as part of his service on the City Council (1991–1993).

Rice is thought to have a good chance in this election because the city of Sterling Heights—his assumed center of voter support—has a much larger population than Switalski's hometown of Roseville. Although Rice served as a member of the nonpartisan city council in the Republican-leaning community of Sterling Heights, in this partisan race he is running as a Republican, and as noted earlier, was unopposed in the primary. He earned a bachelor's degree from Oakland University, located in neighboring Oakland County.

In the past, Rice has been involved in issues focusing on senior citizens, taxes, crime, and the environment. Rice has supported policies that helped seniors obtain affordable housing. In addition, his support for senior citizens included a proposal for a new Sterling Heights senior center that would give seniors quality services when they needed them. During his time on the Sterling Heights City Council, Rice backed a series of tax cut proposals. He became known for advocating tax cuts while maintaining that essential services, including funding for police officers, should not be cut. Today, taxes in Sterling Heights are the lowest they have been in nearly 30 years. Also while serving as a city councilman, Rice championed proposals that sought to hold criminals accountable for their actions and hire more police officers. During Rice's tenure as a City Council member, Sterling Heights has been rated as one of the safest cities in Michigan and in the nation.

However, Rice developed a reputation on the City Council as someone who was a bit difficult to work with. His principled positions occasionally meant that he was unwilling to compromise. This, in part, is a reason why only one of Rice's fellow Sterling Heights City Council members endorsed him in this election; the rest (including the mayor) endorsed Michael Switalski.

CREATING A CAMPAIGN PLAN

The discussion of the candidates for Michigan's 10th State Senate District seat and the surrounding campaign context provides the reader with enough information to begin conducting district and demographic analyses as well as candidate profiles for the simulation exercises in Chapter 3. Supplemental material needed to complete those exercises is also included at the end of this chapter. We provide the following information that will be needed to complete the exercises in Chapter 3:

- *A map of the district.* The map included provides a general location of the district within the state. This map will help you to begin to familiarize yourself with the district and the lay of the land where the campaign will be waged. It will also provide important information in terms of where the district is situated in relation to other communities in the area. A more detailed map of the district can tell you about the kind of district in which you will be working— that is, whether it is urban, suburban, rural, or a combination of the three. This kind of map can also help to determine some aspects of campaign strategy such as whether the candidate will go door-to-door, or whether canvassing of this kind is out of the question because of the district's geographic elements.

- *U.S. Census data on the Michigan 10th State Senate District.* This information will be the beginning of your research into the district and its residents that you will use in several of the exercises in Chapter 3. We have provided you with some of the information you will need, but there is more out there. For example, the Southeast Michigan Council of Governments (SEMCOG) provides up-to-date "community profile" information on communities that is sometimes more current than census data.[2] You will need to use your research skills to go out and find other pertinent data that will help you complete the exercises.

- *Newspaper articles on the campaign.* We have provided a couple of news accounts that preview the race and give some additional description of the candidates and their campaigns. These will also be useful in several of the exercises.

- *Voter data on the district.* We have provided some of the information you will need to collect on the voters of the 10th district by providing election results from 1994 through 2000. Again, you may have to rely on your research skills to complement the given information relating to the voters of this district.

- *Campaign finance information.* Although we have tried to keep this simulation as realistic as possible, we will deviate a bit from the real world here. The Michigan 10th State Senate District is a competitive race; therefore, more money would be spent in this race than in a typical Michigan state senate race. For instance, as in many competitive campaigns, political party organizations may also spend money on this race. More money in a campaign means that more things can be done in the campaign and a wider variety of campaign tactics can be utilized. We supply a budget figure that provides some context for the race (remember that the state's campaign finance law, summarized earlier in this chapter, is also part of this context). This is the figure that must be raised in the fund-raising exercise outlined in Chapter 3. It will also be informative in terms of what other kinds of resources will be available in the campaign. We have taken a realistic figure that would be spent in this race and discounted it slightly. Just about anyone can run a campaign that is flush with cash. The real learning comes from having to decide how to divide up scarce resources in an efficient manner. As we have previously noted, activities related to the raising and spending of campaign funds must be periodically reported to the state. In order to illustrate what goes into these reports, we have provided examples of actual campaign finance reports from the two candidates (these are available on the book's companion Web site). The pages provided also serve as examples of sources from which the candidates raised money and what they spent it on. The budget for each campaign in the Michigan 10th State Senate District is $80,000.

NOTES

1. Of course, candidates can start to campaign before the filing deadline (whether they have officially filed for office or not), but we say the primary season lasts roughly 90 days because the full field of opposition candidates is not known until the deadline passes; a candidate could enter the race late and change the dynamics of the campaign.
2. SEMCOG's Web site can be accessed at http://www.semcog.org.

Supplemental Materials for Michigan's 10th State Senate District

Contents include:

District map

Census data

Voting history

Newspaper articles

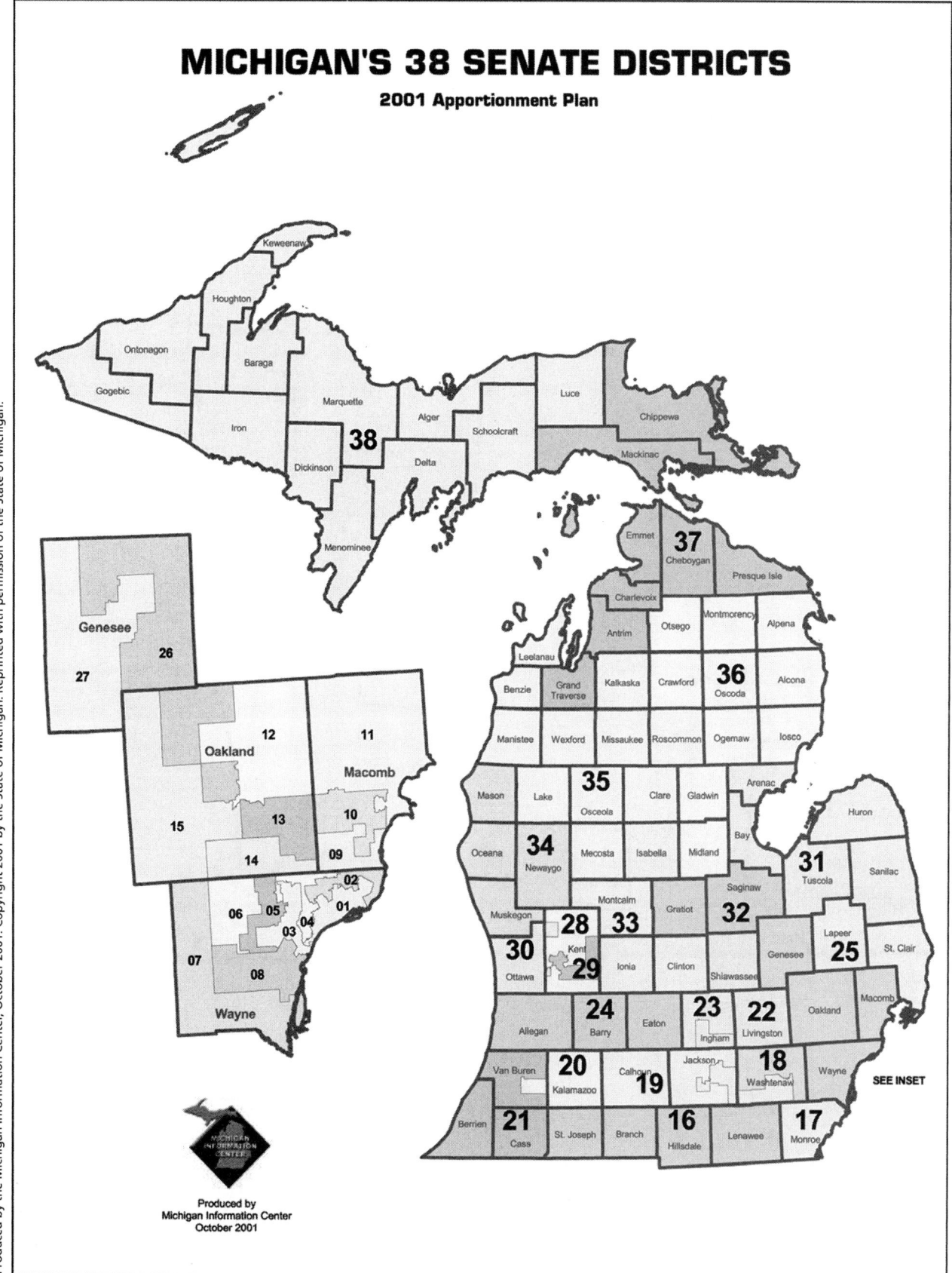

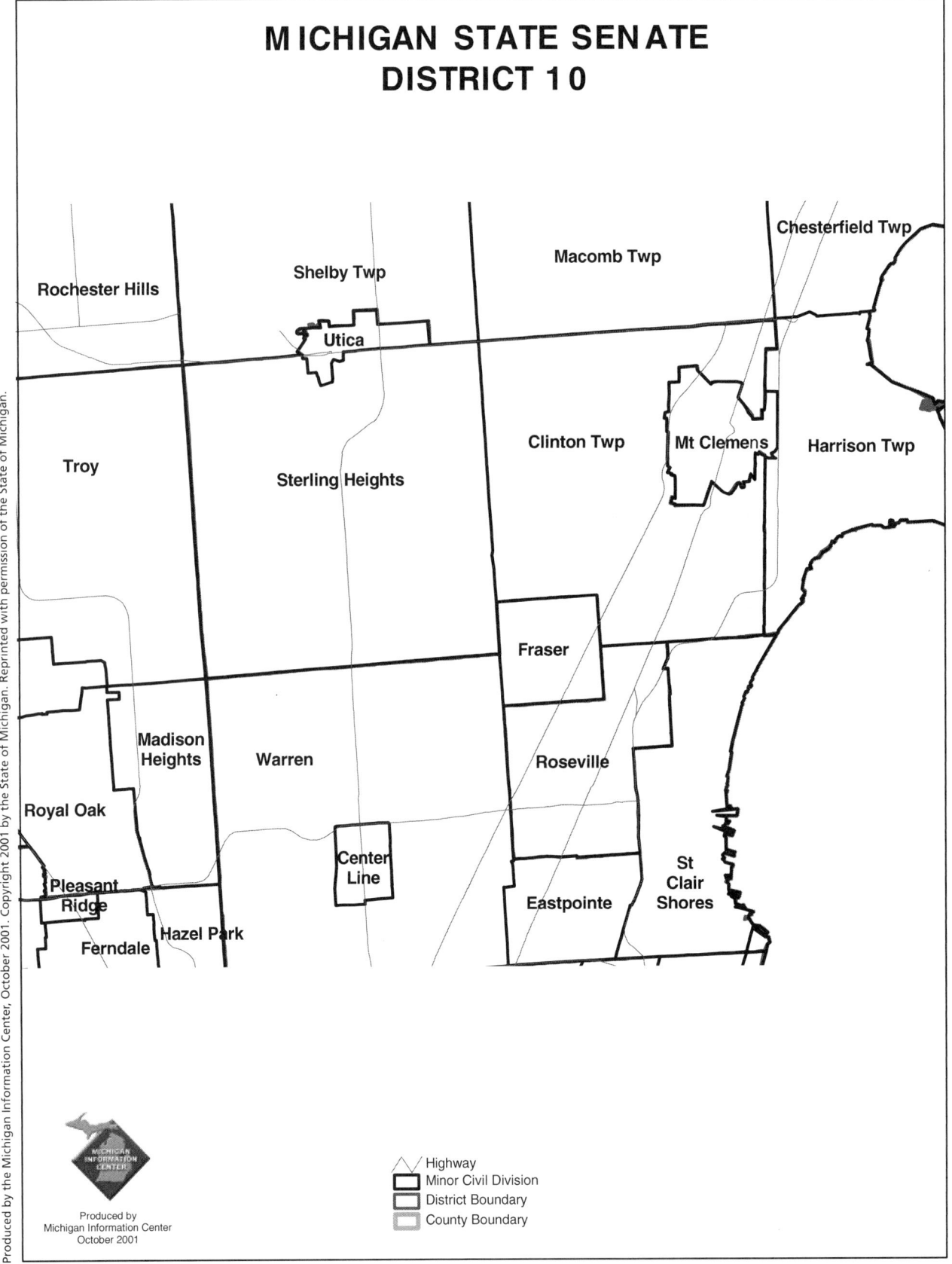

Table DP-1. Profile of General Demographic Characteristics: 2000

Geographic area: Clinton township, Macomb County, Michigan

[For information on confidentiality protection, nonsampling error, and definitions, see text]

Subject	Number	Percent	Subject	Number	Percent
Total population	95,648	100.0	**HISPANIC OR LATINO AND RACE**		
SEX AND AGE			Total population	95,648	100.0
Male	45,939	48.0	Hispanic or Latino (of any race)	1,664	1.7
Female	49,709	52.0	Mexican	1,128	1.2
			Puerto Rican	111	0.1
Under 5 years	5,797	6.1	Cuban	44	-
5 to 9 years	6,101	6.4	Other Hispanic or Latino	381	0.4
10 to 14 years	5,964	6.2	Not Hispanic or Latino	93,984	98.3
15 to 19 years	5,783	6.0	White alone	86,042	90.0
20 to 24 years	6,397	6.7	**RELATIONSHIP**		
25 to 34 years	14,432	15.1	Total population	95,648	100.0
35 to 44 years	15,077	15.8	In households	94,893	99.2
45 to 54 years	13,635	14.3	Householder	40,299	42.1
55 to 59 years	5,009	5.2	Spouse	19,644	20.5
60 to 64 years	3,785	4.0	Child	27,510	28.8
65 to 74 years	7,063	7.4	Own child under 18 years	19,948	20.9
75 to 84 years	5,149	5.4	Other relatives	3,360	3.5
85 years and over	1,456	1.5	Under 18 years	1,050	1.1
Median age (years)	37.3	(X)	Nonrelatives	4,080	4.3
			Unmarried partner	2,041	2.1
18 years and over	74,266	77.6	In group quarters	755	0.8
Male	34,872	36.5	Institutionalized population	553	0.6
Female	39,394	41.2	Noninstitutionalized population	202	0.2
21 years and over	70,790	74.0			
62 years and over	15,875	16.6	**HOUSEHOLD BY TYPE**		
65 years and over	13,668	14.3	Total households	40,299	100.0
Male	5,295	5.5	Family households (families)	25,556	63.4
Female	8,373	8.8	With own children under 18 years	11,313	28.1
			Married-couple family	19,644	48.7
RACE			With own children under 18 years	8,254	20.5
One race	93,898	98.2	Female householder, no husband present	4,395	10.9
White	87,151	91.1	With own children under 18 years	2,379	5.9
Black or African American	4,461	4.7	Nonfamily households	14,743	36.6
American Indian and Alaska Native	276	0.3	Householder living alone	12,407	30.8
Asian	1,605	1.7	Householder 65 years and over	4,371	10.8
Asian Indian	448	0.5			
Chinese	293	0.3	Households with individuals under 18 years	12,072	30.0
Filipino	280	0.3	Households with individuals 65 years and over	9,840	24.4
Japanese	50	0.1			
Korean	197	0.2	Average household size	2.35	(X)
Vietnamese	149	0.2	Average family size	2.98	(X)
Other Asian [1]	188	0.2			
Native Hawaiian and Other Pacific Islander	14	-	**HOUSING OCCUPANCY**		
Native Hawaiian	3	-	Total housing units	41,803	100.0
Guamanian or Chamorro	4	-	Occupied housing units	40,299	96.4
Samoan	7	-	Vacant housing units	1,504	3.6
Other Pacific Islander [2]	-	-	For seasonal, recreational, or occasional use	139	0.3
Some other race	391	0.4			
Two or more races	1,750	1.8	Homeowner vacancy rate (percent)	1.0	(X)
			Rental vacancy rate (percent)	5.3	(X)
Race alone or in combination with one or more other races: [3]			**HOUSING TENURE**		
White	88,716	92.8	Occupied housing units	40,299	100.0
Black or African American	5,011	5.2	Owner-occupied housing units	27,997	69.5
American Indian and Alaska Native	816	0.9	Renter-occupied housing units	12,302	30.5
Asian	1,966	2.1			
Native Hawaiian and Other Pacific Islander	60	0.1	Average household size of owner-occupied units	2.55	(X)
Some other race	953	1.0	Average household size of renter-occupied units	1.90	(X)

- Represents zero or rounds to zero.   (X) Not applicable.
[1] Other Asian alone, or two or more Asian categories.
[2] Other Pacific Islander alone, or two or more Native Hawaiian and Other Pacific Islander categories.
[3] In combination with one or more of the other races listed. The six numbers may add to more than the total population and the six percentages may add to more than 100 percent because individuals may report more than one race.

Source: U.S. Census Bureau, Census 2000.

Table DP-2. Profile of Selected Social Characteristics: 2000

Geographic area: Clinton township, Macomb County, Michigan

[Data based on a sample. For information on confidentiality protection, sampling error, nonsampling error, and definitions, see text]

Subject	Number	Percent	Subject	Number	Percent
SCHOOL ENROLLMENT			**NATIVITY AND PLACE OF BIRTH**		
Population 3 years and over enrolled in school	23,453	100.0	Total population	95,648	100.0
Nursery school, preschool	1,321	5.6	Native	87,797	91.8
Kindergarten	1,281	5.5	Born in United States	87,117	91.1
Elementary school (grades 1-8)	9,656	41.2	State of residence	75,347	78.8
High school (grades 9-12)	5,062	21.6	Different state	11,770	12.3
College or graduate school	6,133	26.2	Born outside United States	680	0.7
			Foreign born	7,851	8.2
EDUCATIONAL ATTAINMENT			Entered 1990 to March 2000	2,820	2.9
Population 25 years and over	65,644	100.0	Naturalized citizen	3,853	4.0
Less than 9th grade	2,475	3.8	Not a citizen	3,998	4.2
9th to 12th grade, no diploma	7,418	11.3	**REGION OF BIRTH OF FOREIGN BORN**		
High school graduate (includes equivalency)	21,504	32.8	Total (excluding born at sea)	7,851	100.0
Some college, no degree	17,157	26.1	Europe	4,605	58.7
Associate degree	5,306	8.1	Asia	1,705	21.7
Bachelor's degree	7,661	11.7	Africa	84	1.1
Graduate or professional degree	4,123	6.3	Oceania	17	0.2
			Latin America	485	6.2
Percent high school graduate or higher	84.9	(X)	Northern America	955	12.2
Percent bachelor's degree or higher	18.0	(X)	**LANGUAGE SPOKEN AT HOME**		
MARITAL STATUS			Population 5 years and over	89,822	100.0
Population 15 years and over	77,787	100.0	English only	79,420	88.4
Never married	21,039	27.0	Language other than English	10,402	11.6
Now married, except separated	41,442	53.3	Speak English less than very well	4,106	4.6
Separated	854	1.1	Spanish	1,388	1.5
Widowed	5,686	7.3	Speak English less than very well	562	0.6
Female	4,776	6.1	Other Indo-European languages	7,151	8.0
Divorced	8,766	11.3	Speak English less than very well	2,617	2.9
Female	5,176	6.7	Asian and Pacific Island languages	1,098	1.2
			Speak English less than very well	603	0.7
GRANDPARENTS AS CAREGIVERS					
Grandparent living in household with one or more own grandchildren under 18 years	1,051	100.0	**ANCESTRY (single or multiple)**		
			Total population	95,648	100.0
			Total ancestries reported	117,044	122.4
Grandparent responsible for grandchildren	306	29.1	Arab	1,869	2.0
			Czech[1]	537	0.6
VETERAN STATUS			Danish	172	0.2
Civilian population 18 years and over	74,214	100.0	Dutch	1,255	1.3
Civilian veterans	9,446	12.7	English	7,323	7.7
			French (except Basque)[1]	5,715	6.0
DISABILITY STATUS OF THE CIVILIAN NONINSTITUTIONALIZED POPULATION			French Canadian[1]	2,258	2.4
			German	22,997	24.0
Population 5 to 20 years	19,166	100.0	Greek	867	0.9
With a disability	1,657	8.6	Hungarian	903	0.9
			Irish[1]	11,162	11.7
Population 21 to 64 years	56,792	100.0	Italian	15,285	16.0
With a disability	8,702	15.3	Lithuanian	415	0.4
Percent employed	59.4	(X)	Norwegian	436	0.5
No disability	48,090	84.7	Polish	17,532	18.3
Percent employed	80.6	(X)	Portuguese	56	0.1
Population 65 years and over	13,254	100.0	Russian	717	0.7
With a disability	5,267	39.7	Scotch-Irish	1,090	1.1
			Scottish	2,060	2.2
RESIDENCE IN 1995			Slovak	736	0.8
Population 5 years and over	89,822	100.0	Subsaharan African	62	0.1
Same house in 1995	51,287	57.1	Swedish	821	0.9
Different house in the U.S. in 1995	36,529	40.7	Swiss	168	0.2
Same county	25,146	28.0	Ukrainian	1,007	1.1
Different county	11,383	12.7	United States or American	3,058	3.2
Same state	8,443	9.4	Welsh	408	0.4
Different state	2,940	3.3	West Indian (excluding Hispanic groups)	54	0.1
Elsewhere in 1995	2,006	2.2	Other ancestries	18,081	18.9

-Represents zero or rounds to zero. (X) Not applicable.

[1]The data represent a combination of two ancestries shown separately in Summary File 3. Czech includes Czechoslovakian. French includes Alsatian. French Canadian includes Acadian/Cajun. Irish includes Celtic.

Source: U.S. Bureau of the Census, Census 2000.

Table DP-3. Profile of Selected Economic Characteristics: 2000

Geographic area: Clinton township, Macomb County, Michigan
[Data based on a sample. For information on confidentiality protection, sampling error, nonsampling error, and definitions, see text]

Subject	Number	Percent	Subject	Number	Percent
EMPLOYMENT STATUS			**INCOME IN 1999**		
Population 16 years and over	76,652	100.0	Households	40,274	100.0
In labor force	51,312	66.9	Less than $10,000	2,349	5.8
Civilian labor force	51,256	66.9	$10,000 to $14,999	1,928	4.8
Employed	48,924	63.8	$15,000 to $24,999	4,124	10.2
Unemployed	2,332	3.0	$25,000 to $34,999	4,781	11.9
Percent of civilian labor force	4.5	(X)	$35,000 to $49,999	6,921	17.2
Armed Forces	56	0.1	$50,000 to $74,999	8,872	22.0
Not in labor force	25,340	33.1	$75,000 to $99,999	5,504	13.7
			$100,000 to $149,999	4,214	10.5
Females 16 years and over	40,382	100.0	$150,000 to $199,999	956	2.4
In labor force	23,613	58.5	$200,000 or more	625	1.6
Civilian labor force	23,590	58.4	Median household income (dollars)	50,067	(X)
Employed	22,728	56.3			
Own children under 6 years	6,858	100.0	With earnings	32,599	80.9
All parents in family in labor force	4,089	59.6	Mean earnings (dollars)[1]	62,209	(X)
			With Social Security income	10,704	26.6
COMMUTING TO WORK			Mean Social Security income (dollars)[1]	12,259	(X)
Workers 16 years and over	48,068	100.0	With Supplemental Security Income	1,151	2.9
Car, truck, or van - - drove alone	43,414	90.3	Mean Supplemental Security Income (dollars)[1]	8,015	(X)
Car, truck, or van - - carpooled	3,221	6.7			
Public transportation (including taxicab)	219	0.5	With public assistance income	843	2.1
Walked	454	0.9	Mean public assistance income (dollars)[1]	2,220	(X)
Other means	226	0.5	With retirement income	8,037	20.0
Worked at home	534	1.1	Mean retirement income (dollars)[1]	16,055	(X)
Mean travel time to work (minutes)[1]	27.2	(X)			
			Families	25,631	100.0
Employed civilian population			Less than $10,000	776	3.0
16 years and over	48,924	100.0	$10,000 to $14,999	483	1.9
OCCUPATION			$15,000 to $24,999	1,811	7.1
Management, professional, and related occupations	15,618	31.9	$25,000 to $34,999	2,369	9.2
Service occupations	6,313	12.9	$35,000 to $49,999	4,203	16.4
Sales and office occupations	14,277	29.2	$50,000 to $74,999	6,427	25.1
Farming, fishing, and forestry occupations	15	-	$75,000 to $99,999	4,566	17.8
Construction, extraction, and maintenance occupations	4,419	9.0	$100,000 to $149,999	3,667	14.3
			$150,000 to $199,999	820	3.2
Production, transportation, and material moving occupations	8,282	16.9	$200,000 or more	509	2.0
			Median family income (dollars)	61,497	(X)
INDUSTRY			Per capita income (dollars)[1]	25,758	(X)
Agriculture, forestry, fishing and hunting, and mining	14	-	*Median earnings (dollars):*		
			Male full-time, year-round workers	48,818	(X)
Construction	3,334	6.8	Female full-time, year-round workers	29,847	(X)

Subject	Number	Percent	Subject	Number below poverty level	Percent below poverty level
Manufacturing	12,824	26.2			
Wholesale trade	1,662	3.4			
Retail trade	5,985	12.2			
Transportation and warehousing, and utilities	1,608	3.3			
Information	997	2.0	**POVERTY STATUS IN 1999**		
Finance, insurance, real estate, and rental and leasing	2,728	5.6	Families	1,079	4.2
			With related children under 18 years	782	6.6
Professional, scientific, management, administrative, and waste management services	4,591	9.4	With related children under 5 years	423	9.3
Educational, health and social services	7,930	16.2	Families with female householder, no husband present	560	13.4
Arts, entertainment, recreation, accommodation and food services	3,571	7.3	With related children under 18 years	478	19.4
Other services (except public administration)	2,209	4.5	With related children under 5 years	296	33.7
Public administration	1,471	3.0			
CLASS OF WORKER			Individuals	5,500	5.8
Private wage and salary workers	43,429	88.8	18 years and over	3,914	5.3
Government workers	3,836	7.8	65 years and over	905	6.8
Self-employed workers in own not incorporated business	1,544	3.2	Related children under 18 years	1,558	7.4
			Related children 5 to 17 years	1,008	6.6
Unpaid family workers	115	0.2	Unrelated individuals 15 years and over	2,112	11.5

-Represents zero or rounds to zero. (X) Not applicable.
[1]If the denominator of a mean value or per capita value is less than 30, then that value is calculated using a rounded aggregate in the numerator. See text.
Source: U.S. Bureau of the Census, Census 2000.

Table DP-4. Profile of Selected Housing Characteristics: 2000
Geographic area: Clinton township, Macomb County, Michigan
[Data based on a sample. For information on confidentiality protection, sampling error, nonsampling error, and definitions, see text]

Subject	Number	Percent	Subject	Number	Percent
Total housing units....................	41,803	100.0	**OCCUPANTS PER ROOM**		
UNITS IN STRUCTURE			Occupied housing units	40,299	100.0
1-unit, detached.............................	20,486	49.0	1.00 or less.................................	39,306	97.5
1-unit, attached.............................	6,034	14.4	1.01 to 1.50.................................	616	1.5
2 units...	179	0.4	1.51 or more................................	377	0.9
3 or 4 units..................................	1,566	3.7			
5 to 9 units..................................	3,694	8.8	Specified owner-occupied units........	23,644	100.0
10 to 19 units...............................	3,534	8.5	**VALUE**		
20 or more units............................	3,686	8.8	Less than $50,000.........................	426	1.8
Mobile home.................................	2,624	6.3	$50,000 to $99,999........................	4,000	16.9
Boat, RV, van, etc..........................	-	-	$100,000 to $149,999.....................	8,261	34.9
			$150,000 to $199,999.....................	7,203	30.5
YEAR STRUCTURE BUILT			$200,000 to $299,999.....................	3,203	13.5
1999 to March 2000........................	680	1.6	$300,000 to $499,999.....................	451	1.9
1995 to 1998.................................	3,682	8.8	$500,000 to $999,999.....................	66	0.3
1990 to 1994.................................	4,426	10.6	$1,000,000 or more........................	34	0.1
1980 to 1989.................................	8,842	21.2	Median (dollars).............................	145,400	(X)
1970 to 1979.................................	11,204	26.8			
1960 to 1969.................................	7,150	17.1	**MORTGAGE STATUS AND SELECTED**		
1940 to 1959.................................	5,115	12.2	**MONTHLY OWNER COSTS**		
1939 or earlier..............................	704	1.7	With a mortgage............................	17,100	72.3
			Less than $300............................	39	0.2
ROOMS			$300 to $499...............................	610	2.6
1 room..	490	1.2	$500 to $699...............................	1,863	7.9
2 rooms.......................................	1,484	3.5	$700 to $999...............................	4,720	20.0
3 rooms.......................................	4,027	9.6	$1,000 to $1,499..........................	6,884	29.1
4 rooms.......................................	8,343	20.0	$1,500 to $1,999..........................	2,195	9.3
5 rooms.......................................	10,848	26.0	$2,000 or more............................	789	3.3
6 rooms.......................................	7,885	18.9	Median (dollars)...........................	1,080	(X)
7 rooms.......................................	4,406	10.5	Not mortgaged.............................	6,544	27.7
8 rooms.......................................	2,466	5.9	Median (dollars)...........................	347	(X)
9 or more rooms............................	1,854	4.4			
Median (rooms).............................	5.1	(X)	**SELECTED MONTHLY OWNER COSTS**		
			AS A PERCENTAGE OF HOUSEHOLD		
Occupied housing units	40,299	100.0	**INCOME IN 1999**		
YEAR HOUSEHOLDER MOVED INTO UNIT			Less than 15.0 percent....................	9,800	41.4
1999 to March 2000........................	7,444	18.5	15.0 to 19.9 percent.......................	4,748	20.1
1995 to 1998.................................	12,019	29.8	20.0 to 24.9 percent.......................	3,098	13.1
1990 to 1994.................................	7,353	18.2	25.0 to 29.9 percent.......................	1,998	8.5
1980 to 1989.................................	7,046	17.5	30.0 to 34.9 percent.......................	1,217	5.1
1970 to 1979.................................	3,834	9.5	35.0 percent or more.....................	2,684	11.4
1969 or earlier..............................	2,603	6.5	Not computed..............................	99	0.4
VEHICLES AVAILABLE			Specified renter-occupied units........	12,267	100.0
None...	2,451	6.1	**GROSS RENT**		
1..	14,912	37.0	Less than $200.............................	636	5.2
2..	16,258	40.3	$200 to $299................................	272	2.2
3 or more.....................................	6,678	16.6	$300 to $499................................	2,299	18.7
			$500 to $749................................	6,394	52.1
HOUSE HEATING FUEL			$750 to $999................................	1,597	13.0
Utility gas.....................................	37,492	93.0	$1,000 to $1,499...........................	586	4.8
Bottled, tank, or LP gas...................	353	0.9	$1,500 or more.............................	229	1.9
Electricity.....................................	2,154	5.3	No cash rent................................	254	2.1
Fuel oil, kerosene, etc.....................	85	0.2	Median (dollars)............................	599	(X)
Coal or coke..................................	-	-			
Wood...	37	0.1	**GROSS RENT AS A PERCENTAGE OF**		
Solar energy..................................	7	-	**HOUSEHOLD INCOME IN 1999**		
Other fuel.....................................	125	0.3	Less than 15.0 percent....................	2,968	24.2
No fuel used..................................	46	0.1	15.0 to 19.9 percent.......................	2,158	17.6
			20.0 to 24.9 percent.......................	1,522	12.4
SELECTED CHARACTERISTICS			25.0 to 29.9 percent.......................	1,395	11.4
Lacking complete plumbing facilities.............	104	0.3	30.0 to 34.9 percent.......................	780	6.4
Lacking complete kitchen facilities................	139	0.3	35.0 percent or more.....................	3,039	24.8
No telephone service...........................	557	1.4	Not computed..............................	405	3.3

-Represents zero or rounds to zero.   (X) Not applicable.

Source: U.S. Bureau of the Census, Census 2000.

Table DP-1. Profile of General Demographic Characteristics: 2000

Geographic area: Roseville city, Michigan

[For information on confidentiality protection, nonsampling error, and definitions, see text]

Subject	Number	Percent	Subject	Number	Percent
Total population	48,129	100.0	**HISPANIC OR LATINO AND RACE**		
SEX AND AGE			Total population	48,129	100.0
Male	23,297	48.4	Hispanic or Latino (of any race)	722	1.5
Female	24,832	51.6	Mexican	462	1.0
			Puerto Rican	61	0.1
Under 5 years	3,140	6.5	Cuban	41	0.1
5 to 9 years	3,260	6.8	Other Hispanic or Latino	158	0.3
10 to 14 years	3,012	6.3	Not Hispanic or Latino	47,407	98.5
15 to 19 years	2,787	5.8	White alone	44,477	92.4
20 to 24 years	2,877	6.0	**RELATIONSHIP**		
25 to 34 years	7,949	16.5	Total population	48,129	100.0
35 to 44 years	7,952	16.5	In households	47,945	99.6
45 to 54 years	5,971	12.4	Householder	19,976	41.5
55 to 59 years	2,035	4.2	Spouse	9,267	19.3
60 to 64 years	1,727	3.6	Child	14,308	29.7
65 to 74 years	3,814	7.9	Own child under 18 years	10,136	21.1
75 to 84 years	2,891	6.0	Other relatives	2,136	4.4
85 years and over	714	1.5	Under 18 years	767	1.6
Median age (years)	36.2	(X)	Nonrelatives	2,258	4.7
			Unmarried partner	1,145	2.4
18 years and over	36,992	76.9	In group quarters	184	0.4
Male	17,533	36.4	Institutionalized population	153	0.3
Female	19,459	40.4	Noninstitutionalized population	31	0.1
21 years and over	35,393	73.5			
62 years and over	8,443	17.5	**HOUSEHOLD BY TYPE**		
65 years and over	7,419	15.4	Total households	19,976	100.0
Male	2,805	5.8	Family households (families)	12,723	63.7
Female	4,614	9.6	With own children under 18 years	5,706	28.6
			Married-couple family	9,267	46.4
RACE			With own children under 18 years	4,098	20.5
One race	47,375	98.4	Female householder, no husband present	2,539	12.7
White	44,968	93.4	With own children under 18 years	1,211	6.1
Black or African American	1,252	2.6	Nonfamily households	7,253	36.3
American Indian and Alaska Native	201	0.4	Householder living alone	6,143	30.8
Asian	785	1.6	Householder 65 years and over	2,516	12.6
Asian Indian	300	0.6			
Chinese	99	0.2	Households with individuals under 18 years	6,229	31.2
Filipino	118	0.2	Households with individuals 65 years and over	5,553	27.8
Japanese	15	-			
Korean	33	0.1	Average household size	2.40	(X)
Vietnamese	57	0.1	Average family size	3.02	(X)
Other Asian [1]	163	0.3			
Native Hawaiian and Other Pacific Islander	15	-	**HOUSING OCCUPANCY**		
Native Hawaiian	2	-	Total housing units	20,519	100.0
Guamanian or Chamorro	6	-	Occupied housing units	19,976	97.4
Samoan	1	-	Vacant housing units	543	2.6
Other Pacific Islander [2]	6	-	For seasonal, recreational, or occasional use	55	0.3
Some other race	154	0.3			
Two or more races	754	1.6	Homeowner vacancy rate (percent)	0.9	(X)
			Rental vacancy rate (percent)	3.3	(X)
Race alone or in combination with one or more other races: [3]			**HOUSING TENURE**		
White	45,679	94.9	Occupied housing units	19,976	100.0
Black or African American	1,426	3.0	Owner-occupied housing units	15,021	75.2
American Indian and Alaska Native	530	1.1	Renter-occupied housing units	4,955	24.8
Asian	919	1.9			
Native Hawaiian and Other Pacific Islander	35	0.1	Average household size of owner-occupied units	2.53	(X)
Some other race	316	0.7	Average household size of renter-occupied units	2.01	(X)

- Represents zero or rounds to zero.   (X) Not applicable.

[1] Other Asian alone, or two or more Asian categories.

[2] Other Pacific Islander alone, or two or more Native Hawaiian and Other Pacific Islander categories.

[3] In combination with one or more of the other races listed. The six numbers may add to more than the total population and the six percentages may add to more than 100 percent because individuals may report more than one race.

Source: U.S. Census Bureau, Census 2000.

Table DP-2. Profile of Selected Social Characteristics: 2000

Geographic area: Roseville city, Michigan

[Data based on a sample. For information on confidentiality protection, sampling error, nonsampling error, and definitions, see text]

Subject	Number	Percent	Subject	Number	Percent
SCHOOL ENROLLMENT			**NATIVITY AND PLACE OF BIRTH**		
Population 3 years and over enrolled in school	10,984	100.0	Total population	48,129	100.0
Nursery school, preschool	653	5.9	Native	45,509	94.6
Kindergarten	664	6.0	Born in United States	45,196	93.9
Elementary school (grades 1-8)	5,193	47.3	State of residence	39,224	81.5
High school (grades 9-12)	2,338	21.3	Different state	5,972	12.4
College or graduate school	2,136	19.4	Born outside United States	313	0.7
			Foreign born	2,620	5.4
EDUCATIONAL ATTAINMENT			Entered 1990 to March 2000	856	1.8
Population 25 years and over	33,081	100.0	Naturalized citizen	1,318	2.7
Less than 9th grade	1,714	5.2	Not a citizen	1,302	2.7
9th to 12th grade, no diploma	6,174	18.7			
High school graduate (includes equivalency)	12,815	38.7	**REGION OF BIRTH OF FOREIGN BORN**		
Some college, no degree	7,998	24.2	Total (excluding born at sea)	2,620	100.0
Associate degree	2,007	6.1	Europe	1,304	49.8
Bachelor's degree	1,770	5.4	Asia	785	30.0
Graduate or professional degree	603	1.8	Africa	-	-
			Oceania	8	0.3
Percent high school graduate or higher	76.2	(X)	Latin America	131	5.0
Percent bachelor's degree or higher	7.2	(X)	Northern America	392	15.0
MARITAL STATUS			**LANGUAGE SPOKEN AT HOME**		
Population 15 years and over	38,671	100.0	Population 5 years and over	45,050	100.0
Never married	10,885	28.1	English only	41,388	91.9
Now married, except separated	19,096	49.4	Language other than English	3,662	8.1
Separated	321	0.8	Speak English less than very well	1,489	3.3
Widowed	3,526	9.1	Spanish	424	0.9
Female	2,904	7.5	Speak English less than very well	142	0.3
Divorced	4,843	12.5	Other Indo-European languages	2,349	5.2
Female	2,766	7.2	Speak English less than very well	956	2.1
			Asian and Pacific Island languages	605	1.3
GRANDPARENTS AS CAREGIVERS			Speak English less than very well	266	0.6
Grandparent living in household with one or more own grandchildren under 18 years	693	100.0	**ANCESTRY (single or multiple)**		
Grandparent responsible for grandchildren	223	32.2	Total population	48,129	100.0
			Total ancestries reported	*58,515*	*121.6*
VETERAN STATUS			Arab	626	1.3
Civilian population 18 years and over	36,946	100.0	Czech[1]	197	0.4
Civilian veterans	4,971	13.5	Danish	138	0.3
			Dutch	512	1.1
DISABILITY STATUS OF THE CIVILIAN NONINSTITUTIONALIZED POPULATION			English	3,652	7.6
			French (except Basque)[1]	3,422	7.1
Population 5 to 20 years	9,590	100.0	French Canadian[1]	1,527	3.2
With a disability	863	9.0	German	11,792	24.5
Population 21 to 64 years	28,021	100.0	Greek	395	0.8
With a disability	5,238	18.7	Hungarian	483	1.0
Percent employed	55.5	(X)	Irish[1]	6,443	13.4
No disability	22,783	81.3	Italian	6,930	14.4
Percent employed	79.3	(X)	Lithuanian	180	0.4
Population 65 years and over	7,269	100.0	Norwegian	153	0.3
With a disability	3,302	45.4	Polish	9,549	19.8
			Portuguese	9	-
RESIDENCE IN 1995			Russian	405	0.8
Population 5 years and over	45,050	100.0	Scotch-Irish	584	1.2
Same house in 1995	27,526	61.1	Scottish	1,113	2.3
Different house in the U.S. in 1995	16,861	37.4	Slovak	209	0.4
Same county	11,670	25.9	Subsaharan African	59	0.1
Different county	5,191	11.5	Swedish	404	0.8
Same state	3,991	8.9	Swiss	38	0.1
Different state	1,200	2.7	Ukrainian	284	0.6
Elsewhere in 1995	663	1.5	United States or American	1,785	3.7
			Welsh	234	0.5
			West Indian (excluding Hispanic groups)	52	0.1
			Other ancestries	7,340	15.3

-Represents zero or rounds to zero.   (X) Not applicable.

[1]The data represent a combination of two ancestries shown separately in Summary File 3. Czech includes Czechoslovakian. French includes Alsatian. French Canadian includes Acadian/Cajun. Irish includes Celtic.

Source: U.S. Bureau of the Census, Census 2000.

Table DP-3. Profile of Selected Economic Characteristics: 2000

Geographic area: Roseville city, Michigan

[Data based on a sample. For information on confidentiality protection, sampling error, nonsampling error, and definitions, see text]

Subject	Number	Percent	Subject	Number	Percent
EMPLOYMENT STATUS			**INCOME IN 1999**		
Population 16 years and over	38,070	100.0	Households	19,999	100.0
In labor force	24,616	64.7	Less than $10,000	1,502	7.5
Civilian labor force	24,598	64.6	$10,000 to $14,999	1,121	5.6
Employed	23,201	60.9	$15,000 to $24,999	2,675	13.4
Unemployed	1,397	3.7	$25,000 to $34,999	2,777	13.9
Percent of civilian labor force	5.7	(X)	$35,000 to $49,999	4,065	20.3
Armed Forces	18	-	$50,000 to $74,999	4,593	23.0
Not in labor force	13,454	35.3	$75,000 to $99,999	2,068	10.3
			$100,000 to $149,999	986	4.9
Females 16 years and over	19,965	100.0	$150,000 to $199,999	131	0.7
In labor force	11,398	57.1	$200,000 or more	81	0.4
Civilian labor force	11,392	57.1	Median household income (dollars)	41,220	(X)
Employed	10,830	54.2			
			With earnings	15,558	77.8
Own children under 6 years	3,608	100.0	Mean earnings (dollars)[1]	49,129	(X)
All parents in family in labor force	2,054	56.9	With Social Security income	6,033	30.2
			Mean Social Security income (dollars)[1]	12,035	(X)
COMMUTING TO WORK			With Supplemental Security Income	746	3.7
Workers 16 years and over	22,618	100.0	Mean Supplemental Security Income (dollars)[1]	6,790	(X)
Car, truck, or van - - drove alone	19,944	88.2	With public assistance income	477	2.4
Car, truck, or van - - carpooled	1,753	7.8	Mean public assistance income (dollars)[1]	2,516	(X)
Public transportation (including taxicab)	217	1.0	With retirement income	4,231	21.2
Walked	253	1.1	Mean retirement income (dollars)[1]	13,895	(X)
Other means	171	0.8			
Worked at home	280	1.2	Families	12,792	100.0
Mean travel time to work (minutes)[1]	24.2	(X)	Less than $10,000	514	4.0
			$10,000 to $14,999	374	2.9
Employed civilian population 16 years and over	23,201	100.0	$15,000 to $24,999	1,155	9.0
OCCUPATION			$25,000 to $34,999	1,560	12.2
Management, professional, and related occupations	4,527	19.5	$35,000 to $49,999	2,907	22.7
Service occupations	3,740	16.1	$50,000 to $74,999	3,648	28.5
Sales and office occupations	6,725	29.0	$75,000 to $99,999	1,621	12.7
Farming, fishing, and forestry occupations	32	0.1	$100,000 to $149,999	833	6.5
Construction, extraction, and maintenance occupations	3,154	13.6	$150,000 to $199,999	122	1.0
Production, transportation, and material moving occupations	5,023	21.6	$200,000 or more	58	0.5
			Median family income (dollars)	49,244	(X)
INDUSTRY			Per capita income (dollars)[1]	19,823	(X)
Agriculture, forestry, fishing and hunting, and mining	39	0.2	**Median earnings (dollars):**		
			Male full-time, year-round workers	40,113	(X)
Construction	1,988	8.6	Female full-time, year-round workers	26,281	(X)
Manufacturing	5,649	24.3			
Wholesale trade	1,017	4.4			
Retail trade	3,270	14.1			
Transportation and warehousing, and utilities	897	3.9			
Information	350	1.5			

Subject	Number below poverty level	Percent below poverty level
POVERTY STATUS IN 1999		
Families	776	6.1
With related children under 18 years	582	9.4
With related children under 5 years	269	10.7
Families with female householder, no husband present	458	17.4
With related children under 18 years	381	28.5
With related children under 5 years	185	40.3
Individuals	3,781	7.9
18 years and over	2,650	7.2
65 years and over	424	5.8
Related children under 18 years	1,086	9.9
Related children 5 to 17 years	797	10.1
Unrelated individuals 15 years and over	1,489	15.9

(Industry continued:)

Subject	Number	Percent
Finance, insurance, real estate, and rental and leasing	1,273	5.5
Professional, scientific, management, administrative, and waste management services	2,016	8.7
Educational, health and social services	3,141	13.5
Arts, entertainment, recreation, accommodation and food services	1,852	8.0
Other services (except public administration)	1,176	5.1
Public administration	533	2.3
CLASS OF WORKER		
Private wage and salary workers	20,621	88.9
Government workers	1,548	6.7
Self-employed workers in own not incorporated business	992	4.3
Unpaid family workers	40	0.2

-Represents zero or rounds to zero. (X) Not applicable.

[1]If the denominator of a mean value or per capita value is less than 30, then that value is calculated using a rounded aggregate in the numerator. See text.

Source: U.S. Bureau of the Census, Census 2000.

Table DP-4. Profile of Selected Housing Characteristics: 2000

Geographic area: Roseville city, Michigan

[Data based on a sample. For information on confidentiality protection, sampling error, nonsampling error, and definitions, see text]

Subject	Number	Percent	Subject	Number	Percent
Total housing units	20,519	100.0	**OCCUPANTS PER ROOM**		
UNITS IN STRUCTURE			Occupied housing units	19,976	100.0
1-unit, detached	15,332	74.7	1.00 or less	19,501	97.6
1-unit, attached	1,053	5.1	1.01 to 1.50	361	1.8
2 units	284	1.4	1.51 or more	114	0.6
3 or 4 units	570	2.8			
5 to 9 units	1,464	7.1	Specified owner-occupied units	14,284	100.0
10 to 19 units	721	3.5	**VALUE**		
20 or more units	1,043	5.1	Less than $50,000	510	3.6
Mobile home	52	0.3	$50,000 to $99,999	7,142	50.0
Boat, RV, van, etc	-	-	$100,000 to $149,999	6,037	42.3
			$150,000 to $199,999	502	3.5
YEAR STRUCTURE BUILT			$200,000 to $299,999	86	0.6
1999 to March 2000	54	0.3	$300,000 to $499,999	7	-
1995 to 1998	490	2.4	$500,000 to $999,999	-	-
1990 to 1994	566	2.8	$1,000,000 or more	-	-
1980 to 1989	1,679	8.2	Median (dollars)	97,800	(X)
1970 to 1979	2,653	12.9			
1960 to 1969	4,242	20.7	**MORTGAGE STATUS AND SELECTED**		
1940 to 1959	9,529	46.4	**MONTHLY OWNER COSTS**		
1939 or earlier	1,306	6.4	With a mortgage	10,098	70.7
			Less than $300	84	0.6
ROOMS			$300 to $499	731	5.1
1 room	80	0.4	$500 to $699	1,984	13.9
2 rooms	607	3.0	$700 to $999	4,377	30.6
3 rooms	1,807	8.8	$1,000 to $1,499	2,534	17.7
4 rooms	3,034	14.8	$1,500 to $1,999	324	2.3
5 rooms	8,042	39.2	$2,000 or more	64	0.4
6 rooms	4,493	21.9	Median (dollars)	845	(X)
7 rooms	1,581	7.7	Not mortgaged	4,186	29.3
8 rooms	584	2.8	Median (dollars)	261	(X)
9 or more rooms	291	1.4			
Median (rooms)	5.1	(X)	**SELECTED MONTHLY OWNER COSTS**		
			AS A PERCENTAGE OF HOUSEHOLD		
Occupied housing units	19,976	100.0	**INCOME IN 1999**		
YEAR HOUSEHOLDER MOVED INTO UNIT			Less than 15.0 percent	5,688	39.8
1999 to March 2000	2,787	14.0	15.0 to 19.9 percent	2,753	19.3
1995 to 1998	5,420	27.1	20.0 to 24.9 percent	2,049	14.3
1990 to 1994	3,066	15.3	25.0 to 29.9 percent	1,183	8.3
1980 to 1989	3,048	15.3	30.0 to 34.9 percent	698	4.9
1970 to 1979	2,205	11.0	35.0 percent or more	1,780	12.5
1969 or earlier	3,450	17.3	Not computed	133	0.9
VEHICLES AVAILABLE			Specified renter-occupied units	4,934	100.0
None	1,410	7.1	**GROSS RENT**		
1	7,674	38.4	Less than $200	231	4.7
2	7,782	39.0	$200 to $299	226	4.6
3 or more	3,110	15.6	$300 to $499	1,171	23.7
			$500 to $749	2,333	47.3
HOUSE HEATING FUEL			$750 to $999	688	13.9
Utility gas	18,081	90.5	$1,000 to $1,499	84	1.7
Bottled, tank, or LP gas	171	0.9	$1,500 or more	20	0.4
Electricity	1,431	7.2	No cash rent	181	3.7
Fuel oil, kerosene, etc	51	0.3	Median (dollars)	569	(X)
Coal or coke	-	-			
Wood	25	0.1	**GROSS RENT AS A PERCENTAGE OF**		
Solar energy	-	-	**HOUSEHOLD INCOME IN 1999**		
Other fuel	143	0.7	Less than 15.0 percent	996	20.2
No fuel used	74	0.4	15.0 to 19.9 percent	747	15.1
			20.0 to 24.9 percent	565	11.5
SELECTED CHARACTERISTICS			25.0 to 29.9 percent	573	11.6
Lacking complete plumbing facilities	69	0.3	30.0 to 34.9 percent	404	8.2
Lacking complete kitchen facilities	31	0.2	35.0 percent or more	1,337	27.1
No telephone service	318	1.6	Not computed	312	6.3

-Represents zero or rounds to zero.   (X) Not applicable.

Source: U.S. Bureau of the Census, Census 2000.

Table DP-1. Profile of General Demographic Characteristics: 2000

Geographic area: Sterling Heights city, Michigan

[For information on confidentiality protection, nonsampling error, and definitions, see text]

Subject	Number	Percent	Subject	Number	Percent
Total population	124,471	100.0	**HISPANIC OR LATINO AND RACE**		
SEX AND AGE			Total population	124,471	100.0
Male	60,970	49.0	Hispanic or Latino (of any race)	1,665	1.3
Female	63,501	51.0	Mexican	890	0.7
			Puerto Rican	152	0.1
Under 5 years	7,729	6.2	Cuban	58	-
5 to 9 years	8,326	6.7	Other Hispanic or Latino	565	0.5
10 to 14 years	8,758	7.0	Not Hispanic or Latino	122,806	98.7
15 to 19 years	8,153	6.6	White alone	111,743	89.8
20 to 24 years	7,595	6.1	**RELATIONSHIP**		
25 to 34 years	17,786	14.3	Total population	124,471	100.0
35 to 44 years	20,087	16.1	In households	123,273	99.0
45 to 54 years	18,621	15.0	Householder	46,319	37.2
55 to 59 years	7,462	6.0	Spouse	27,959	22.5
60 to 64 years	5,316	4.3	Child	40,377	32.4
65 to 74 years	7,266	5.8	Own child under 18 years	28,422	22.8
75 to 84 years	5,398	4.3	Other relatives	5,504	4.4
85 years and over	1,974	1.6	Under 18 years	1,295	1.0
Median age (years)	37.0	(X)	Nonrelatives	3,114	2.5
			Unmarried partner	1,518	1.2
18 years and over	94,506	75.9	In group quarters	1,198	1.0
Male	45,450	36.5	Institutionalized population	672	0.5
Female	49,056	39.4	Noninstitutionalized population	526	0.4
21 years and over	90,125	72.4			
62 years and over	17,577	14.1	**HOUSEHOLD BY TYPE**		
65 years and over	14,638	11.8	Total households	46,319	100.0
Male	5,781	4.6	Family households (families)	33,392	72.1
Female	8,857	7.1	With own children under 18 years	15,248	32.9
			Married-couple family	27,959	60.4
RACE			With own children under 18 years	12,862	27.8
One race	121,359	97.5	Female householder, no husband present	3,955	8.5
White	112,899	90.7	With own children under 18 years	1,842	4.0
Black or African American	1,614	1.3	Nonfamily households	12,927	27.9
American Indian and Alaska Native	260	0.2	Householder living alone	11,160	24.1
Asian	6,123	4.9	Householder 65 years and over	3,915	8.5
Asian Indian	2,410	1.9			
Chinese	890	0.7	Households with individuals under 18 years	16,118	34.8
Filipino	1,350	1.1	Households with individuals 65 years and over	10,252	22.1
Japanese	59	-			
Korean	488	0.4	Average household size	2.66	(X)
Vietnamese	435	0.3	Average family size	3.21	(X)
Other Asian [1]	491	0.4			
Native Hawaiian and Other Pacific Islander	45	-	**HOUSING OCCUPANCY**		
Native Hawaiian	5	-	Total housing units	47,547	100.0
Guamanian or Chamorro	9	-	Occupied housing units	46,319	97.4
Samoan	-	-	Vacant housing units	1,228	2.6
Other Pacific Islander [2]	31	-	For seasonal, recreational, or occasional use	132	0.3
Some other race	418	0.3			
Two or more races	3,112	2.5	Homeowner vacancy rate (percent)	0.9	(X)
			Rental vacancy rate (percent)	3.7	(X)
Race alone or in combination with one or more other races: [3]			**HOUSING TENURE**		
White	115,818	93.0	Occupied housing units	46,319	100.0
Black or African American	1,895	1.5	Owner-occupied housing units	36,584	79.0
American Indian and Alaska Native	690	0.6	Renter-occupied housing units	9,735	21.0
Asian	6,779	5.4			
Native Hawaiian and Other Pacific Islander	100	0.1	Average household size of owner-occupied units	2.87	(X)
Some other race	2,416	1.9	Average household size of renter-occupied units	1.88	(X)

- Represents zero or rounds to zero.   (X) Not applicable.

[1] Other Asian alone, or two or more Asian categories.

[2] Other Pacific Islander alone, or two or more Native Hawaiian and Other Pacific Islander categories.

[3] In combination with one or more of the other races listed. The six numbers may add to more than the total population and the six percentages may add to more than 100 percent because individuals may report more than one race.

Source: U.S. Census Bureau, Census 2000.

Table DP-2. Profile of Selected Social Characteristics: 2000

Geographic area: Sterling Heights city, Michigan

[Data based on a sample. For information on confidentiality protection, sampling error, nonsampling error, and definitions, see text]

Subject	Number	Percent	Subject	Number	Percent
SCHOOL ENROLLMENT			**NATIVITY AND PLACE OF BIRTH**		
Population 3 years and over enrolled in school	33,141	100.0	Total population	124,471	100.0
Nursery school, preschool	2,024	6.1	Native	103,325	83.0
Kindergarten	1,588	4.8	Born in United States	102,519	82.4
Elementary school (grades 1-8)	13,955	42.1	State of residence	89,147	71.6
High school (grades 9-12)	7,401	22.3	Different state	13,372	10.7
College or graduate school	8,173	24.7	Born outside United States	806	0.6
EDUCATIONAL ATTAINMENT			Foreign born	21,146	17.0
Population 25 years and over	83,774	100.0	Entered 1990 to March 2000	8,380	6.7
Less than 9th grade	5,368	6.4	Naturalized citizen	11,165	9.0
9th to 12th grade, no diploma	8,059	9.6	Not a citizen	9,981	8.0
High school graduate (includes equivalency)	24,468	29.2	**REGION OF BIRTH OF FOREIGN BORN**		
Some college, no degree	19,738	23.6	Total (excluding born at sea)	21,146	100.0
Associate degree	6,905	8.2	Europe	8,690	41.1
Bachelor's degree	13,166	15.7	Asia	10,823	51.2
Graduate or professional degree	6,070	7.2	Africa	283	1.3
			Oceania	71	0.3
Percent high school graduate or higher	84.0	(X)	Latin America	352	1.7
Percent bachelor's degree or higher	23.0	(X)	Northern America	927	4.4
MARITAL STATUS			**LANGUAGE SPOKEN AT HOME**		
Population 15 years and over	99,643	100.0	Population 5 years and over	116,666	100.0
Never married	25,527	25.6	English only	89,680	76.9
Now married, except separated	59,788	60.0	Language other than English	26,986	23.1
Separated	541	0.5	Speak English less than very well	11,548	9.9
Widowed	6,210	6.2	Spanish	1,167	1.0
Female	5,163	5.2	Speak English less than very well	361	0.3
Divorced	7,577	7.6	Other Indo-European languages	14,278	12.2
Female	4,573	4.6	Speak English less than very well	5,980	5.1
			Asian and Pacific Island languages	3,217	2.8
GRANDPARENTS AS CAREGIVERS			Speak English less than very well	1,522	1.3
Grandparent living in household with one or more own grandchildren under 18 years	2,128	100.0	**ANCESTRY (single or multiple)**		
Grandparent responsible for grandchildren	641	30.1	Total population	124,471	100.0
			Total ancestries reported	150,391	120.8
VETERAN STATUS			Arab	4,598	3.7
Civilian population 18 years and over	94,390	100.0	Czech[1]	767	0.6
Civilian veterans	10,085	10.7	Danish	223	0.2
DISABILITY STATUS OF THE CIVILIAN NONINSTITUTIONALIZED POPULATION			Dutch	1,438	1.2
			English	9,264	7.4
Population 5 to 20 years	26,441	100.0	French (except Basque)[1]	5,744	4.6
With a disability	1,809	6.8	French Canadian[1]	2,679	2.2
			German	24,814	19.9
Population 21 to 64 years	75,563	100.0	Greek	1,086	0.9
With a disability	11,064	14.6	Hungarian	1,322	1.1
Percent employed	63.8	(X)	Irish[1]	11,949	9.6
No disability	64,499	85.4	Italian	16,556	13.3
Percent employed	79.5	(X)	Lithuanian	405	0.3
			Norwegian	556	0.4
Population 65 years and over	13,924	100.0	Polish	26,123	21.0
With a disability	5,659	40.6	Portuguese	92	0.1
			Russian	886	0.7
RESIDENCE IN 1995			Scotch-Irish	1,654	1.3
Population 5 years and over	116,666	100.0	Scottish	2,765	2.2
Same house in 1995	70,154	60.1	Slovak	937	0.8
Different house in the U.S. in 1995	42,685	36.6	Subsaharan African	93	0.1
Same county	23,413	20.1	Swedish	758	0.6
Different county	19,272	16.5	Swiss	135	0.1
Same state	15,567	13.3	Ukrainian	1,405	1.1
Different state	3,705	3.2	United States or American	4,357	3.5
Elsewhere in 1995	3,827	3.3	Welsh	436	0.4
			West Indian (excluding Hispanic groups)	29	-
			Other ancestries	29,320	23.6

-Represents zero or rounds to zero. (X) Not applicable.

[1]The data represent a combination of two ancestries shown separately in Summary File 3. Czech includes Czechoslovakian. French includes Alsatian. French Canadian includes Acadian/Cajun. Irish includes Celtic.

Source: U.S. Bureau of the Census, Census 2000.

Table DP-3. Profile of Selected Economic Characteristics: 2000

Geographic area: Sterling Heights city, Michigan

[Data based on a sample. For information on confidentiality protection, sampling error, nonsampling error, and definitions, see text]

Subject	Number	Percent	Subject	Number	Percent
EMPLOYMENT STATUS			**INCOME IN 1999**		
Population 16 years and over	97,973	100.0	Households	46,381	100.0
In labor force	66,726	68.1	Less than $10,000	2,157	4.7
Civilian labor force	66,659	68.0	$10,000 to $14,999	1,795	3.9
Employed	64,340	65.7	$15,000 to $24,999	3,749	8.1
Unemployed	2,319	2.4	$25,000 to $34,999	4,473	9.6
Percent of civilian labor force	3.5	(X)	$35,000 to $49,999	6,497	14.0
Armed Forces	67	0.1	$50,000 to $74,999	10,773	23.2
Not in labor force	31,247	31.9	$75,000 to $99,999	8,087	17.4
			$100,000 to $149,999	6,977	15.0
Females 16 years and over	50,557	100.0	$150,000 to $199,999	1,321	2.8
In labor force	30,264	59.9	$200,000 or more	552	1.2
Civilian labor force	30,256	59.8	Median household income (dollars)	60,494	(X)
Employed	29,206	57.8			
Own children under 6 years	9,301	100.0	With earnings	38,941	84.0
All parents in family in labor force	5,208	56.0	Mean earnings (dollars)[1]	67,316	(X)
			With Social Security income	11,318	24.4
COMMUTING TO WORK			Mean Social Security income (dollars)[1]	12,429	(X)
Workers 16 years and over	63,247	100.0	With Supplemental Security Income	1,049	2.3
Car, truck, or van - - drove alone	57,460	90.9	Mean Supplemental Security Income (dollars)[1]	7,402	(X)
Car, truck, or van - - carpooled	3,951	6.2	With public assistance income	963	2.1
Public transportation (including taxicab)	204	0.3	Mean public assistance income (dollars)[1]	3,113	(X)
Walked	412	0.7	With retirement income	8,828	19.0
Other means	215	0.3	Mean retirement income (dollars)[1]	15,075	(X)
Worked at home	1,005	1.6			
Mean travel time to work (minutes)[1]	25.4	(X)	Families	33,548	100.0
			Less than $10,000	835	2.5
Employed civilian population 16 years and over	64,340	100.0	$10,000 to $14,999	640	1.9
			$15,000 to $24,999	1,855	5.5
OCCUPATION			$25,000 to $34,999	2,373	7.1
Management, professional, and related occupations	22,844	35.5	$35,000 to $49,999	4,350	13.0
Service occupations	7,889	12.3	$50,000 to $74,999	8,302	24.7
Sales and office occupations	19,213	29.9	$75,000 to $99,999	7,088	21.1
Farming, fishing, and forestry occupations	51	0.1	$100,000 to $149,999	6,395	19.1
Construction, extraction, and maintenance occupations	4,927	7.7	$150,000 to $199,999	1,231	3.7
Production, transportation, and material moving occupations	9,416	14.6	$200,000 or more	479	1.4
			Median family income (dollars)	70,140	(X)
INDUSTRY			Per capita income (dollars)[1]	24,958	(X)
			Median earnings (dollars):		
Agriculture, forestry, fishing and hunting, and mining	53	0.1	Male full-time, year-round workers	51,207	(X)
Construction	3,226	5.0	Female full-time, year-round workers	31,489	(X)
Manufacturing	16,639	25.9			
Wholesale trade	2,471	3.8	Subject	Number below poverty level	Percent below poverty level
Retail trade	9,105	14.2			
Transportation and warehousing, and utilities	1,583	2.5			
Information	1,475	2.3			
Finance, insurance, real estate, and rental and leasing	4,091	6.4	**POVERTY STATUS IN 1999**		
			Families	1,335	4.0
Professional, scientific, management, administrative, and waste management services	6,774	10.5	With related children under 18 years	970	6.0
Educational, health and social services	9,651	15.0	With related children under 5 years	475	7.8
Arts, entertainment, recreation, accommodation and food services	4,777	7.4	Families with female householder, no husband present	526	13.8
Other services (except public administration)	2,372	3.7	With related children under 18 years	476	24.3
Public administration	2,123	3.3	With related children under 5 years	242	41.9
CLASS OF WORKER			Individuals	6,480	5.2
Private wage and salary workers	56,779	88.2	18 years and over	4,457	4.8
Government workers	5,021	7.8	65 years and over	1,041	7.5
Self-employed workers in own not incorporated business	2,376	3.7	Related children under 18 years	1,944	6.6
			Related children 5 to 17 years	1,304	5.9
Unpaid family workers	164	0.3	Unrelated individuals 15 years and over	1,947	12.0

-Represents zero or rounds to zero.   (X) Not applicable.

[1]If the denominator of a mean value or per capita value is less than 30, then that value is calculated using a rounded aggregate in the numerator. See text.

Source: U.S. Bureau of the Census, Census 2000.

Table DP-4. Profile of Selected Housing Characteristics: 2000

Geographic area: Sterling Heights city, Michigan

[Data based on a sample. For information on confidentiality protection, sampling error, nonsampling error, and definitions, see text]

Subject	Number	Percent	Subject	Number	Percent
Total housing units....................	47,547	100.0	**OCCUPANTS PER ROOM**		
UNITS IN STRUCTURE			Occupied housing units...............	46,319	100.0
1-unit, detached.............................	32,602	68.6	1.00 or less..................................	44,839	96.8
1-unit, attached	3,022	6.4	1.01 to 1.50	885	1.9
2 units	134	0.3	1.51 or more................................	595	1.3
3 or 4 units	1,411	3.0			
5 to 9 units	4,658	9.8	Specified owner-occupied units........	33,272	100.0
10 to 19 units...............................	1,459	3.1	**VALUE**		
20 or more units	2,542	5.3	Less than $50,000.........................	183	0.6
Mobile home..................................	1,714	3.6	$50,000 to $99,999.......................	1,726	5.2
Boat, RV, van, etc	5	-	$100,000 to $149,999....................	10,431	31.4
			$150,000 to $199,999....................	15,124	45.5
YEAR STRUCTURE BUILT			$200,000 to $299,999....................	4,610	13.9
1999 to March 2000	1,196	2.5	$300,000 to $499,999....................	1,139	3.4
1995 to 1998	3,386	7.1	$500,000 to $999,999....................	35	0.1
1990 to 1994	2,890	6.1	$1,000,000 or more.......................	24	0.1
1980 to 1989	7,763	16.3	Median (dollars)............................	160,700	(X)
1970 to 1979	16,915	35.6			
1960 to 1969	11,604	24.4	**MORTGAGE STATUS AND SELECTED**		
1940 to 1959	3,284	6.9	**MONTHLY OWNER COSTS**		
1939 or earlier	509	1.1	With a mortgage	24,669	74.1
			Less than $300	32	0.1
ROOMS			$300 to $499	592	1.8
1 room..	486	1.0	$500 to $699	1,956	5.9
2 rooms.......................................	1,358	2.9	$700 to $999	6,170	18.5
3 rooms.......................................	4,044	8.5	$1,000 to $1,499	11,029	33.1
4 rooms.......................................	5,731	12.1	$1,500 to $1,999	3,707	11.1
5 rooms.......................................	9,140	19.2	$2,000 or more	1,183	3.6
6 rooms.......................................	13,063	27.5	Median (dollars).........................	1,140	(X)
7 rooms.......................................	6,583	13.8	Not mortgaged..............................	8,603	25.9
8 rooms.......................................	4,512	9.5	Median (dollars).........................	332	(X)
9 or more rooms	2,630	5.5			
Median (rooms)	5.7	(X)	**SELECTED MONTHLY OWNER COSTS**		
			AS A PERCENTAGE OF HOUSEHOLD		
Occupied housing units	46,319	100.0	**INCOME IN 1999**		
YEAR HOUSEHOLDER MOVED INTO UNIT			Less than 15.0 percent.....................	14,416	43.3
1999 to March 2000	7,696	16.6	15.0 to 19.9 percent	6,458	19.4
1995 to 1998	12,981	28.0	20.0 to 24.9 percent	4,270	12.8
1990 to 1994	7,323	15.8	25.0 to 29.9 percent	2,657	8.0
1980 to 1989	7,949	17.2	30.0 to 34.9 percent	1,528	4.6
1970 to 1979	7,143	15.4	35.0 percent or more	3,725	11.2
1969 or earlier	3,227	7.0	Not computed................................	218	0.7
VEHICLES AVAILABLE			Specified renter-occupied units	9,725	100.0
None	2,563	5.5	**GROSS RENT**		
1..	13,293	28.7	Less than $200	407	4.2
2..	20,521	44.3	$200 to $299	370	3.8
3 or more.....................................	9,942	21.5	$300 to $499	905	9.3
			$500 to $749	4,990	51.3
HOUSE HEATING FUEL			$750 to $999	1,966	20.2
Utility gas	43,586	94.1	$1,000 to $1,499	459	4.7
Bottled, tank, or LP gas	213	0.5	$1,500 or more	375	3.9
Electricity.....................................	2,348	5.1	No cash rent.................................	253	2.6
Fuel oil, kerosene, etc	29	0.1	Median (dollars)............................	644	(X)
Coal or coke..................................	-	-			
Wood..	4	-	**GROSS RENT AS A PERCENTAGE OF**		
Solar energy..................................	-	-	**HOUSEHOLD INCOME IN 1999**		
Other fuel.....................................	76	0.2	Less than 15.0 percent.....................	2,406	24.7
No fuel used..................................	63	0.1	15.0 to 19.9 percent	1,504	15.5
			20.0 to 24.9 percent	1,356	13.9
SELECTED CHARACTERISTICS			25.0 to 29.9 percent	1,024	10.5
Lacking complete plumbing facilities	118	0.3	30.0 to 34.9 percent	695	7.1
Lacking complete kitchen facilities.............	72	0.2	35.0 percent or more	2,357	24.2
No telephone service	215	0.5	Not computed................................	383	3.9

-Represents zero or rounds to zero. (X) Not applicable.

Source: U.S. Bureau of the Census, Census 2000.

Table DP-1. Profile of General Demographic Characteristics: 2000

Geographic area: Utica city, Michigan

[For information on confidentiality protection, nonsampling error, and definitions, see text]

Subject	Number	Percent	Subject	Number	Percent
Total population	4,577	100.0	**HISPANIC OR LATINO AND RACE**		
SEX AND AGE			Total population	4,577	100.0
Male	2,204	48.2	Hispanic or Latino (of any race)	96	2.1
Female	2,373	51.8	Mexican	67	1.5
			Puerto Rican	8	0.2
Under 5 years	234	5.1	Cuban	-	-
5 to 9 years	243	5.3	Other Hispanic or Latino	21	0.5
10 to 14 years	301	6.6	Not Hispanic or Latino	4,481	97.9
15 to 19 years	299	6.5	White alone	4,232	92.5
20 to 24 years	324	7.1	**RELATIONSHIP**		
25 to 34 years	709	15.5	Total population	4,577	100.0
35 to 44 years	744	16.3	In households	4,465	97.6
45 to 54 years	693	15.1	Householder	1,952	42.6
55 to 59 years	223	4.9	Spouse	854	18.7
60 to 64 years	145	3.2	Child	1,306	28.5
65 to 74 years	271	5.9	Own child under 18 years	895	19.6
75 to 84 years	271	5.9	Other relatives	160	3.5
85 years and over	120	2.6	Under 18 years	50	1.1
Median age (years)	37.3	(X)	Nonrelatives	193	4.2
			Unmarried partner	79	1.7
18 years and over	3,616	79.0	In group quarters	112	2.4
Male	1,731	37.8	Institutionalized population	45	1.0
Female	1,885	41.2	Noninstitutionalized population	67	1.5
21 years and over	3,451	75.4			
62 years and over	742	16.2	**HOUSEHOLD BY TYPE**		
65 years and over	662	14.5	Total households	1,952	100.0
Male	241	5.3	Family households (families)	1,184	60.7
Female	421	9.2	With own children under 18 years	531	27.2
			Married-couple family	854	43.8
RACE			With own children under 18 years	356	18.2
One race	4,502	98.4	Female householder, no husband present	260	13.3
White	4,292	93.8	With own children under 18 years	146	7.5
Black or African American	42	0.9	Nonfamily households	768	39.3
American Indian and Alaska Native	17	0.4	Householder living alone	667	34.2
Asian	117	2.6	Householder 65 years and over	210	10.8
Asian Indian	74	1.6			
Chinese	2	-	Households with individuals under 18 years	565	28.9
Filipino	6	0.1	Households with individuals 65 years and over	434	22.2
Japanese	1	-			
Korean	25	0.5	Average household size	2.29	(X)
Vietnamese	4	0.1	Average family size	2.96	(X)
Other Asian [1]	5	0.1			
Native Hawaiian and Other Pacific Islander	-	-	**HOUSING OCCUPANCY**		
Native Hawaiian	-	-	Total housing units	2,005	100.0
Guamanian or Chamorro	-	-	Occupied housing units	1,952	97.4
Samoan	-	-	Vacant housing units	53	2.6
Other Pacific Islander [2]	-	-	For seasonal, recreational, or occasional use	11	0.5
Some other race	34	0.7			
Two or more races	75	1.6	Homeowner vacancy rate (percent)	0.2	(X)
			Rental vacancy rate (percent)	3.0	(X)
Race alone or in combination with one or more other races: [3]			**HOUSING TENURE**		
White	4,362	95.3	Occupied housing units	1,952	100.0
Black or African American	55	1.2	Owner-occupied housing units	1,052	53.9
American Indian and Alaska Native	39	0.9	Renter-occupied housing units	900	46.1
Asian	129	2.8			
Native Hawaiian and Other Pacific Islander	1	-	Average household size of owner-occupied units	2.60	(X)
Some other race	71	1.6	Average household size of renter-occupied units	1.92	(X)

- Represents zero or rounds to zero.   (X) Not applicable.

[1] Other Asian alone, or two or more Asian categories.

[2] Other Pacific Islander alone, or two or more Native Hawaiian and Other Pacific Islander categories.

[3] In combination with one or more of the other races listed. The six numbers may add to more than the total population and the six percentages may add to more than 100 percent because individuals may report more than one race.

Source: U.S. Census Bureau, Census 2000.

Table DP-2. Profile of Selected Social Characteristics: 2000

Geographic area: Utica city, Michigan

[Data based on a sample. For information on confidentiality protection, sampling error, nonsampling error, and definitions, see text]

Subject	Number	Percent	Subject	Number	Percent
SCHOOL ENROLLMENT			**NATIVITY AND PLACE OF BIRTH**		
Population 3 years and over enrolled in school	1,174	100.0	Total population	4,577	100.0
Nursery school, preschool	69	5.9	Native	3,982	87.0
Kindergarten	44	3.7	Born in United States	3,981	87.0
Elementary school (grades 1-8)	428	36.5	State of residence	3,328	72.7
High school (grades 9-12)	258	22.0	Different state	653	14.3
College or graduate school	375	31.9	Born outside United States	1	-
			Foreign born	595	13.0
EDUCATIONAL ATTAINMENT			Entered 1990 to March 2000	361	7.9
Population 25 years and over	3,195	100.0	Naturalized citizen	185	4.0
Less than 9th grade	193	6.0	Not a citizen	410	9.0
9th to 12th grade, no diploma	420	13.1	**REGION OF BIRTH OF FOREIGN BORN**		
High school graduate (includes equivalency)	944	29.5	Total (excluding born at sea)	595	100.0
Some college, no degree	758	23.7	Europe	367	61.7
Associate degree	294	9.2	Asia	159	26.7
Bachelor's degree	418	13.1	Africa	-	-
Graduate or professional degree	168	5.3	Oceania	-	-
			Latin America	11	1.8
Percent high school graduate or higher	80.8	(X)	Northern America	58	9.7
Percent bachelor's degree or higher	18.3	(X)	**LANGUAGE SPOKEN AT HOME**		
MARITAL STATUS			Population 5 years and over	4,344	100.0
Population 15 years and over	3,798	100.0	English only	3,759	86.5
Never married	1,031	27.1	Language other than English	585	13.5
Now married, except separated	1,915	50.4	Speak English less than very well	269	6.2
Separated	8	0.2	Spanish	30	0.7
Widowed	339	8.9	Speak English less than very well	17	0.4
Female	250	6.6	Other Indo-European languages	493	11.3
Divorced	505	13.3	Speak English less than very well	224	5.2
Female	362	9.5	Asian and Pacific Island languages	34	0.8
			Speak English less than very well	19	0.4
GRANDPARENTS AS CAREGIVERS			**ANCESTRY (single or multiple)**		
Grandparent living in household with one or more own grandchildren under 18 years	69	100.0	Total population	4,577	100.0
Grandparent responsible for grandchildren	17	24.6	Total ancestries reported	5,210	113.8
			Arab	11	0.2
VETERAN STATUS			Czech[1]	16	0.3
Civilian population 18 years and over	3,610	100.0	Danish	23	0.5
Civilian veterans	442	12.2	Dutch	86	1.9
			English	452	9.9
DISABILITY STATUS OF THE CIVILIAN NONINSTITUTIONALIZED POPULATION			French (except Basque)[1]	330	7.2
			French Canadian[1]	68	1.5
Population 5 to 20 years	905	100.0	German	1,250	27.3
With a disability	41	4.5	Greek	17	0.4
Population 21 to 64 years	2,769	100.0	Hungarian	24	0.5
With a disability	602	21.7	Irish[1]	432	9.4
Percent employed	66.6	(X)	Italian	367	8.0
No disability	2,167	78.3	Lithuanian	6	0.1
Percent employed	80.4	(X)	Norwegian	44	1.0
Population 65 years and over	624	100.0	Polish	676	14.8
With a disability	260	41.7	Portuguese	-	-
			Russian	62	1.4
RESIDENCE IN 1995			Scotch-Irish	23	0.5
			Scottish	92	2.0
			Slovak	21	0.5
Population 5 years and over	4,344	100.0	Subsaharan African	-	-
Same house in 1995	2,330	53.6	Swedish	42	0.9
Different house in the U.S. in 1995	1,676	38.6	Swiss	8	0.2
Same county	1,028	23.7	Ukrainian	16	0.3
Different county	648	14.9	United States or American	180	3.9
Same state	583	13.4	Welsh	23	0.5
Different state	65	1.5	West Indian (excluding Hispanic groups)	-	-
Elsewhere in 1995	338	7.8	Other ancestries	941	20.6

-Represents zero or rounds to zero.   (X) Not applicable.

[1]The data represent a combination of two ancestries shown separately in Summary File 3. Czech includes Czechoslovakian. French includes Alsatian. French Canadian includes Acadian/Cajun. Irish includes Celtic.

Source: U.S. Bureau of the Census, Census 2000.

Table DP-3. Profile of Selected Economic Characteristics: 2000

Geographic area: Utica city, Michigan

[Data based on a sample. For information on confidentiality protection, sampling error, nonsampling error, and definitions, see text]

Subject	Number	Percent	Subject	Number	Percent
EMPLOYMENT STATUS			**INCOME IN 1999**		
Population 16 years and over	3,732	100.0	Households	1,953	100.0
In labor force	2,562	68.6	Less than $10,000	197	10.1
Civilian labor force	2,562	68.6	$10,000 to $14,999	90	4.6
Employed	2,397	64.2	$15,000 to $24,999	303	15.5
Unemployed	165	4.4	$25,000 to $34,999	249	12.7
Percent of civilian labor force	6.4	(X)	$35,000 to $49,999	284	14.5
Armed Forces	-	-	$50,000 to $74,999	414	21.2
Not in labor force	1,170	31.4	$75,000 to $99,999	228	11.7
Females 16 years and over	1,979	100.0	$100,000 to $149,999	146	7.5
In labor force	1,201	60.7	$150,000 to $199,999	28	1.4
Civilian labor force	1,201	60.7	$200,000 or more	14	0.7
Employed	1,113	56.2	Median household income (dollars)	38,683	(X)
Own children under 6 years	263	100.0	With earnings	1,623	83.1
All parents in family in labor force	149	56.7	Mean earnings (dollars)[1]	50,683	(X)
			With Social Security income	447	22.9
COMMUTING TO WORK			Mean Social Security income (dollars)[1]	9,746	(X)
Workers 16 years and over	2,349	100.0	With Supplemental Security Income	32	1.6
Car, truck, or van - - drove alone	2,071	88.2	Mean Supplemental Security Income (dollars)[1]	5,686	(X)
Car, truck, or van - - carpooled	180	7.7	With public assistance income	56	2.9
Public transportation (including taxicab)	7	0.3	Mean public assistance income (dollars)[1]	2,509	(X)
Walked	42	1.8	With retirement income	281	14.4
Other means	25	1.1	Mean retirement income (dollars)[1]	15,326	(X)
Worked at home	24	1.0			
Mean travel time to work (minutes)[1]	24.9	(X)	Families	1,193	100.0
			Less than $10,000	51	4.3
Employed civilian population 16 years and over	2,397	100.0	$10,000 to $14,999	6	0.5
OCCUPATION			$15,000 to $24,999	156	13.1
Management, professional, and related occupations	700	29.2	$25,000 to $34,999	90	7.5
Service occupations	365	15.2	$35,000 to $49,999	164	13.7
Sales and office occupations	673	28.1	$50,000 to $74,999	357	29.9
Farming, fishing, and forestry occupations	-	-	$75,000 to $99,999	193	16.2
Construction, extraction, and maintenance occupations	277	11.6	$100,000 to $149,999	134	11.2
Production, transportation, and material moving occupations	382	15.9	$150,000 to $199,999	28	2.3
			$200,000 or more	14	1.2
			Median family income (dollars)	57,156	(X)
INDUSTRY			Per capita income (dollars)[1]	21,615	(X)
Agriculture, forestry, fishing and hunting, and mining	-	-	**Median earnings (dollars):**		
Construction	214	8.9	Male full-time, year-round workers	36,912	(X)
Manufacturing	584	24.4	Female full-time, year-round workers	26,353	(X)

Subject	Number below poverty level	Percent below poverty level
INDUSTRY (continued)		
Wholesale trade — 31 (1.3)		
Retail trade — 278 (11.6)		
Transportation and warehousing, and utilities — 63 (2.6)		
Information — 40 (1.7)		
Finance, insurance, real estate, and rental and leasing — 111 (4.6)		
POVERTY STATUS IN 1999		
Families	57	4.8
With related children under 18 years	49	8.4
With related children under 5 years	23	10.6
Families with female householder, no husband present	30	14.7
With related children under 18 years	30	22.1
With related children under 5 years	4	26.7
Individuals	316	7.0
18 years and over	252	7.1
65 years and over	108	17.3
Related children under 18 years	64	6.7
Related children 5 to 17 years	35	4.8
Unrelated individuals 15 years and over	165	16.9

Additional INDUSTRY data:
- Professional, scientific, management, administrative, and waste management services: 362, 15.1
- Educational, health and social services: 414, 17.3
- Arts, entertainment, recreation, accommodation and food services: 169, 7.1
- Other services (except public administration): 91, 3.8
- Public administration: 40, 1.7

CLASS OF WORKER
- Private wage and salary workers: 2,172, 90.6
- Government workers: 174, 7.3
- Self-employed workers in own not incorporated business: 51, 2.1
- Unpaid family workers: -, -

-Represents zero or rounds to zero. (X) Not applicable.

[1]If the denominator of a mean value or per capita value is less than 30, then that value is calculated using a rounded aggregate in the numerator. See text.

Source: U.S. Bureau of the Census, Census 2000.

Table DP-4. Profile of Selected Housing Characteristics: 2000
Geographic area: Utica city, Michigan

[Data based on a sample. For information on confidentiality protection, sampling error, nonsampling error, and definitions, see text]

Subject	Number	Percent	Subject	Number	Percent
Total housing units..................	2,005	100.0	**OCCUPANTS PER ROOM**		
UNITS IN STRUCTURE			Occupied housing units...............	1,952	100.0
1-unit, detached.............................	921	45.9	1.00 or less.................	1,878	96.2
1-unit, attached.............................	316	15.8	1.01 to 1.50.................	40	2.0
2 units.......................................	48	2.4	1.51 or more.................	34	1.7
3 or 4 units..................................	99	4.9			
5 to 9 units..................................	219	10.9	Specified owner-occupied units........	997	100.0
10 to 19 units................................	226	11.3	**VALUE**		
20 or more units.............................	173	8.6	Less than $50,000.................	64	6.4
Mobile home.................................	3	0.1	$50,000 to $99,999.................	116	11.6
Boat, RV, van, etc...........................	-	-	$100,000 to $149,999.................	353	35.4
			$150,000 to $199,999.................	350	35.1
YEAR STRUCTURE BUILT			$200,000 to $299,999.................	114	11.4
1999 to March 2000.........................	6	0.3	$300,000 to $499,999.................	-	-
1995 to 1998.................................	21	1.0	$500,000 to $999,999.................	-	-
1990 to 1994.................................	107	5.3	$1,000,000 or more.................	-	-
1980 to 1989.................................	89	4.4	Median (dollars).................	145,800	(X)
1970 to 1979.................................	607	30.3			
1960 to 1969.................................	487	24.3	**MORTGAGE STATUS AND SELECTED**		
1940 to 1959.................................	483	24.1	**MONTHLY OWNER COSTS**		
1939 or earlier.............................	205	10.2	With a mortgage.................	747	74.9
			Less than $300.................	12	1.2
ROOMS			$300 to $499.................	29	2.9
1 room.......................................	16	0.8	$500 to $699.................	94	9.4
2 rooms......................................	67	3.3	$700 to $999.................	197	19.8
3 rooms......................................	279	13.9	$1,000 to $1,499.................	302	30.3
4 rooms......................................	422	21.0	$1,500 to $1,999.................	84	8.4
5 rooms......................................	454	22.6	$2,000 or more.................	29	2.9
6 rooms......................................	356	17.8	Median (dollars).................	1,056	(X)
7 rooms......................................	236	11.8	Not mortgaged.................	250	25.1
8 rooms......................................	101	5.0	Median (dollars).................	327	(X)
9 or more rooms.............................	74	3.7			
Median (rooms).............................	5.0	(X)	**SELECTED MONTHLY OWNER COSTS**		
			AS A PERCENTAGE OF HOUSEHOLD		
Occupied housing units...............	1,952	100.0	**INCOME IN 1999**		
YEAR HOUSEHOLDER MOVED INTO UNIT			Less than 15.0 percent.................	420	42.1
1999 to March 2000.........................	319	16.3	15.0 to 19.9 percent.................	173	17.4
1995 to 1998.................................	601	30.8	20.0 to 24.9 percent.................	113	11.3
1990 to 1994.................................	294	15.1	25.0 to 29.9 percent.................	111	11.1
1980 to 1989.................................	344	17.6	30.0 to 34.9 percent.................	68	6.8
1970 to 1979.................................	296	15.2	35.0 percent or more.................	112	11.2
1969 or earlier.............................	98	5.0	Not computed.................	-	-
VEHICLES AVAILABLE			Specified renter-occupied units........	884	100.0
None...	150	7.7	**GROSS RENT**		
1...	896	45.9	Less than $200.................	16	1.8
2...	644	33.0	$200 to $299.................	-	-
3 or more....................................	262	13.4	$300 to $499.................	394	44.6
			$500 to $749.................	406	45.9
HOUSE HEATING FUEL			$750 to $999.................	43	4.9
Utility gas..................................	1,816	93.0	$1,000 to $1,499.................	-	-
Bottled, tank, or LP gas.....................	12	0.6	$1,500 or more.................	-	-
Electricity..................................	93	4.8	No cash rent.................	25	2.8
Fuel oil, kerosene, etc.....................	20	1.0	Median (dollars).................	507	(X)
Coal or coke.................................	-	-			
Wood...	-	-	**GROSS RENT AS A PERCENTAGE OF**		
Solar energy.................................	-	-	**HOUSEHOLD INCOME IN 1999**		
Other fuel...................................	-	-	Less than 15.0 percent.................	243	27.5
No fuel used.................................	11	0.6	15.0 to 19.9 percent.................	134	15.2
			20.0 to 24.9 percent.................	79	8.9
SELECTED CHARACTERISTICS			25.0 to 29.9 percent.................	68	7.7
Lacking complete plumbing facilities........	3	0.2	30.0 to 34.9 percent.................	41	4.6
Lacking complete kitchen facilities..........	-	-	35.0 percent or more.................	277	31.3
No telephone service........................	35	1.8	Not computed.................	42	4.8

-Represents zero or rounds to zero. (X) Not applicable.

Source: U.S. Bureau of the Census, Census 2000.

Table 4.1 Michigan's 10th State Senate District Voting History, 1994–2000.

	1994		1996		1998		2000	
registered voters	175,495		184,259		191,825		181,690	
voter turnout	88,128		107,274		86,693		116,378	
turnout percentage	50.2%		58.2%		45.2%		64.0%	
Election Results								
	votes	percent	votes	percent	votes	percent	votes	percent
President								
Republican			41,571	39.8%			54,038	47.1%
Democrat			52,563	50.4%			58,612	51.1%
			94,134				112,650	
Governor								
Republican	60,392	70.1%			57,405	70.9%		
Democrat	25,747	29.8%			23,513	29.1%		
	86,139				80,918			
Secretary of State								
Republican	33,087	38.9%			62,682	75.9%		
Democrat	51,851	61.0%			19,890	24.0%		
	84,938				82,572			
U.S. Senate								
Republican	47,789	61.2%	42,923	42.1%			53,803	48.9%
Democrat	30,269	38.7%	58,807	57.8%			56,185	51.0%
	78,058		101,730				109,988	
U.S. House								
Republican	36,940	43.9%	43,535	44.0%	36,685	45.1%	36,017	33.5%
Democrat	47,055	56.0%	55,308	55.9%	44,673	54.9%	71,507	66.5%
	83,995		98,843		81,358		107,524	
State Senate								
Republican	45,288	55.7%			41,307	52.1%		
Democrat	35,946	44.2%			37,917	47.8%		
	81,234				79,224			
State House								
Republican	40,238	49.8%	47,010	47.5%	42,945	54.6%	51,954	48.7%
Democrat	40,454	50.1%	51,853	52.5%	35,742	45.4%	54,803	51.3%
	80,692		98,863		78,687		106,757	

The number of registered voters in this district for this election is: 181,237.

Rice, Switalski Race-Off Is Main Event for Macomb Ballot*
By Chad Selweski
The Macomb Daily
October 1, 2002

More than 140 candidates will appear on ballots across Macomb County in November but Macomb's main event shapes up as a stare-down between two men: Steve Rice and Michael Switalski.

Switalski, a Democratic state representative from Roseville, and Rice, the Republican nominee and a Sterling Heights councilman, will butt heads in a coveted state Senate District where anything goes.

The newly drawn 10th District is labeled a toss-up, a 50-50 split between Republicans and Democrats. The district, which should remain a political battleground for the next decade, consists of Sterling Heights, Clinton Township, Roseville and Utica.

Switalski, 47, should hold the early advantage because of his legislative experience and his convincing win in the August primary over former state representative Sharon Gire.

But Rice, unopposed in the GOP primary, hopes to deliver a body blow to Switalski, who has not faced a major challenge in a fall contest since 1992.

"This is the first time he's had a serious fall general election. His record will come out in this campaign. He has to address his (House) votes," said Rice, 44. "He continues to send money elsewhere, not to his district."

Rice's portrayal of Switalski as too liberal targets the representative's vote for partial-birth abortions, which could become an issue in the heavily Catholic 10th District. Rice is pro-life; Switalski is pro-choice.

But Switalski calls the House vote on partial-birth abortions a partisan manipulation by the GOP, as lawmakers knew the courts would strike down the legislation. Federal jurists set aside the Michigan law.

Rice served on the Sterling Heights City Council from 1985 to 1993, including two years as the city's part-time mayor. He was defeated in the 1993 election, returned to the council in 1995, and won re-election four years later.

Switalski has never lost an election. He served on the Roseville City Council from 1989 to 1992, first won election to the county Board of Commissioners in 1992 and served three terms, then was elected to the state House in 1998 and 2000.

A member of the House Appropriations Committee, Switalski said lawmakers knew the main issue in January for the new Legislature will be a $1 billion budget deficit.

"The biggest issue is the slowing economy and the state budget deficit," he said. "The one-time fixes we've seen won't solve our problems. I think I was ahead of my time (in 2001) by calling for a freeze on spending and tax cuts."

Switalski has emphasized his fiscally conservative stands—a 40-hour work requirement for welfare recipients and no tax hikes—but Rice said his opponent's labor union backing makes him suspect.

"If Detroit comes calling, doesn't he start spending and doing whatever (liberal interest groups) require? He'll do as he's told to do," Rice said.

Taxes, a proposed "tweaking" of Proposal A and water rate increases are issues that Rice opposes. He sees a separation between himself and Switalski on all three fronts.

As the campaign heats up, Clinton Township could shape up as the key battleground in the 10th District. But Switalski has shown an eagerness to challenger Rice's Sterling Heights base and Rice has been campaigning in Switalski's back yard of Roseville.

Rice emphasizes that his town has won recognition as one of the nation's best-managed, safest and most livable cities. But five of Rice's six colleagues on City Council have endorsed Switalski for Senate.

Rice has also raised the prospect that the Switalski brothers—"all on the taxpayer dole"—could become a campaign issue. Mark Switalski is a Macomb County circuit judge and Matt Switalski, an assistant prosecutor, is running in November for a circuit court seat.

Michael Switalski views his brothers as an asset, not a liability. His campaign consists entirely of folksy newsletters that contain the former sports reporter's writings about his large family and his Lansing experiences.

Switalski's unconventional methods have been questioned by political analysts, who say he fails to target key voters and stress "hot button" issues.

"That's total garbage," he said. "That's what's wrong with conventional campaigning. I think there's a hunger out there among voters for . . . something that makes a connection, rather than slogans and brochures with glossy pictures."

* Reprinted with permission from *The Macomb Daily*.

Nasty Tone Sours Legislative Races*
By Chad Selweski
The Macomb Daily
November 2, 2002

To say that two local races for the Legislature have heated up in the final days of [the] campaign . . . would only hint at the fuse that's burning.

The candidates' temperament has reached the boiling point, and voters are doing a slow burn trying to sort through all the negative advertising pointed their way.

In the 24th District House race, the battle between Republican Jack Brandenburg of Harrison Township and Democrat Frank Benson of St. Clair Shores has apparently come down to this: Who has the more damning criminal record?

In the 10th District Senate race, Democrat Michael Switalski of Roseville is trying to defend himself from a GOP onslaught while Republican Steve Rice of Sterling Heights tries to stay above the fray.

The increasingly nasty 24th District race features campaign literature and cable television advertising that crudely focuses exclusively on the candidates' character.

The Michigan Democratic Party started this war three weeks ago by declaring Brandenburg a "dangerous" candidate because of his conviction last year in Ohio on a disorderly conduct charge. The attack centers around a case in which a family was victimized by threatening phone calls and vandalism.

On Thursday, the state Republican Party hit back with literature calling Benson "risky" because of two drinking-and-driving convictions and a marijuana possession conviction—all dating back more than 20 years.

Benson, 45, a union official, was also convicted of malicious destruction of property in 1998 after a picket line incident in Warren in which he smashed the grille of a car with his fist. Both candidates had hoped to avoid a campaign based on their checkered pasts but now, with the state GOP and Democrats lighting the fuse, it seems voters are asked to cast their ballots based on the past, not the issues.

Brandenburg, 51, has lashed out at the Lansing-based parties for allowing the race to degenerate into a mudslinging contest.

"I have four teen-age kids and Benson has three teen-agers. Who do you think is going to suffer?" the Mount Clemens business owner said. "This is all happening because both parties are acting like idiots. I think it's pathetic. It's gotten totally out of hand."

Brandenburg has responded with cable TV ads that suggest Benson's record is much more serious than his. Benson, an admitted alcoholic who has been sober for more than 20 years, has responded with literature that stresses his volunteer role in city and school programs that council drug and alcohol abusers.

"I feel sorry for the voters at this point," said Benson, a former St. Clair Shores city council member. "They're really tired of all this bashing. Most people are fed up with the whole process."

In the 10th Senate District, the candidates have no convictions to explain, but Switalski is painting GOP literature as a crime.

The state representative is crying foul after coming under a barrage of GOP attacks that he believes have distorted his record and lied about his stand on the issues.

Republican literature designed to boost Rice's candidacy suggests that Switalski would alter Proposal A and raise property taxes. Switalski has consistently opposed changes to Proposal A.

The GOP ad campaign claims that Switalski has a history of raising taxes. But the Roseville Democrat, in 14 years as a city councilman, county commissioner and state representative, has never voted for a tax increase.

"I hope the voters can see through this," said Switalski, 47.

Rice offers no comment on the GOP attacks regarding tax issues.

"I can't be pleased with every single thing that every independent campaign does for me in this election," said Rice, 44 . . .

* Reprinted with permission from *The Macomb Daily*.

5

Texas's 32nd State House District

The state house member serving the 32nd State House District in Texas represents constituents living in Calhoun, Aransas, and San Patricio counties as well as part of Nueces County, all of which are in the Gulf Coast region of Texas.[1] A small section of the city of Corpus Christi, which lies in the southernmost part of the district in Nueces County, is also included in the 32nd District. The most dramatic feature of the district is the presence of the Gulf of Mexico as its eastern border (Calhoun County itself has 500 miles of coastline), the effects of which are very important, both politically and economically, to the district.

The Gulf Coast area is known for its impact on Texas's economy in several areas, the most important being the oil and petrochemical industry (Maxwell et al. 2004). Because of the oil industry, which got its start in the area with a well named Spindletop that was drilled near Beaumont in 1901, the entire region experienced a nearly continuous economic boom for most of the twentieth century (Crain and Perkins 2003). In addition to the petrochemical industry, the area's location on the Gulf of Mexico has led to the region becoming one of the most important shipping centers in the United States. Access to the Gulf allows businesses in the region to ship their goods to markets around the world.

The region that houses the 32nd State House District has also benefited economically from a large influx of residents from both inside and outside of Texas. Drawn by the economic opportunity in the region, a wave of jobseekers arrived from East Texas as well as from other areas of the United States (including the Great Lakes and Mid-Atlantic states) (Maxwell et al. 2004; Crain and Perkins 2003). This has given the region a diverse and modern feel, as its residents are made up of individuals ranging from those who hail from rural Texas towns to white-collar professionals from northern states. However, as the oil boom began to decline, the region was hit hard by falling oil and other petrochemical prices in the 1980s and 1990s.

The politics of Texas are shaped by, among other things, its population, its history, its economy, and its culture, which is a mixture of the Old South and the western frontier. The politics in Texas are also affected by what some have called the Texas Creed, "which incorporates the same five ideas that comprise the American Creed—individualism, liberty, equality, constitutionalism, and democracy" (Haag, Keith, and Pebbles 2003, 44). Texans are deeply committed to their state and their way of life. So much so that "woe to the politician who does not publicly embrace the myth that Texas is the most wonderful place to live that has ever existed on the planet!" (Kraemer, Newell, and Prindle 2003, 20). More importantly for our purposes here, "the issue that has dominated Texas politics and government has always been economics" (Haag et al. 2003, 33).

Until the end of the twentieth century, the Texas economy relied on producing, processing, and shipping its goods and products to outside markets. For much of its history, "the Texas economy was dependent on external demand and the prices paid for three products: cotton, cattle, and petroleum" (Haag et al. 2003, 33). For instance, "King Cotton," as it was called, was grown across Texas then barged down Texas rivers to the Gulf of Mexico where it was shipped to the rest of the United States and Europe. More recently, during the 1980s the Reynolds Metal Company operated a plant on Corpus Christi Bay where they extracted alumina from the raw material bauxite, which was brought to the region from places like Africa, Australia, and Brazil. And in San Patricio County, sorghum grain, cotton, corn, vegetables, and feed crops are shipped all over, which helps drive the district's economy (Guthrie 2004). In the nineteenth century, however, cattle constituted the economic heartbeat of Texas. There was a huge demand for beef in more developed areas, which made Texas an economically vibrant area, as it drew investment and people to the state.

Although cotton and cattle have been and remain important in Texas—today the average cotton harvest yields roughly 5 million bales of lint and 2 million tons of cottonseed, and Texas remains the number one cattle state with about 14 million head—the biggest economic impact was felt through the petroleum and petrochemical industry. "At its peak in the early 1980s, the Texas petroleum industry employed half a million workers earning more than $11 billion annually. By that time, the state's oil business had expanded into gasoline refineries, petrochemical plants, and factories for manufacturing a wide range of tools and equipment used in drilling, transporting, and refining operations" (Brown et al. 2001, 11). In other words, the Texas economy of the twentieth century was defined by the oil business. The Gulf Coast region, arguably, has felt the impact of this sector of the economy more than any other area in the state. In San Patricio County alone, where the oil business was the main mechanism driving the economy during the mid-1900s, over 16 million barrels of oil were produced in 1956 with a grand total of nearly 500 million being produced between 1930 and 1990 (Guthrie 2004).

Texas generated a gross state product (GSP) of $799 billion in 2002. However, not much of that was a result of the oil industry. Early in the twenty-first century, the oil and gas industry accounted for only about 10 percent of the state's economy (Brown et al. 2001). The 32nd State House District has also seen this economic weakening, as oil production in San Patricio County fell to about 3.5 million barrels by 1982 and roughly 2 million in 1990 (Guthrie 2004). This relative decline in the oil business has not stopped Texans from moving forward, however. The Texas economy of today is more diverse than ever before, as it reaches more markets, both nationally and internationally, than ever in the state's history. "Furthermore, the economic regions of Texas that were most dependent on oil and natural gas—the Gulf Coast, West Texas, and portions of South Texas—have substantially altered their economies" (Haag et al. 2003, 56).

Much of the reinvention of the Texas economy occurred because of its expansion to more global markets. This has mainly been possible because of the North American Free Trade Agreement (NAFTA), which was passed by the U.S. Congress and signed into law by President Bill Clinton in 1993. NAFTA removed many trade barriers between the United States and Mexico (as well as Canada) and allows Texans to trade more easily with their neighbors to the south. "In 2000, Texas exports reached $100 billion, growing by 66 percent since 1993, and accounting for 13.8 percent of Texas's gross product" (Haag et al. 2003, 58). Four industries accounted for roughly two-thirds of the exports Texas shipped to other countries—electronics, industrial machinery, chemicals and petrochemicals, and transportation equipment. NAFTA will continue to be an important part of a healthy Texas economy, as it will continue to open up more markets for Texas goods. It will also have a great impact on Texas politics, as there are negatives that are associated with NAFTA; companies and industries not only can ship their goods to other nations, but can also send jobs to other countries. As noted in Chapters 4 and 6, the effects of NAFTA can negatively impact a number of individuals even as it helps others.

The long-term health of the Texas economy, however, will be affected by NAFTA as it creates a number of opportunities. "Economic experts predict that the Texas economy will continue to diversify over the next 35 years. Jobs in service industries, both tourism and retail trade, and in important businesses will greatly expand . . . The outlook for new jobs in Texas is bright, but many of these new jobs, especially in trade and services, will be in low-paying occupations, limiting the growth of wages and income" (Crain and Perkins 2003, 17). To remain strong, the Texas economy will have to confront its challenges head on, and continue to adapt and change as it has throughout its long history of success.

THE TEXAS POLITICAL CONTEXT

Today, Texas is known and thought of as a Republican state through and through. However, this has not always been the case. In fact, Texas used to be heavily Democratic. So much so that the state was considered a one-party state because Democrats won nearly every election, and Republicans could not seem to break the lock Democrats had on the state legislature or the governor's office. In fact, prior to 1978, Republicans only ran poorly funded, token candidates in most races across the state (Maxwell et al. 2004). After making some gains in the 1960s and 1970s—U.S. Senator John Tower was elected for terms through the 1960s and 1970s, and the GOP was able to capture two of the state's congressional seats in 1966 (one victorious candidate was future President George H. W. Bush)—Republicans were still at a disadvantage politically, as the Democrats made up over 90 percent and nearly 90 percent, respectively, of the state senate and state house. Even as recently as 1986, Texas was still a solidly Democratic state, as 80 percent of the state senators were on the Democratic side of the aisle along with almost two-thirds of their state house colleagues.

The results of recent elections illustrate not only that Texas is a two-party state, but that it leans to the GOP; since the 1996 elections, Republicans have won control of every statewide elective office in Texas. Also in 1996, more Texans voted in the Republican primary than voted in the Democratic primary, which speaks to a shift in party preferences among Texans. Republicans have held the governorship since 1994 when a relatively inexperienced politician, George W. Bush, defeated sitting governor Ann Richards. Bush went on to win re-election in 1998 before successfully running for president of the United States. Texas's current governor, Republican Rick Perry, replaced Bush after he resigned his post.[2] Moreover, many popular Texas Democrats try to distance themselves from more traditional Democrats nationally because of their more liberal positions on many issues; these positions simply would not be acceptable in Texas (Maxwell et al. 2004). In other words, even the Democrats in Texas are conservative. "Twenty years ago, when average Texans reached the point on the ballot where they were no longer familiar with the candidates, they automatically voted Democrat. Today, faced with the same proposition, they vote Republican" (Benson, Clinkscale, and Giardino 2004, 102). The Texas legislature is a slightly different story, however. As of 2001, Republicans controlled 16 of the state senate's 31 seats (51.6 percent), but only 72 of the 150 seats in the state house (48 percent).

Still, Texas politics will remain intriguing well into the future. As some observers have noted, the state's "long Democratic heritage, coupled with its conservatism . . . will make elective politics one of the most interesting games in town for years to come" (Benson et al. 2004, 103). Texas's upcoming election campaigns will be interesting for another reason as well: the growing importance of Hispanic Americans in the electoral process. The 2000 census estimated the Hispanic population of the state to be 6.6 million, or nearly one-third of Texas's population (in San Patricio County, this figure rises to 48 percent). This is a marked increase from 1990 when the Hispanic population numbered only 4.3 million. "By 2020, it is estimated that, as a percentage of the population, Hispanic Texans will equal Anglos (42 percent), and by 2030, Hispanics will constitute a majority of the state's population" (Benson et al. 2004, 29).

"By 2001, Hispanics had achieved considerable political clout in Texas. In that year, there were 1,828 Hispanic elected public officials in Texas" (Haag et al. 2003, 38). Of those Hispanic Americans serving in elected positions, 98 percent were Democrats. Although this is an impressive record, Hispanic voters will hold even more electoral power in current and future elections because they are a relatively new constituency that has yet to be fully tapped by either of the major parties. In a time when the United States as a whole is evenly divided on policy issues and in which party it supports, Hispanic Americans may be the voting group that holds the key to either the Democrats or the Republicans creating a substantial majority for their party. The party that can make significant inroads in the Hispanic community will have a powerful and growing group of voters in their corner. An example of efforts to court Hispanic voters is the fact that during his gubernatorial re-election campaign in 1998 and his presidential run in 2000, George W. Bush often spoke Spanish to groups of potential voters who were of Hispanic descent. In addition, both national parties frequently create television commercials in both English and Spanish, and even target those ads on Spanish-language television. Currently, only slightly less than 42 percent of Hispanics in Texas consider themselves Democrats. However, this does not necessarily translate into good news for the GOP; over 31 percent of Hispanics in Texas report that they are Independents. It will be critical to both political parties' electoral fortunes to continue to try to make gains in this community.

Candidates for state house seats in Texas run every two years, whereas those running for state senate seats run every four, with one-half of the senators up for re-election every two years. These contests are held in every even-numbered year (2000, 2002, 2004, and so on), whereas elections for governor and other statewide offices are held in presidential midterm years (1998, 2002, 2006, and so on).[3] Texas does not have term limits in place, and it is unlikely that they will ever be adopted because Texas does not employ the initiative process that allows citizens to vote on matters of public policy, which tends to be how term limits are imposed (Haag et al. 2003). Like Michigan and North Carolina, Texas uses a single-member district, winner-take-all, plurality system, where the candidate who garners the most votes on Election Day is declared the winner.

The two- and four-year terms of house members and senators in Texas are not very different from legislators' terms in other states. However, once state legislators get to Austin and the state capital, legislative activities are very different from what most Americans are used to in terms of the activity of their legislators. Texas employs a part-time legislature, which meets only for 140 days every two years, or biennially. The Texas system was meant to encourage "citizen legislators" to serve in the state capital. "Biennial legislatures were common in the nineteenth and into the twentieth century, out of the belief that 'citizen' legislators could tend to the affairs of the state in a short period of time, then return to their jobs and families. Today, Texas is the only large, urban state that uses biennial sessions" (Haag et al. 2003, 242).

What this means for Texas politics is that those individuals who serve in the state legislature are elected public officials only for a short time every two years; they must have a career outside of politics to make a living. In fact, state legislators are paid only $7,200 per year, plus a small per diem to cover expenses when in Austin. Although Texas legislators are not what we would usually classify as "career politicians," in that politics is not their main way of earning a living, they are in the sense that once elected most tend to stay; in 2000, there was only a 7 percent turnover in the state house.

Texas Primary and General Elections

As in nearly every other state in the U.S., candidates seeking elective office in Texas must compete in both primary and general election contests, with the primary determining which candidates from their respective political parties will face each other in the general election.[4] Unlike most states, in order for candidates to be placed on the primary ballot in Texas, they must file the appropriate paperwork with the chair of their county party. This requirement is a function of the section of the Texas Election Code that gives the responsibility of conducting primaries to each party's county executive committee. As a practical matter, however, primaries are executed by the county clerk or county elections administrator. Texas primaries are held on the second Tuesday in March, with the filing deadline usually in early January. Candidates wishing to run for their party's nomination must, along with their paperwork, either submit a filing fee ($750 for state house and $1,250 for state senate) or provide a nominating petition signed by 500 qualified voters.

Primaries in Texas are technically closed; however, operationally they are open primaries. Texans do not record their party affiliation when they register to vote, as is required in North Carolina and several other states. Rather, Texans can vote in either party's primary; this is what makes the primaries essentially open. "A person can be standing in line to vote in the Democratic primary, change his mind, and go to the Republican primary" (Benson et al. 2004, 70). The only restriction is that once a voter participates in one party's primary, she may not take part in another party's primary or convention. "Furthermore, a person who votes in one party's primary cannot cross over and vote in the other party's runoff . . ." (see the discussion of runoffs that follows) (Benson et al. 2004, 70).

Another interesting and strategically important aspect of the Texas primary system is that to be nominated by one's party, a candidate must garner 50 percent plus one (a simple majority) of the votes cast on Election Day. For instance, suppose there are four candidates seeking the Democratic nomination for the fall election and the four candidates split the vote 45 percent, 30 percent, 20 percent, and 5 percent. No candidate has received a majority of votes, so in Texas, as in many other southern states, a second primary is held. In Texas, the runoff primary is held roughly one month later on the second Tuesday in April with the top two vote-getters squaring off in a head-to-head race. The winner here goes on to represent his party in the general election.

Texas stands out from other states in that no other state holds primaries for offices such as state legislature or for the U.S. Congress as early. In effect, this produces the longest general election season in the United States; it lasts from early March (or early April if there is a runoff required) until early November—a full eight months! This is a lengthy period for the party nominees to battle one another for the right to serve as an elected public official. One consequence of this long general election period is that it increases the cost of campaigns in Texas; candidates need to spend more money over this period simply to keep their campaigns up and running and their candidacies viable.

As noted earlier, Texans head to the polls in even-numbered years to elect all their representatives (as opposed to states like New Jersey that hold elections for offices such as governor in odd-numbered years). Texas holds its statewide elections on the same day as all federal elections—the first Tuesday after the first Monday in November. Also noted earlier, state house members and half of the state senators are elected every two years and the governor and other statewide officers are elected every four years. One point to note is that gubernatorial and other statewide elections are held in the presidential off-year purposely so as to minimize the influence of presidential elections on the outcome of state campaigns.

Because of the large Hispanic population in Texas, ballots for all elections are printed in both Spanish and English, thanks to a law approved by the legislature and signed by the governor in 1975. According to that law, any county that has a Mexican-American population greater than 5 percent of the total population must provide bilingual ballots and other election materials. The format of the ballot—punch card, optical scan, and so on—is not uniform across

Texas. Instead, each county is responsible for determining the format of the ballot.

A final important point about elections in Texas is that in 1991 the Texas legislature approved a process that allows Texans to vote *before* the formal Election Day. Early voting allows voters to cast their ballots up to 17 days prior to either the primary or general election (and 10 days before a runoff primary). However, no early voting is allowed within 4 days of any Election Day. In other words, voters have a two-week period in which they can cast their ballots, for first primaries and general elections, before the calendar Election Day. Early voting in Texas is not similar to absentee balloting or the vote-by-mail system in Oregon. Rather, voters wishing to cast their ballots early must make a trip to the polls as they would on Election Day; during the period of early voting, special polling places such as courthouses, the county clerk's office, as well as other, more traditional polling places like schools and police stations are made available. Although there has not been a meaningful increase in the number of Texans who cast ballots—one of the goals of the early voting system—it has made voting easier and voters have taken advantage. Consider the following figures: in 1992, about one quarter of all votes were cast early; in 1996, roughly one-third of all votes were cast before Election Day; and in 2000, almost 39 percent of all voters went to the polls before Election Day.

It is obvious from these figures that early voting can cause large headaches for candidates and their campaigns in Texas. A common strategy used in campaigns across the United States has been to make a strong final push for votes in the last few days of a campaign leading up to Election Day. This is made more difficult in Texas because there are potentially 15 separate Election Days from which each voter may choose. As only one example of the problems this can create for campaigns, any resource used to communicate with voters who have already voted has been wasted.[5]

Fund-Raising and Campaign Finance Law in Texas

Fund-raising in Texas state campaigns is very different from fund-raising in either Michigan or North Carolina. Several laws apply to the regulation of campaign finance in Texas, with the most recent being the Texas Campaign Reporting and Disclosure Act of 1973 and the 1991 Ethics Law. The 1973 Act created provisions for the reporting and disclosure of the raising and spending of campaign-related funds. In rules similar to those in other states, every candidate for office and every political committee must, among other things, file periodic reports with the state disclosing all contributions and disbursements over $50 (since 2000, candidates for statewide and legislative positions have been required to file these reports electronically). The 1991 Ethics Law "was designed to regulate and moderate the impact of private wealth on public policy in campaigns and at other levels of Texas politics" (Kraemer et al. 2003, 132); it also created an Ethics Commission that hears complaints, levies fines, receives candidate campaign finance filings, and reports severe violations of campaign finance practices.

The difference between Texas and many other states is not in what is *included* in the regulation of fund-raising and campaign finance practices; it lies in what is *excluded*. In Texas, there are no limits placed on how much money an individual, party, or political action committee (PAC) can give to a

> **BOX 5.1 Texas at a Glance**
>
> | | | |
> |---|---|---|
> | 2000 population | | 20,851,820 |
> | U.S. Congressional districts | | 32 |
> | State Senate districts | | 31 |
> | State House districts | | 150 |
> | State Senate district population (avg.) | | 672,639 |
> | State House district population (avg.) | | 139,012 |
> | Full-time legislature | | No |
> | Term limits | | None |
> | Voter registration by party | | No |
> | Campaign finance contribution limits (per candidate per election) | House | Senate |
> | *Source:* | | |
> | Individual | Unlimited | Unlimited |
> | PAC | Unlimited | Unlimited |
> | Party | Unlimited | Unlimited |

candidate for office; judicial candidates, however, are limited (depending on the office being sought) in the amount they may take from individual donors, thanks to the 1995 Judicial Campaign Fairness Act.

Because of the unlimited nature of campaign contributions in Texas, campaigns in the state are usually expensive endeavors. Because of the lack of limitations on contributions, "Individual contributions of $5,000 to $10,000 or more are common in campaigns for major state offices" (Kraemer et al. 2003, 128). The expensive nature of Texas campaigns—because of the long general election period and the unlimited contributions that are allowed—has been reflected in the amount of money spent by candidates in Texas. For many years, candidates for governor and the U.S. Senate have spent millions on their races—in 1990, Republican Clayton Williams reportedly spent $20 million in his effort to defeat the sitting Democratic governor, Ann Richards, and lost. In 2002, Democrat Tony Sanchez spent nearly $70 million (mostly from his own pocket), only to lose handily to Governor Rick Perry, who spent just shy of $30 million. Although races for the state legislature are not multimillion-dollar affairs, they too are expensive. "It is not unusual for a candidate in a competitive race for the state house to spend between $100,000 and $200,000" (Maxwell 2004, 92). One observer has noted that: "Money doesn't just talk in Texas elections: it does tap dances and sings the state anthem in three-part harmony" (Northcott 1982, 18).

THE CAMPAIGN

In the election being contested in this simulation, the Texas 32nd State House District is a hotly contested incumbent-versus-challenger race. The incumbent candidate, Republican State Representative Gene Seaman, is running for a fourth term of office. Democrat Josephine Miller, a sitting and popular county judge, is challenging him. The 32nd is a targeted state house race and both political parties have said they are committed to putting as many resources into the campaign as are needed to win. Even though the Democrats still maintain a majority in the state house prior to this race, the 32nd is seen as a possible "pick-up" for the Democrats, meaning that the party feels this could be one race where the challenger candidate could defeat the incumbent. However, on the Republican side, they must hold the 32nd if they have any chance of being able to take over control of the state house and elect a Republican speaker.

For this simulation, the 32nd District has recently been redistricted—the new boundaries have greatly reshaped the politics of the race. As noted earlier, the district fully includes the counties of Aransas, Calhoun, and San Patricio; it also includes portions of Nueces County and the city of Corpus Christi. The redistricting process created the new district by replacing Jackson County with San Patricio County. Therefore, San Patricio is an entirely new area in which the incumbent must campaign. Another consequence of the redistricting process was that the newly created 32nd District put two incumbent house members in the same district; when San Patricio County was included in the district, Democrat Judy Hawley, the sitting representative from the district that included that county, would have been forced to run against Representative Seaman. Seaman was counting on an easy re-election campaign after Hawley decided not to run; only after Hawley said she would not run did Miller throw the proverbial hat into the ring.

Part of what makes this a competitive race is that the incumbent, Seaman, is from Nueces County (only 15 percent of which is in the district) whereas the challenger, Miller, is from San Patricio County (which makes up 44 percent of the district's voting age population). In total, the district has a population of 145,780. The area is considered to be a politically competitive battleground. Seaman narrowly won the old 32nd District in 1996, but has been unopposed since. Moreover, the newly added county of San Patricio leans to the GOP, but that is the home of the challenger candidate, who happened to win her judicial re-election campaign with 65 percent of the vote against a GOP candidate in 1994 and has had no challenger since 1998.

Both the Seaman and Miller campaigns will raise a good deal of money for this race, which also signals the competitiveness of the campaign. As noted earlier, both political party organizations can be expected to be active as well; it is likely that they will each contribute to their candidates directly as well as spend money on their behalf.

The race for the 32nd District is being contested in a context that includes hotly contested races for the U.S. Senate, governor, and lieutenant governor, as well as a number of other races at both the state and federal level.

The Candidates

Gene Seaman (R) Gene Seaman, a 72-year-old resident of Corpus Christi, is a homebuilder by trade, owns a financial planning business, and is involved in real estate development. However, he has been a political activist for over 30 years, first as a GOP party leader in Nueces County, and then as a state representative. After first being elected to the 32nd State House District seat in 1996, he has been unopposed ever since. Early in life, Seaman served in the Merchant Marines and the U.S. Army, where he entered Officer Candidate School and eventually attained the rank of captain. Seaman enrolled in The American College (a school focused on financial services education) in 1957, where he went on to earn four designations and degrees.

In the state house, Seaman sits on the important Insurance and Economic Development Committees. One newspaper has said that Seaman's record in the legislature "is strong and he has played an integral part in passing legislation on key issues such as insurance and education" (Powell 2002a, A1). Representative Seaman's voting record while in the state house has been viewed as a mixture between moderate and conservative. For instance, Seaman earned an "A" rating from the Texas Association of Business and Chambers of Commerce for his voting record on key business issues, which the organization says have supported Texas businesses and created jobs.

Seaman has also become known as someone who does not let his conservative-leaning voting record affect every aspect of his politics. Before this election, Seaman endorsed one of his Democratic colleagues, Representative Vilma Luna from the neighboring 33rd State House District, for re-election. Endorsing another incumbent for re-election, even if it is someone of the opposing party, was seen as a pragmatic move on Seaman's part, as he argued the region would be better served by two representatives with seniority rather than one senior member and a freshman member.

Seaman is seen as a fairly effective legislator. During the legislative session prior to this election, Seaman authored, jointly authored, or sponsored 65 house bills, and sponsored or jointly sponsored eight senate bills. Of these, Seaman introduced, as the primary sponsor or author, 18 bills in the house. Seven of these bills passed the house, 4 also passed the senate and were presented to the governor for signature or veto where 2 were signed and 2 were vetoed.

Representative Seaman has also earned the endorsements of the Texas Hospital Association, the Texas Association of Business, and the Nueces County members of the Texas Farm Bureau. The Texas Abortion and Reproductive Rights Action League reports that Seaman is pro-life; the Texas Alliance for Life concurs. In addition, one local newspaper said that Seaman "has tirelessly pressed his causes" while in office (Corpus Christi Caller-Times 2002).

Josephine Miller (D) Josephine Miller, a 60-year-old resident of Sinton (in San Patricio County) and former schoolteacher and librarian, has been a San Patricio County judge for 12 years. Prior to winning her seat on the bench, she served 8 years on the Sinton City Council (including a term as chairperson). She was a founding member of the San Patricio County Economic Development Corporation, and has also served on the Regional Metropolitan Planning Organization as well as many other regional and state commissions dealing with issues such as transportation, education, jails, water, and health. Miller earned her bachelor's degree from the University of Texas.

Originally, Miller was not interested in running for the 32nd District's seat in the state legislature. However, after the last redistricting plan was put in place, which put two incumbents in the same district when San Patricio County was added to the 32nd, and when the incumbent representing San Patricio County, Judy Hawley, decided not to run against fellow incumbent Representative Seaman, Miller decided to enter the race. In fact, Republican John Barrett, who serves on the Coastal Coordination Council, was one of the first to encourage Miller to run.

Judge Miller is seen as a moderate Democrat and a very experienced individual with the right mix of skills to be an effective legislator. When she entered her post as county judge, San Patricio had an overcrowded jail and a run-down courthouse. During Miller's 12 years on the job, the courthouse has been renovated and expanded, and other problems have been fixed. Also during this time, Miller has led regional efforts to bring economic development to the county and protect the military assets that are in place in the area (Powell 2002b). Miller has been described as a consensus builder who can get people of different opinions to work together toward a compromise. She is also seen as someone who could step right into the legislature and perform well because of her wide range of experiences. State Senator Judith Zaffirini (D) said that if Miller is elected, she would not be a true freshman in the state house because she has represented the area on the state Democratic committee, which has helped her to gain important insight into how the state government actually works (Powell 2002b). Zaffirini has also called Miller a "leader" who has "experience and insight into the issues of the region," and has described her as someone "who would be a passionate leader for the area she represents" (Powell 2002b, A1).

Judge Miller earned a great deal of attention, and with that, important name recognition and some popularity, through her leadership in response to a recent crisis in the general area of the district, including Nueces and San Patricio Counties. Torrential rains created serious flood conditions in the area of the upper basin of the Nueces River, which had spread to lower-lying areas along the river all the way down to Nueces Bay. The flooding was so severe that some areas were declared federal disaster areas shortly after the flooding started. Miller was one of the first to call for residents in the area to be evacuated from their homes. Miller also became a key leader in responding to the crisis when the emergency management coordinator resigned in the wake of a scandal involving the Red Cross. She, along with the sheriff's department, became the link between government and citizens to let residents know what was happening.

Judge Miller has been endorsed by the San Patricio County members of the Texas Farm Bureau. The Texas Abortion and Reproductive Rights Action League reports that Miller is pro-choice.

CREATING A CAMPAIGN PLAN

The discussion of the candidates for Texas's 32nd State House District seat and the surrounding campaign context provides the reader with enough information to begin conducting district and demographic analyses as well as candidate profiles for the simulation exercises in Chapter 3. Supplemental material needed to complete those exercises is also included at the end of this chapter. We provide the following information that will be needed to complete the exercises in Chapter 3:

- *A map of the district.* The map included provides a general location of the district within the state. This map will help you to begin to familiarize yourself with the district and the lay of the land where the campaign will be waged; however, this map does not provide all the geographic details that your team will want to know. It will also provide important information in terms of where the district is situated in relation to other communities in the area. A more detailed map of the district can tell you about the kind of district in which you will be working—that is, whether it is urban, suburban, rural, or a combination of the three. This kind of map can also help to determine some aspects of campaign strategy such as whether the candidate will go door-to-door, or whether canvassing of this kind is out of the question because of the district's geographic elements.

- *U.S. Census Bureau data on the 32nd State House District.* This information will be the beginning of your research into the district and its residents that you will use in several of the exercises in Chapter 3. We have provided you with some of the information you will need, but there is more out there. For example, an organization named Texas Economic Development (TxED) provides up-to-date "community profile" information on communities around the state that is sometimes more current than census data.[6] You will need to use your research skills to go out and find other pertinent data that will help you complete the exercises.

- *Newspaper articles on the campaign.* We have provided a couple of news accounts that preview the race and give some additional description of the candidates and their campaigns. These will also be useful in several of the exercises.

- *Voter data on the district.* We have provided some of the information you will need to collect on the voters of the 32nd District by providing election results from 1994 through 2000. Again, you may have to rely on your research skills to complement the given information relating to the voters of this district.

- *Campaign finance information.* Although we have tried to keep this simulation as realistic as possible, we will deviate a bit from the real world here. The Texas 32nd State House District is a competitive race; therefore, more money would be spent in this race than in a typical Texas state house race. For instance, as in many competitive campaigns, political party organizations may also spend money on this race. More money in a campaign means that more things can be done in the campaign and a wider variety of campaign tactics can be utilized. We supply a budget figure that provides some context for the race (remember that the state's campaign finance law, summarized earlier in this chapter, is also part of this context). This is the figure that must be raised in the fund-raising exercise outlined in Chapter 3. It will also be informative in terms of what other kinds of resources will be available in the campaign. We have taken a realistic figure that would be spent in this race and discounted it slightly. Just about anyone can run a campaign that is flush with cash. The real learning comes from having to decide how to divide up scarce resources in an efficient manner. As we have previously noted, activities related to the raising and spending of campaign funds must be periodically reported to the state. In order to illustrate what goes into these reports, we have provided examples of actual campaign finance reports from the two candidates (available on the book's companion web site). The pages provided also serve as examples of sources from which the candidates raised money and what they spent it on. The budget for each campaign in the Texas 32nd State House District is $125,000.

NOTES

1. There are several ways of characterizing the different geographic areas that make up the entire state of Texas. One geographic categorization divides the state into the following areas: Panhandle, West, North, East, Central, Gulf Coast, South, Southwest, and German Hill Country (Maxwell et al. 2004). Another classification includes two large geographic zones—the Gulf Lowlands and the Western Highlands—with each divided into several other specific and distinct areas (Benson, Clinkscale, and Giardino 2004). The one commonality is that the area that comprises the 32nd District is squarely in the Gulf Coast region, no matter how one slices the geographic divisions.

2. Perry became governor because he was the sitting lieutenant governor at the time; in cases like this the lieutenant governor ascends to the governorship.

3. This is with one exception; some state senators serve only two-year terms. This happens only after redistricting has occurred in the wake of the decennial census, and is done so that after the census and the new districts have been created, senators remain on staggered terms of office. In such a scenario, senators draw lots to see who will serve a two-year term and who will serve a four-year term.

4. This is unless a party's gubernatorial candidate received less than 20 percent of the vote in the previous gubernatorial election. In this case, the party can choose to hold a primary or a party convention to pick its candidate. When a party's gubernatorial candidate receives less than 2 percent of the vote, the party is required to choose their next slate of nominees by party convention.

5. When going through the exercises in this race, be sure to consider how early voting will affect your responses; especially important will be the paid and earned media, and get-out-the-vote aspects of the exercises.

6. Texas Economic Development's (TxED) Web site can be accessed at http://community.txed.state.tx.us/

Supplemental Materials for Texas' 32nd State House District

Contents include:

    District map
    Census data
    Voting history
    Newspaper articles

Texas State House Districts

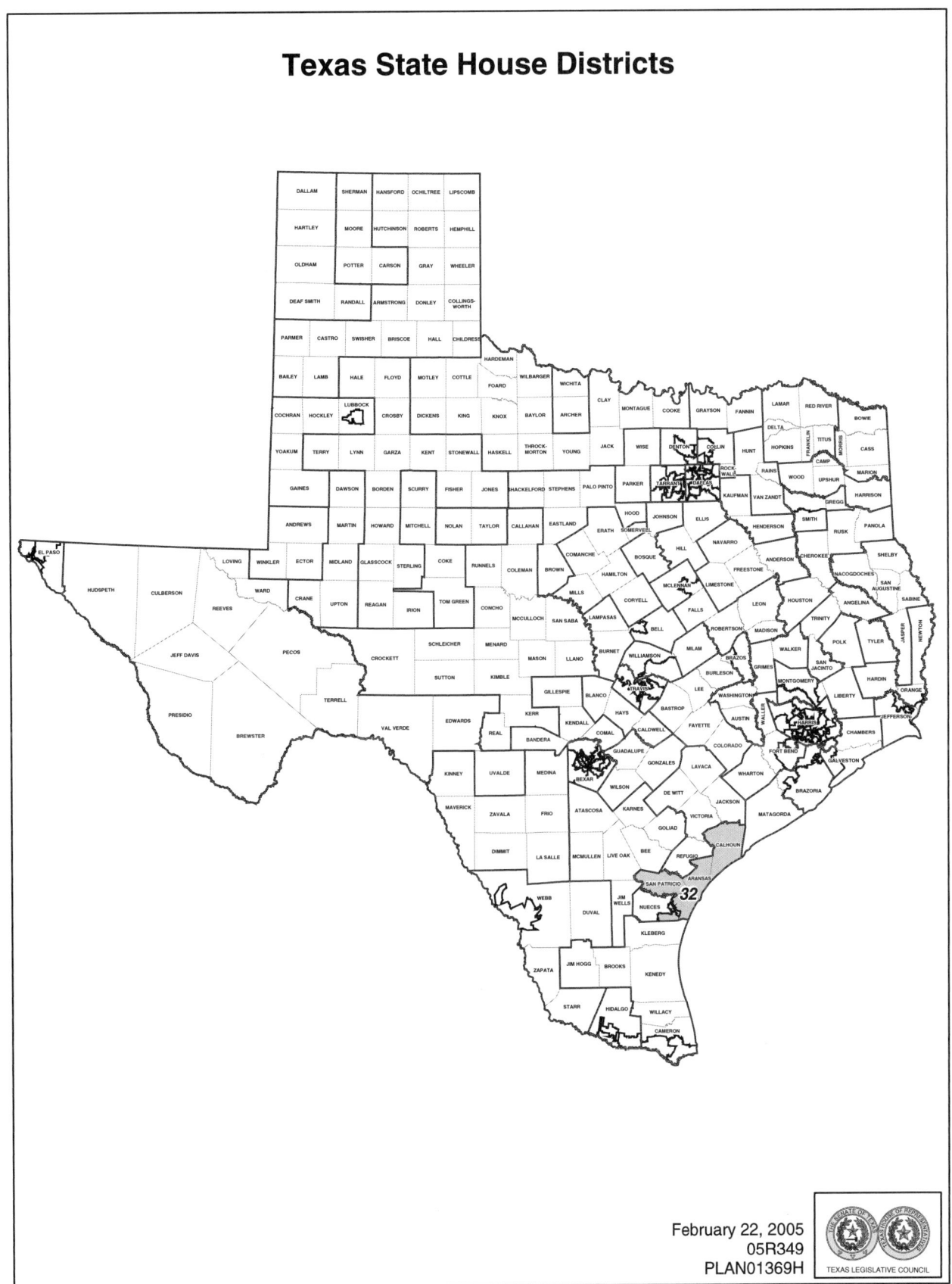

February 22, 2005
05R349
PLAN01369H

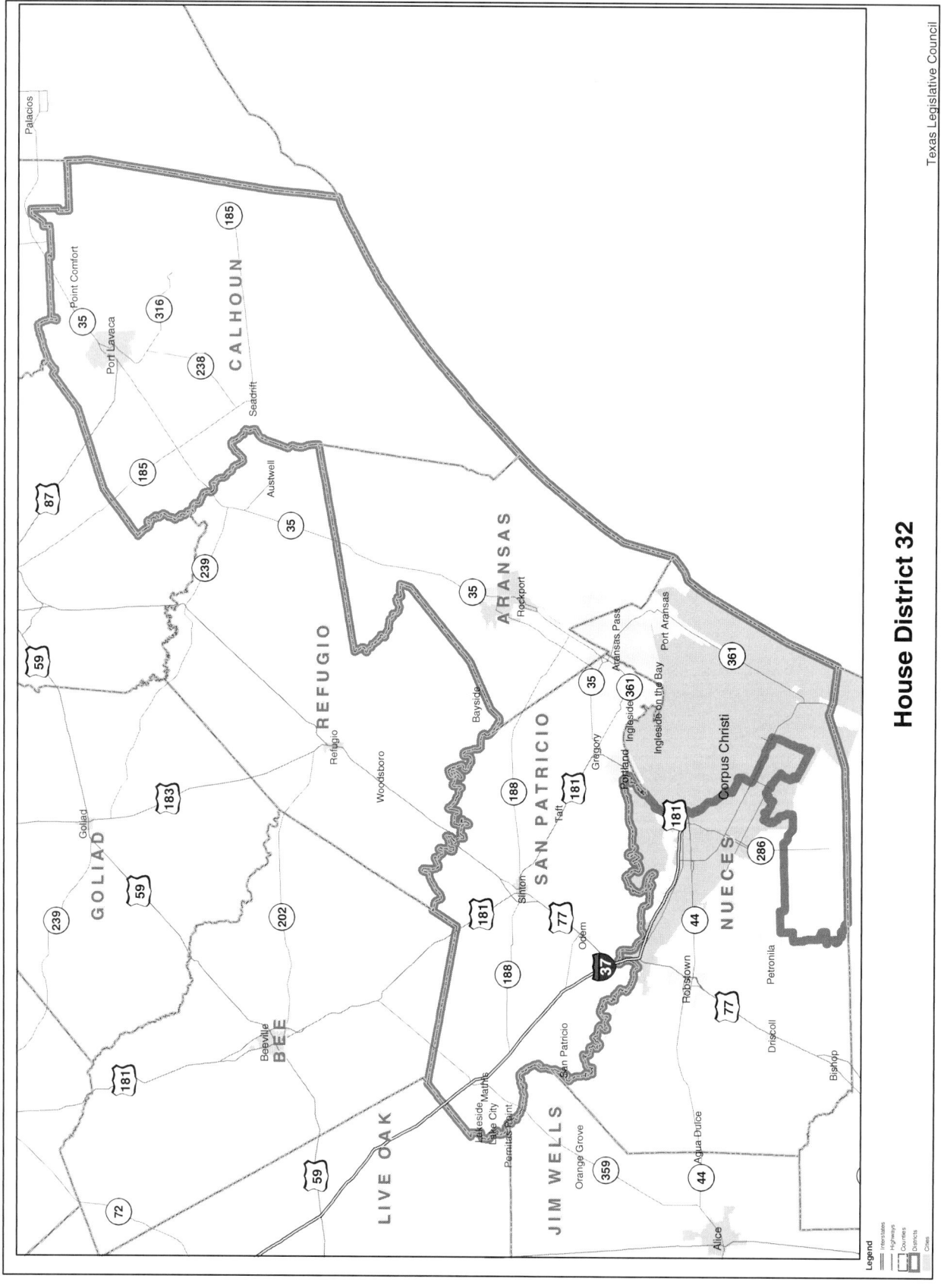

House District 32

SF 405	POPULATION AND HOUSEHOLD PROFILE			TEXAS LEGISLATIVE COUNCIL		
DATA: 2000 & 1990 CENSUS, SF3, SF1	TEXAS HOUSE OF REPRESENTATIVES DISTRICT 32			05/29/03		PAGE 1
PLAN01369H						
	—— 2000 CENSUS ——			—— 1990 CENSUS ——		
	TOTAL	PERCENT	STATE	TOTAL	PERCENT	STATE
SELECTED POPULATION CHARACTERISTICS						
TOTAL POPULATION	145,423		20,851,820	118,735		16,986,510
AGE						
0-5	12,884	8.9%	9.3%	11,345	9.6%	9.9%
6-17	27,713	19.1%	18.9%	23,704	20.0%	18.6%
18-64	86,920	59.8%	61.8%	69,982	58.9%	61.4%
65+	17,906	12.3%	9.9%	13,704	11.5%	10.1%
PLACE OF BIRTH/CITIZENSHIP						
U.S. NATIVE	137,683	94.7%	86.1%	114,043	96.1%	91.0%
NATIVE TEXAN	97,716	67.2%	62.2%	85,011	71.6%	64.7%
FOREIGN BORN	7,658	5.3%	13.9%	4,636	3.9%	9.0%
NONCITIZEN	4,282	2.9%	9.5%	2,629	2.2%	5.9%
URBAN POPULATION	113,867	78.3%	82.5%	74,686	62.9%	80.3%
RURAL POPULATION	31,474	21.7%	17.5%	43,993	37.1%	19.7%
MOVED SINCE 1995 (2000 CENSUS)						
OR 1985 (1990 CENSUS)						
TO DIFFERENT LOCATION WITHIN TEXAS	49,842	37.0%	39.5%	42,392	38.7%	41.0%
TO TEXAS FROM ANOTHER STATE OR COUNTRY	18,359	13.6%	10.9%	9,654	8.8%	9.8%
ABILITY TO SPEAK ENGLISH						
SPEAKS OTHER THAN ENGLISH AT HOME	40,817	30.3%	31.2%	37,365	34.1%	25.4%
DOES NOT SPEAK ENGLISH WELL	5,033	3.7%	7.4%	5,570	5.1%	5.2%
SELECTED HOUSEHOLD CHARACTERISTICS						
TOTAL NUMBER OF HOUSEHOLDS	52,510		7,393,354	41,583		6,070,937
AVERAGE NUMBER OF PERSONS PER HOUSEHOLD	2.7		2.7	2.8		2.7
HOUSEHOLDS BY COMPOSITION						
1 PERSON	11,487	21.9%	23.7%	8,739	21.0%	23.9%
2 PERSONS	17,719	33.7%	30.5%	13,233	31.8%	30.1%
3 OR 4 PERSONS	16,654	31.7%	32.4%	13,529	32.5%	33.0%
5 OR MORE PERSONS	6,650	12.7%	13.4%	6,082	14.6%	12.9%
PERSONS BY HOUSEHOLD TYPE & GROUP QUARTERS						
FAMILY HOUSEHOLDS	125,416	86.2%	84.5%	105,553	88.9%	85.4%
NONFAMILY HOUSEHOLDS	16,892	11.6%	12.8%	11,587	9.8%	12.3%
GROUP QUARTERS	3,115	2.1%	2.7%	1,595	1.3%	2.3%
FAMILIES WITH CHILDREN						
SINGLE-PARENT FAMILIES	4,637	24.8%	26.5%	3,829	22.2%	24.7%
CHILDREN WITH ALL PARENTS WORKING	21,946	57.6%	59.6%	17,632	52.7%	61.0%

ANALYSIS USES 99.4% OF DISTRICT POPULATION

SF 405 DATA: 2000 & 1990 CENSUS, SF3, SF1 PLAN01369H	EDUCATION AND EMPLOYMENT PROFILE TEXAS HOUSE OF REPRESENTATIVES DISTRICT 32			TEXAS LEGISLATIVE COUNCIL 05/29/03 PAGE 2		
	2000 CENSUS			1990 CENSUS		
	TOTAL	PERCENT	STATE	TOTAL	PERCENT	STATE
SELECTED EDUCATION CHARACTERISTICS						
POPULATION AGE 3+ ENROLLED IN SCHOOL						
PORTION AGE 3–5 IN PRESCHOOL	2,622	41.7%	40.3%	1,766	29.7%	35.8%
IN ELEMENTARY OR HIGH SCHOOL	30,625	22.0%	21.9%	24,910	22.0%	20.4%
PORTION OF THESE IN PUBLIC SCHOOL	28,865	94.3%	93.1%	24,242	97.3%	94.5%
IN COLLEGE	6,934	5.0%	6.0%	5,813	5.1%	7.4%
EDUCATIONAL ATTAINMENT						
BACHELOR'S DEGREE OR HIGHER (Age 25+)	17,723	19.4%	23.2%	11,475	15.7%	20.3%
DID NOT GRADUATE HIGH SCHOOL (Age 25+)	21,232	23.3%	24.3%	23,672	32.3%	27.9%
HIGH SCHOOL DROPOUTS (Age 16–19)	839	9.1%	12.5%	977	13.4%	12.9%
SELECTED LABOR CHARACTERISTICS (Age 16+)						
LABOR FORCE STATUS						
IN ARMED FORCES	4,305	3.9%	0.7%	1,238	1.4%	1.0%
IN CIVILIAN LABOR FORCE	61,591	56.2%	62.9%	51,345	58.6%	64.9%
NOT IN LABOR FORCE	43,765	39.9%	36.4%	35,016	40.0%	34.0%
CIVILIAN LABOR FORCE						
EMPLOYED						
TOTAL EMPLOYED	57,451	93.3%	93.9%	47,193	91.9%	92.9%
ANGLO EMPLOYED	47,631	94.0%	95.0%	39,503	93.2%	94.2%
BLACK EMPLOYED	1,256	89.4%	89.5%	844	83.9%	86.6%
HISPANIC EMPLOYED	19,020	90.6%	91.3%	15,118	87.6%	89.1%
UNEMPLOYED						
TOTAL UNEMPLOYED	4,140	6.7%	6.1%	4,152	8.1%	7.1%
ANGLO UNEMPLOYED	3,041	6.0%	5.0%	2,904	6.8%	5.8%
BLACK UNEMPLOYED	149	10.6%	10.5%	162	16.1%	13.4%
HISPANIC UNEMPLOYED	1,982	9.4%	8.7%	2,133	12.4%	10.9%
EMPLOYMENT SECTOR						
PRIVATE SECTOR	41,489	72.2%	78.0%	34,118	72.3%	76.7%
GOVERNMENT SECTOR	10,327	18.0%	14.6%	7,851	16.6%	15.2%
SELF-EMPLOYED	5,332	9.3%	7.1%	4,821	10.2%	7.6%
WORKED IN 1999 (2000 CENSUS) OR 1989 (1990 CENSUS)						
WORKED AT ALL	72,345	66.0%	69.7%	56,595	64.6%	70.4%
WORKED 50–52 WEEKS	44,689	40.8%	45.3%	31,421	35.9%	43.1%

ANALYSIS USES 99.4% OF DISTRICT POPULATION

SF 405	INCOME AND HOUSING PROFILE			TEXAS LEGISLATIVE COUNCIL		
DATA: 2000 & 1990 CENSUS, SF3, SF1	TEXAS HOUSE OF REPRESENTATIVES DISTRICT 32			05/29/03		PAGE 3
PLAN01369H						
	2000 CENSUS			1990 CENSUS		
	TOTAL	PERCENT	STATE	TOTAL	PERCENT	STATE
SELECTED INCOME CHARACTERISTICS						
PER CAPITA INCOME	$18,831		$19,617	$11,621		$12,904
ANNUAL HOUSEHOLD INCOME						
LESS THAN $10,000	5,874	11.2%	10.4%	8,483	20.4%	17.7%
$10,000 TO $24,999	11,553	22.0%	20.2%	12,581	30.3%	28.6%
$25,000 TO $49,999	15,983	30.5%	30.0%	13,014	31.4%	32.3%
$50,000 OR MORE	19,041	36.3%	39.5%	7,419	17.9%	21.4%
POVERTY						
POPULATION LIVING IN POVERTY	22,700	16.0%	15.4%	25,607	21.9%	18.1%
FAMILIES WITH CHILDREN LIVING IN POVERTY	3,661	17.8%	16.6%	4,374	24.9%	19.2%
PORTION THAT ARE SINGLE PARENT FAMILIES	2,020	55.2%	54.3%	1,833	41.9%	49.1%
PORTION OF POPULATION 65+ IN POVERTY	2,178	12.6%	12.8%	2,260	17.3%	18.4%
HOUSEHOLD INCOME INCLUDES						
SOCIAL SECURITY	14,416	27.5%	21.6%	11,015	26.5%	22.1%
PUBLIC ASSISTANCE	1,739	3.3%	3.2%	3,360	8.1%	6.7%
SELECTED HOUSING CHARACTERISTICS						
AGE OF HOUSING						
BUILT BETWEEN 1990 AND 2000 (2000 CENSUS) OR BETWEEN 1980 AND 1990 (1990 CENSUS)	13,992	21.2%	20.7%	15,504	27.8%	29.7%
BUILT BEFORE 1960	11,853	17.9%	21.7%	13,971	25.0%	28.1%
OCCUPIED BY						
RENTER	16,431	31.3%	36.2%	14,110	34.0%	39.1%
OWNER	36,045	68.7%	63.8%	27,380	66.0%	60.9%
VACANT	13,574	20.6%	9.4%	14,291	25.6%	13.4%
AVERAGE RENT PER MONTH	$568		$616	$390	$428	
AVERAGE VALUE OF OWNER-OCCUPIED HOUSING	$98,271		$109,639	$65,388	$73,543	
VALUE OF OWNER-OCCUPIED HOUSING						
LESS THAN $50,000	7,826	27.9%	22.7%	9,994	47.0%	39.7%
BETWEEN $50,000 AND $100,000	11,439	40.8%	40.6%	8,400	39.5%	42.5%
MORE THAN $100,000	8,782	31.3%	36.7%	2,865	13.5%	17.8%
PORTION OF TOTAL INCOME SPENT ON HOUSING BY						
RENTERS						
35+ PERCENT	3,911	23.9%	27.1%	3,555	25.6%	27.3%
LESS THAN 20 PERCENT	5,480	33.5%	34.1%	4,566	32.9%	32.9%
OWNERS						
35+ PERCENT	3,817	13.6%	13.6%	2,825	13.3%	12.8%
LESS THAN 20 PERCENT	16,787	59.9%	59.0%	13,212	62.1%	57.3%

ANALYSIS USES 99.4% OF DISTRICT POPULATION

Data: 2000 Census

TEXAS HOUSE OF REPRESENTATIVES DISTRICTS
POPULATION ANALYSIS

	POPULATION					
	TOTAL	ANGLO	BLACK	HISP	B+H	OTHER
DISTRICT 32	145,780	82,524	4,639	54,244	58,518	4,738
Aransas	22,497	16,596	373	4,571	4,915	986
Calhoun	20,647	10,774	596	8,448	9,000	873
Nueces (PART)	35,498	24,405	1,514	8,044	9,482	1,611
San Patricio	67,138	30,749	2,156	33,181	35,121	1,268

Source: Texas Legislative Council

Data: 2000 Census

TEXAS HOUSE OF REPRESENTATIVES DISTRICT 32
CITIES AND CENSUS DESIGNATED PLACES (CDP)

COUNTY	CITY	SPLIT % POP	TOTAL POPULATION
Aransas	Aransas Pass		867
	Fulton		1,553
	Rockport		7,385
Calhoun	Point Comfort		781
	Port Lavaca		12,035
	Seadrift		1,352
Nueces	Aransas Pass		70
	Corpus Christi	11.5%	31,844
	Ingleside		0
	Port Aransas		3,370
	Portland	100.0%	0
San Patricio	Aransas Pass		7,201
	Corpus Christi	11.5%	4
	Del Sol-Loma Linda CDP		726
	Doyle CDP		285
	Edgewater-Paisano CDP		182
	Edroy CDP		420
	Falman-County Acres CDP		289
	Gregory		2,318
	Ingleside		9,388
	Ingleside on the Bay		659
	Lake City		526
	Lakeshore Gardens-Hidden Acres CDP		720
	Lakeside (San Patricio)		333
	Mathis		5,034
	Morgan Farm Area CDP		484
	Odem		2,499
	Portland	100.0%	14,827
	Rancho Chico CDP		309
	St. Paul CDP		542
	San Patricio	84.6%	269
	Sinton		5,676
	Taft		3,396
	Taft Southwest CDP		1,721
	Tradewinds CDP		163
	CITY TOTAL:		117,228
	NONCITY TOTAL:		28,552
	DISTRICT TOTAL:		145,780

Source: Texas Legislative Council

Table 5.1 Texas's 32nd State House District Voting History, 1994–2000

	1994		1996		1998		2000	
Registered voters	85,623		86,335		86,569		86,590	
Voter turnout	35,994		44,891		32,567		48,161	
Turnout percentage	42.1%		51.9%		37.6%		55.6%	
Election Results	Votes	Percent	Votes	Percent	Votes	Percent	Votes	Percent
President								
Republican			19,900	48.2%			27,199	57.6%
Democrat			21,351	51.8%			20,045	42.4%
			41,251				47,244	
U.S. Senate								
Republican	19,984	58.5%	22,843	52.6%			29,364	63.4%
Democrat	14,179	41.5%	20,658	47.4%			16,980	36.6%
	34,163		43,501				46,344	
U.S. House								
Republican	20,589	65.3%	25,463	59.8%	17,732	58.8%	25,333	58.4%
Democrat	10,942	34.7%	17,116	40.2%	12,425	41.2%	18,045	41.6%
	31,531		42,579		30,157		43,378	
Governor								
Republican	17,218	49.3%			20,093	66.9%		
Democrat	17,760	50.7%			9,933	33.1%		
	34,978				30,025			
Lieutenant Governor								
Republican	10,359	30.4%			12,541	42.9%		
Democrat	23,736	69.6%			16,725	57.1%		
	34,095				29,266			
Attorney General								
Republican	13,447	40.9%			13,466	46.1%		
Democrat	19,395	59.1%			15,724	53.9%		
	32,842				29,191			
State Senate								
Republican	15,344	46.2%			13,137	43.8%		
Democrat	17,867	53.8%			16,856	56.2%		
	33,211				29,993			
State House								
Republican	17,140	49.5%	20,970	50.8%	not included because in some areas one candidate was unopposed		not included because in some areas one candidate was unopposed	
Democrat	17,487	50.5%	20,311	49.2%				
	34,627		41,281					
State Board of Education								
Republican	13,371	41.0%			13,617	47.0%		
Democrat	19,205	59.0%			15,342	53.0%		
	32,576				28,959			
Commissioner of Agriculture								
Republican	19,242	59.7%			15,762	55.3%		
Democrat	13,010	40.3%			12,771	44.7%		
	32,252				28,533			

The number of registered voters in this district for this election is: 86,432.

Seaman Points to His Role in Helping to Pass Key Bills*
By Jaime Powell
Corpus Christi Caller-Times
October 7, 2002

Gene Seaman has been in politics for 30 years, first as a Republican Party leader in Nueces County, then as a state legislator. He plans to continue his political career by running for his fourth term, in the redrawn District 32.

Seaman owns a financial planning business and is involved in real estate development.

As a legislator, Seaman said, his record is strong and he has played an integral part in passing legislation on key issues such as insurance and education. His voting record has been aligned with the moderate and conservative Republicans who are his contemporaries.

Those strong, longstanding Republican ties do not prevent him from endorsing his Democratic colleague, Rep. Vilma Luna of Corpus Christi, over Republican Lauro Cuellar for District 33. That's a gesture in favor of a strong regional delegation with seniority, Seaman says.

In District 33, just like in his own District 32, vote for the incumbent, he says.

The Texas Association of Business and Chambers of Commerce, which represents more than 140,000 Texas employers and 200 Chambers of Commerce, gave him an "A" for his voting record in supporting Texas businesses and for creating and maintaining Texas jobs.

The score was based on Seaman's votes on business issues such as health care, transportation and education.

Seaman said the number one issue facing Texas is insurance reform.

Because he has a seat on the House Committee on Insurance, he said, he is qualified to move legislation that will fix insurance problems.

"It's the biggest issue of all," Seaman said.

"It is bigger than the budget deficit because it affects every single individual in the state."

John Smithee, R-Amarillo, chairman of the insurance committee, said Seaman has carried several insurance bills and seems knowledgeable about insurance issues.

"He has been a player in most of the insurance matters that have come before the House. I know that there will be a lot of legislation filed this session, particularly with homeowners. It is likely that he could have some legislation that could impact on that."

Seaman also sits on the House Committee on Economic Development. As a committee member, he said, he has developed a broader knowledge of economic development issues that could benefit the area.

Limiting lawsuits is another of Seaman's pet issues, and he has won an endorsement from an interest group, Texans for Lawsuit Reform Political Action Committee, because of it.

20-percent passage rate

His passage rate for bills he has filed is 20 percent. Forty percent of the bills he has filed did not receive a hearing.

Last session Seaman authored, jointly authored or sponsored 65 House bills and either sponsored or jointly sponsored eight Senate bills, he said.

Jointly authoring a bill means that there is a primary author.

If the bill is popular, such as the CHIPS program that insures needy children, other politicians sign on as co-authors.

The co-authors build support for the legislation and in turn take home credit for major pieces of legislation for lending their name and support.

In his three legislative sessions, of 57 House bills he has filed personally, 11 passed and 46 died or were killed. Twenty-two of the 46 failed bills never received hearings.

Last session Seaman was either the primary sponsor or author of 21 bills.

Eighteen were House bills he filed. Three were Senate bills he sponsored, which passed.

A Senate bill sponsor in the House is chosen by a senator whose bill has passed the Senate and wants it taken through the House.

Seven of those bills passed the House. Of his four House bills, the governor vetoed two. Seven of Seaman's bills never had a committee hearing. Five died in committee.

The two House bills Seaman authored, which passed, created a County Court of Law in Aransas County and created the Texana Groundwater Conservation District.

Perry vetoed bill

Seaman remembered one veto from last session, which was a career and technology bill. Seaman said Gov. Rick Perry vetoed it because of politics and the Eagle Forum, a conservative group that disagrees with technology programs for students.

The other vetoed bill would have created a county employment development board in certain counties to develop programs for rural economic assistance for career training.

Aransas County Sheriff Mark Gilliam said he has worked extensively with Seaman and voters need to look at Seaman's overall involvement in local matters and the state government, not just the numbers.

Because Seaman co-authored and was the joint author of many bills, he was very effective for the area, Gilliam said.

"His opponents have said he does not get much accomplished, but I have sat down with him and he has shown me legislation he has been involved in," Gilliam said.

"He has the support in Austin to get things done. It does not have to be just legislation he presents, but legislation he is involved in."

Seaman said he is not necessarily a better candidate than his challenger, San Patricio County Judge Josephine Miller, but he has experience as a legislator and he claims that is what counts.

"I am an incumbent," he said.

"The difference is between someone who wants the job and someone who holds it."

Courting other counties

Because only about 15 percent of Seaman's home base in Nueces County is included in District 32, to win he will have to make a strong showing in San Patricio, Aransas and Calhoun counties.

Gilliam, a Republican, said that he expects a majority of the voters in Aransas County to support Seaman.

Seaman said the other counties in the district would pull for him as well because the voters understand what it means to have a senior representative.

He wouldn't say how much money he plans to spend campaigning.

"We are going to put into this race whatever it takes to win," Seaman said.

He said all signs also point to the Republicans controlling the House in the next term. Seaman claims 82 to 88 House seats will be held by his party, leaving between 62 and 68 to the Democrats.

A high-percentage controlling interest for the Republicans would mean that Speaker of the House Pete Laney would be replaced by a Republican, Seaman said.

"Somewhere in that range is where it will fall," Seaman said. "If it is 80 (Republicans) to 70 (Democrats) Laney will remain as speaker. If it is above that, Laney is out."

Under a Republican speaker, Seaman said, he's likely to chair a committee. Committee chairmen can control whether a bill dies or goes to the floor for a full House vote.

"The Republican shift will mean that the legislation that has been bottled up for years under the Democrats will be up for vote," he said.

"We need a Republican there when that happens."

Seaman also pointed to the relationships he has made with other legislators and his ability to cross party lines as two of the main reasons for voters to stick with the status quo and vote for him.

"It takes one or two sessions to understand the process," he said. "We cannot afford to train somebody new."

* Reprinted with permission from the *Corpus Christi Caller-Times*.

Miller Touts Experience, Successes in San Patricio*
By Jaime Powell
Corpus Christi Caller-Times
October 7, 2002

San Patricio County had an overcrowded jail, a rundown courthouse and a waste disposal problem that resulted in a $618,000 fine when Josephine Miller became county judge 12 years ago.

The experience Miller brought to the table was eight years on the Sinton City Council and a career as a school librarian.

Now, the courthouse is renovated and has been expanded, as has the jail. The waste site has been closed. A juvenile detention center has been built. And Miller has led regional efforts for economic development, water supply and protection of military assets.

When redistricting threw San Patricio County into House District 32, Miller was intrigued. She said she knew that it opened the door for someone from San Patricio County. She thought she'd stand a good chance against the incumbent, Gene Seaman, a Republican from Corpus Christi.

But she wouldn't have run against Judy Hawley, the incumbent representative from San Patricio County whose district had been paired with Seaman's.

When Hawley, a friend of Miller, decided not to run, Miller said, all she needed was a push.

She got that from the political leadership in San Patricio County, both Democratic and Republican.

District 32 consists of Eastern Nueces and all of Aransas, Calhoun, and San Patricio counties and has a total population of 145,780. San Patricio County has 67,318 of those people.

When it became clear that Seaman was not going to have a viable challenger, John Barrett, a Republican appointee to the Coastal Coordination Council, was one of the people telling Miller to run. Barrett had considered running against Seaman in the primary, but bowed out because of ill health.

San Patricio County Commissioner Gordon Porter said he was worried what kind of leadership the county would field when Hawley stepped down. He was relieved when Miller said she would run.

"It is going to be a close race, but there are no flies on her when it comes to working," Porter said. "If she carries it, it will be a lot of San Patricio doing it. She has widespread support here."

Though figures from the Texas Legislative Council indicate that San Patricio County leans toward a Republican majority, Miller carried

65 percent of the vote against Republican challenger Charlie McEntire in 1994 and had no challenger in 1998.

Miller describes herself as a consensus-builder, prepared for state politics and already well connected in Austin.

Knows Zaffirini

One of those connections is state Sen. Judith Zaffirini, D-Laredo, who will rank fourth in seniority in the Senate this term.

She has known and worked with Miller since the 1980s and said that if Miller is elected, she won't be a true freshman. Miller has represented the senatorial district on the state Democratic committee and gained insight into how state government works, Zaffirini said.

"Her experience as a leader and her experience and insight into the issues of the region are everything," Zaffirini said.

"She brings that insight to the race. She is also so articulate."

"She has the capacity to express herself with passion while remaining totally under control. She would be a passionate leader for the area she represents."

Miller said there are big issues facing the Legislature. She said she has a working knowledge of most of them because of her experience as a county judge.

As a legislator faced with a budget deficit . . . , Miller said, she would pursue better sales tax collection, do away with franchise tax loopholes and partner with state and local government to get more federal matching funds, especially for education.

Miller said her number one priority would be finding effective funding strategies for education.

One avenue she would explore is drawing down more federal dollars.

Education top priority

"We have all looked at the sin taxes and I think that the sales tax will get looked at," Miller said. "Something as enormous to fund as education, you look at something broad-based that hits everyone a little bit. I think they (legislators) will look at traditional funding and those are some of the things."

"Thirty percent of the budget is federal money," she said. "Could we increase that? I think it is something we need to look at."

To deal with the looming insurance crisis statewide, Miller said she would work to stop insurance companies from selling unregulated policies. She said she also would place rate regulation back into the state's hands. Miller also said adjusters and mold remediators need to be licensed.

Porter said Miller's ability to organize and build consensus has helped San Patricio County and would help state government.

When she took office and the county needed a jail expansion, courthouse renovation and a juvenile center, she enlisted experienced friends and hired a budget consultant.

The county issued $7 million in certificates of obligation and raised taxes about 8 cents. In 1996, the county lowered the tax rate seven-tenths of a cent and hasn't raised it since.

"She has the ability to get people from diverse opinions working to the center," he said.

Zaffirini agreed. When San Patricio County was redistricted and added to Zaffirini's Senate district, Miller fought it.

Fought for link to city

"She was one of the few who fought redistricting and fought to keep San Pat with Corpus Christi without offending me," Zaffirini said. "The minute the decision was made and San Pat was moved, she immediately called me and said she looked forward to working with me. It was not a surprise because I know her. That is how she works."

Porter said the economic growth in the county is also a direct result of Miller's diligence.

"On the state level she will be able to help in education and economic development," he said. "I think she will be able to bring that to the table in Austin."

Of the growth countywide, 75 percent to 80 percent is in Porter's precinct, which runs east of Gregory and includes refineries and industry at Ingleside and Aransas Pass.

"The plants and offshore industries are growing every day," Porter said.

"She has worked on tax abatements, worked on trying to get people in here, and advocating."

"From January through June I've raised more money than the incumbent," she said. "Lots of that has been from small contributions."

Since June, Miller said, she has raised around $45,000.00 more. "I am going to spend everything I have raised," she said "That is about $120,000."

*Reprinted with permission from the *Corpus Christi Caller-Times*.

6

North Carolina's 115th State House District

In North Carolina, the State Senate and State House collectively are called the General Assembly, with 50 and 120 seats respectively. The 115th State House District sits in the mountain region of western North Carolina, and is entirely located within Buncombe County. The district includes the southeast portion of the region's largest city, Asheville, and some surrounding communities, along with some smaller communities in the largely rural area to the east of the city.

The geography and economy of North Carolina have been important influences on the state's politics. The Tar Heel state is roughly divided into three geographic areas—the Coastal Plain, the Piedmont, and the Mountain regions. The Coastal Plain region (in the eastern portion of the state) has traditionally been home to most of the state's tobacco farms, but also a relatively large proportion of the state's African American population (Luebke 1998). The Piedmont region (in the center of the state) has become the most urbanized in the state, as it contains Raleigh-Durham-Chapel Hill (an area which also includes the "research triangle," named, in part, because of the colleges and universities in the three communities) as well as the state's largest city, Charlotte. The Mountain region (in the westernmost portion of the state) has continued to be dominated by small towns and rural areas, with the exception of Asheville.

North Carolina's economy has experienced substantial change since World War II. In the 30-year period after the war, agricultural employment in the state dropped dramatically from 42 percent of the total jobs in the state to 8 percent, while manufacturing employment increased from 20 percent to 40 percent (Luebke 1998). Despite its reputation as an agricultural state—especially tobacco farming, but also livestock such as hogs and turkeys—North Carolina actually has ranked the highest in manufacturing jobs among all of the southern states (Luebke 1998). Even at its peak, the tobacco industry never employed more people than the textile industry. Tobacco as a proportion of the state's economy (as well as the number of jobs and acreage planted) has decreased since the 1990s, but the tobacco industry remains a potent political force in the state. Another component of the state's traditional economy—the textile industry located primarily in the Piedmont region—has also seen many jobs disappear in the last 30 years. Since 1973, North Carolina's textile and apparel industries combined have lost 60 percent of their jobs—about 230,000 in all. The problems have only escalated in recent years; beginning in the mid-1990s, these industries were losing about 15,000 jobs each year (Walden 2003). Much like Michigan's automobile workers, this industry and its employees were deeply affected by international trade agreements such as the North American Free Trade Agreement (NAFTA). These agreements helped consumers by creating a drop in clothing prices, but also eliminated thousands of jobs in North Carolina as well as in the United States generally.

State politics in North Carolina is not divided so much by political party, or even ideological descriptions such as "liberal" and "conservative." Rather, state political debate emerging from the 1960s has been divided into two broad philosophical camps: "modernists" and "traditionalists" (Luebke 1998, 19). Modernists support economic growth and are accepting of the social change that can occur with that growth. They see public education as an important vehicle for economic growth and economic diversity (that is, a move away from the "old economy," which was dependent on low-wage industries such as textiles and clothing). This view also tends to support a more active state government (and thus a need to fund government), as economic growth is considered to be a product of an expanded economic capacity through public education (high school as well as colleges and universities) and infrastructure (that is, highways, airports, and improved utilities including power, sewers, and water). Modernists tend to be most prominent in the metropolitan areas of the Piedmont region, and often include groups linked to interests such as banking, insurance, the media, teachers, utilities, developers, and high technology firms.

The traditionalist view is rooted in rural North Carolina. Its standard-bearers in the state's economy are tobacco farmers, and textile, clothing, and furniture makers. This is, in part, because these industries relied on low-wage workers and a traditional paternalistic social order that did not support labor unions. Traditionalist economic and social policies, based heavily on fundamentalist religion, support a deferential relationship between employer and employee, as well as husband and wife. To some traditionalists, it is wrong for any movement or organization—such as those supporting civil rights, equal rights, affirmative action, and labor unions—to challenge the established social order.

THE NORTH CAROLINA POLITICAL CONTEXT

The partisan changes that have occurred in North Carolina since the early 1980s have been similar to those seen throughout much of the United States. As Republicans began gaining voter support and winning legislative seats during this time, the "solid South" (that is, solidly Democratic) shifted toward greater parity between the major parties.

TABLE 6.1 Party Registration, North Carolina Voters (in percent)

	Democrat	Republican	Unaffiliated
1984	70	26	4
1990	64	31	6
1996	54	34	12
2000	51	34	16

SOURCE: North Carolina State Board of Elections.

This type of shift occurred in places like Michigan and Texas, but is seen in North Carolina as well. Because North Carolina requires individuals to declare their partisanship when they register to vote, trends in party affiliation over time can be tracked. The movement away from the Democratic Party beginning in the mid-1980s is palpable (see Table 6.1). Indeed, as part of the "Reagan revolution" of the 1980s, the Republicans in North Carolina gained more state legislative seats here than any other state in the United States (Luebke 1998). In fact, as a result of the 1994 elections, Republicans gained majority status in the state house. However, that being said, the margins have been small and the majority has swung back and forth between the parties since the mid-1990s. In some legislative sessions, the number of house seats held by the two parties was so close that a shared speakership arrangement was created between the parties where the leaders of both parties each would hold power in controlling some aspects of the chamber (see Chapter 1). Also illustrative of the close electoral and political divide in the state is the loose grip both parties have had on the governor's mansion, and the shift in the congressional delegation towards the GOP. Over the past 25 years, both Republicans and Democrats have been elected to serve as governor; Democrat Jim Hunt served four terms, first serving two terms from 1977 to 1985, and again from 1993 to 2001, with Republican James Martin serving from 1985 to 1993; Democrat Mike Easley has occupied the governor's mansion since 2001.

As in Texas (see Chapter 5), there are no term limits for state legislators in North Carolina. In the early 1990s—along with efforts in many other states at the same time—a proposal for term limits was introduced in the General Assembly but died before any significant action was taken. Also like Texans, North Carolinians do not have an opportunity to place the issue on the ballot through citizen initiative. Therefore, it is unlikely that term limits will be implemented. Ironically, a separate effort has been made to *increase* the current two-year terms of state house members to four years. However, this proposal has not made much headway either.

Candidates for both the North Carolina State Senate and State House run every two years in even-numbered years. However, prior to 2000, North Carolina employed a system for selecting its representatives that resembled that of many European nations more than other state legislatures in the United States. Specifically, North Carolina utilized a multimember district system. Under this method, more than one representative is elected in a geographic area. This is opposed to the single-member districts of Michigan, Texas, and most other states in the U.S. The state house district now known as District 115 used to be District 51, from which three representatives were elected. For the 2000 election, District 51 was divided into State House

Districts 114, 115, and 116; and ever since, North Carolina has used the more familiar single-member district, winner-take-all, plurality system, in which the candidate in the general election who garners of the most votes represents the entire district.

Without a legislative term limits provision, legislative redistricting decisions can be quite controversial. North Carolina has been the subject of much interest regarding redistricting. Beginning in the 1960s, 40 of its 100 counties were subject to the provisions of the federal Voting Rights Act, which was designed to protect the voting rights of minority group members. Later, the 1993 U.S. Supreme Court decision in *Shaw v. Reno* ruled that some so-called "benign gerrymandering" redistricting decisions involving race (that is, those districts drawn to create "majority–minority" districts and encourage the election of minority candidates) were unconstitutional. The *Shaw* case involved the 12th Congressional District in North Carolina, which, as originally drawn, ran like a serpent from Wake County (which includes the city of Raleigh) in the northern Piedmont region to Mecklenburg County (which includes Charlotte) in the southern Piedmont. The court ruled in the *Shaw* case that this district did not meet constitutional muster because the redistricting plan relied too heavily on the racial background of area residents.

Although redistricting in North Carolina perhaps has received more national attention than most other states, the rules and customs influencing these decisions are similar to those in many other states. First, each voting district (whether for the U.S. House or state legislatures) should contain approximately the same number of people as the others for the same office. After the 2000 census, for instance, that meant that each North Carolina State House District would have about 67,000 people. Districts should also avoid crossing existing boundaries (that is, county lines) when possible, and an incumbent's residence should remain in his previous district. North Carolina is similar to other states in another way as well; redistricting decisions create a large percentage of "safe districts" with very few competitive seats.

North Carolina Primary and General Elections

The primary and general election processes in North Carolina are typical of elections in many southern states, in that a primary election may create the need for a runoff (or second primary) election. North Carolina election law provides for primary elections to be held the Tuesday after the first Monday in May; the runoff primary, if necessary, is held four weeks later. The state's general elections are held on the same day as federal elections—the first Tuesday after the first Monday in November in even-numbered years. As noted previously, North Carolina requires voters to declare their party affiliation when they register to vote. Therefore, the state operates a closed primary system of elections where only those voters registered with a party may vote in that party's primary elections.

Until 1990, the state used a runoff primary (like the one employed in Texas) if a party's nominee did not win a majority vote in the first primary election. The top two candidates then ran in a second primary. However, because the runoff was criticized as discriminatory to minority candidates, the General Assembly changed the rules so that if a candidate won a "substantial plurality" (defined as at least 40 percent of the vote) in the primary, no runoff would be necessary and that candidate would serve as his party's nominee (Fleer 1994, 168).

Without a runoff primary, the time between the first primary and the November general election is fairly long—approximately six months (five if a runoff is required). This has a major impact on campaign strategies, especially campaign fund-raising and strategic expenditures such as campaign communications, because six months can be a long time for a state legislative campaign to stay active. However, most campaign activity is likely to occur fairly close to Election Day, when voters begin to pay more attention to elections in general. This means that candidates for these relatively lower-level offices also must compete with candidates for the U.S. House, and sometimes U.S. Senate, governor, or president of the United States, for voters' attention.

Party organizations in the state can provide substantial assistance to their candidates. Services such as candidate recruitment, public opinion polling, campaign management training, voter registration, and fund-raising are common party activities. The parties in North Carolina, as in other states, tend to focus their efforts on major offices and targeted state legislative campaigns (Fleer 1994).

Fund-Raising and Campaign Finance Law in North Carolina

The North Carolina General Assembly enacted significant campaign finance reforms in 1975 for candidates seeking state office, during the same era when the Federal Election Campaign Act of 1971 and its Amendments (1974, 1976, and 1979) imposed reforms on federal candidates. Many states adopted statutes similar to the federal laws in the post-Watergate era, as public awareness about campaign finance reform was relatively high and many reform-minded candidates won office at both national and state levels. The North Carolina law provides for contribution limits, disclosure of campaigns' financial activities, and public financing of political parties and selected statewide candidates.

North Carolina's State Board of Elections (SBOE) is responsible for administering elections in the state. The Campaign Finance Office of the SBOE serves as the repository for all campaign finance-related documentation including the reports that candidates, political action committees (PACs), and political parties are required to submit. The State Board of Elections also collects and maintains data on voter registration by party and voter statistics, such as turnout and election results.

All candidates for office must form a candidate committee and appoint a treasurer, who maintains the committee's financial records and is responsible for campaign finance reporting. North Carolina requires that candidates file quarterly campaign finance reports during election years and semiannual reports (that is, at the end of January and the end of July) in nonelection years, should the campaign organization operate between election years. In addition, reports are available ten days before a given election. There is no overall requirement for electronic filing by candidates running for state office, but those candidates who receive more than $5,000 during an election must file electronically. A candidate committee that does not intend to raise or spend more than $3,000 can file a waiver reporting form (called the Certification of Threshold), which exempts the committee from the reporting requirements.

According to North Carolina law, campaign contributions from both individuals and PACs may not exceed $4,000 per candidate per election, although there are no contribution or expenditure limits for state political party committees. Primary and general elections are treated separately for these purposes; therefore, individuals and PACs can contribute a total of $8,000 to a candidate; if a second (runoff) primary must be held, another $4,000 maximum contribution is allowed. Under state law, corporations, business enterprises, labor unions, professional associations, out-of-state PACs, and insurance companies are prohibited from contributing to a candidate in North Carolina.

Regardless of the contribution's size or source, all donations made to candidate committees must be reported. Contributions from North Carolina residents that individually total less than $100 may be combined on an aggregated contributions list, but once the $100 threshold has been reached, the contributor's name, address, and occupation must be reported along with the contribution.[1] Contributions in any amount from an out-of-state resident must include the name, address, and occupation of the contributor.

In 1988, the state created a North Carolina Candidates Fund, designed as a public financing mechanism for candidates running for the Council of State offices (governor, lieutenant governor, attorney general, state treasurer, and five other statewide offices). Although the presidential public financing system at the federal level is driven by voluntary contributions on individuals' tax returns that do not increase the taxpayer's liability (that is, a check-off system), North Carolina employs a tax add-on system for its candidates fund, which allows taxpayers to designate some (or even all) of their state tax refund to support these campaigns (Fleer 1994).[2] In 2002, the state created a public financing mechanism for judicial races in North Carolina, which is funded through a state income tax check-off system. Candidates agreeing to receive public funds also agree to overall expenditure limits for their campaigns.

The North Carolina Political Parties Financing Fund is also a tax check-off system that provides public funding to state party organizations for party-building activities, candidate support, and support to local parties. Public financing of political party organizations, along with voter registration by party and a closed primary system, all point to a context that can help create and maintain a relatively strong state political party system. In turn, political party organizations (both state and local) can be active in providing campaign funds to selected candidates. This is especially important when a district is competitive and only a few seats are needed to retain or obtain a majority in the legislature.

BOX 6.1   North Carolina at a Glance

2000 population		8,049,313
U.S. Congressional districts		12
State Senate districts		50
State House districts		120
State Senate district population (avg.)		160,986
State House district population (avg.)		67,078
Full-time legislature		No
Term limits		No
Voter registration by party		Yes
Campaign finance contribution limits (per candidate per election)	*House*	*Senate*
Source:		
Individual	$4,000	$4,000
PAC	$4,000	$4,000
Party	Unlimited	Unlimited

THE CAMPAIGN

In the election being contested in this simulation, the campaign for the North Carolina 115th State House District seat is a competitive incumbent-versus-challenger contest. The incumbent is a Republican who was appointed to fill the remaining months in the term of a seat vacated by a fellow Republican who was tapped to fill a position in the governor's cabinet. The anticipated closeness of the election is in large part due to the nature of the district, which was drawn to include part of the city of Asheville (with a population of approximately 70,000), which has a Democratic voting base, as well as a surrounding rural area that is mostly Republican. The district consists of 10 precincts in Asheville, all 5 precincts in Black Mountain, and a few others from areas in Buncombe County located east of the city of Asheville.

In the primary election, Democrat Bruce Goforth beat his opponent Michael Morgan by a 3-to-1 margin, taking 74.5 percent of the vote. Republican Mark Crawford—the incumbent who had been appointed to fill the seat—ran unopposed in his party's primary. Because this is a marginal district and because the incumbent is seen as vulnerable, there is considerable interest in this campaign. The general election campaign in this district is a targeted race. In the previous legislative elections, the Republicans and Democrats held almost exactly the same number of seats. As noted previously, the balance of party power in the state house was so even that the chamber voted to have a shared speakership arrangement between a Democrat and Republican leader. Either political party could achieve majority status with a shift in one or two seats. As such, each election is crucial—especially in those districts that are as competitive as the 115th State House District.

The Candidates

D. Bruce Goforth (D) Bruce Goforth is a 60-year-old businessman from Fairview, located just outside of Asheville, and is the owner of Goforth Building Inc., an Asheville construction company. Goforth has two daughters and five grandchildren, and has been married to his wife for over 40 years. A high school graduate with no college training, he has served two terms on the Buncombe County Board of Education. He is a Buncombe County native and has been active in a number of civic, community, and trade organizations, such as the Lions Club, a local Home Builders Association, the Asheville Board of Realtors, and his local Baptist church. His experience as a local homebuilder for many years has put him in contact with many of the district's residents. Mr. Goforth has neither run for nor served in the General Assembly before.

He has served as president of the Democratic Men's Club in Buncombe County and considers himself a "conservative Democrat" (Goforth 2003). He has supported the use of money awarded to the state in a lawsuit against tobacco companies to fund a prescription drug benefit program for seniors. In addition, during his two terms as a member of the Buncombe County Board of Education, the board greatly expanded funding for public schools, including construction of several new school buildings in the county. In this regard, Goforth may be considered a "modernist" by North Carolina standards (see the relevant discussion in the first section of this chapter). For this election, he was endorsed by the North Carolina Association of Educators. Goforth is known for supporting a plan for regional economic development in western North Carolina, and endorsing fiscal responsibility in the state government's budget.

Mark Crawford (R) Mark Crawford is a 41-year-old resident of Black Mountain, a town of approximately 7,600 located east of Asheville. Crawford is a local real estate agent, and has also served as a substitute teacher in Black Mountain. He has been active in his community, having served for several seasons as a coach of the girls' and boys' soccer teams at Owen High School. He is a graduate of the U.S. Military Academy at West Point and served in Iraq during the Gulf War in the early 1990s. His own educational accomplishments at West Point and his work in the local schools underscore his belief in the importance of education. While a state representative, Crawford became known for taking positions favoring lower taxes and smaller government. He believes that voluntary, nongovernmental organizations (for example, religious organizations and charitable groups) can help serve those in need without too much governmental involvement.

Crawford has previously run for Buncombe County School Board Chairman and twice has run as alderman in his home town of Black Mountain. In each of those races Crawford lost. Because Crawford has lost all of his previous elections, and because he is an incumbent only because of an appointment he received to finish the term of his predecessor, he is afraid that his opponent will try to make his lack of electoral success a campaign issue. Although he could be considered a "favorite son" of Black Mountain in this election, the town did not support him in his two attempts to become town alderman.

Though he was not elected in three previous bids for elective office, Crawford is running as the incumbent against Bruce Goforth because he replaced State Representative Lanier Cansler through a vote of Republican committee members.[3] In the middle of his term, Representative Cansler was appointed by the governor to serve as deputy director of the North Carolina Department of Health and Human Services. Although incumbency brings with it a number of perks for the individual's next campaign, it also means that the individual has a roll-call voting record to defend. According to a study conducted by the North Carolina Center for Public Policy, Mark Crawford's record as a legislator placed him 116th out of 120 state legislators in terms of effectiveness. This rating system is based on effectiveness rankings as judged by fellow state legislators and lobbyists. Moreover, Representative Crawford has not supported legislation that would continue to fund Smart Start, a program begun by former Governor James Hunt that promoted educational excellence in the state and focused on early intervention strategies.

CREATING A CAMPAIGN PLAN

The discussion of the candidates for North Carolina's 115th State House District seat and the surrounding campaign context provides the reader with enough information to begin conducting district and demographic analyses as well as candidate profiles for the simulation exercises in Chapter 3. Supplemental material needed to complete those exercises is also included at the end of this chapter. We provide the following information that will be needed to complete the exercises in Chapter 3:

- *A map of the district.* The map included provides a general location of the district within the state. This map will help you to begin to familiarize yourself with the district and the lay of the land where the campaign will be waged. It will also provide important information in terms of where the district is situated in relation to other communities in the area. A more detailed map of the district can tell you about the kind of district in which you will be working—that is, whether it is urban, suburban, rural, or a combination of the three. This kind of map can also help to determine some aspects of campaign strategy such as whether the candidate will go door-to-door, or whether canvassing of this kind is out of the question because of the district's geographic elements.

- *U.S. Census data on the 115th North Carolina House District.* This information will be the beginning of your research into the district and its residents that you will use in several of the exercises in Chapter 3. We have provided you with some of the information you will need, but there is more out there. You will need to use your research skills to go out and find other pertinent data that will help you complete the exercises.

- *Newspaper articles on the campaign.* In reading other case chapters in this book, the reader will notice that newspaper articles about the races in those chapters have been included as supplemental material. That is not the case in this chapter. There simply was no coverage in the local newspapers of the race between Mark Crawford and Bruce Goforth. This is a fact of life in many lower-level campaigns; as noted in Chapter 1, the media often do not pay much attention to them. Those involved in campaigns at this level will have to deal with the fact that earned media (see Chapters 2 and 3) may not come easily to their campaign.

- *Voter data on the district.* We have provided some of the information you will need to collect on the voters of the 115th District by providing election results from 1994 through 2000. Again, you may have to rely on your research skills to complement the given information relating to the voters of this district.

- *Campaign finance information.* Although we have tried to keep this simulation as realistic as possible, we will deviate a bit from the real world here. The North Carolina 115th State House District is a competitive race; therefore, more money would be spent in this race than in a typical North Carolina state house race. For instance, as in many competitive campaigns, political party organizations may also spend money on this race. More money in a campaign means that more things can be done in the campaign and a wider variety of campaign tactics can be utilized. We supply a budget figure that provides some context for the race (remember that the state's campaign finance law summarized earlier in this chapter is also part of this context). This is the figure that must be raised in the fund-raising exercise outlined in Chapter 3. It will also be informative in terms of what other kinds of resources will be available in the campaign. We have taken a realistic figure that would be spent in this race and discounted it slightly. Just about anyone can run a campaign that is flush with cash. The real learning comes from having to decide how to divide up scarce resources in an efficient manner. As we have previously noted, activities related to the raising and spending of campaign funds must be periodically reported to the state. In order to illustrate what goes into these reports, we have provided examples of actual campaign finance reports from the two candidates. (These are available on the book's companion Web site.) The pages provided also serve as examples of sources from which the candidates raised money and what they spent it on. The budget for each campaign in the 115th North Carolina State House District is $60,000.

NOTES

1. See the campaign finance reports on this book's companion Web site for an example of aggregated contributions reporting.
2. In the federal system, partial public funding through matching funds is provided to presidential candidates for the primary election and full public funding is provided in the general election. See the Federal Election Commission's Web site (http://www.fec.gov) for more on public financing at the federal level. The main difference is that in North Carolina, the voluntary contribution is made from an individual's refund, whereas on a federal tax return there is a box that allows individuals to designate $3 from their tax liability to the public financing fund.
3. In North Carolina, vacant state legislative seats are filled via a recommendation to the governor by a political party's executive committee, a group of about 50 people.

Supplemental Materials for North Carolina's 115th State House District

Contents include:

District map

Census data

Voting history

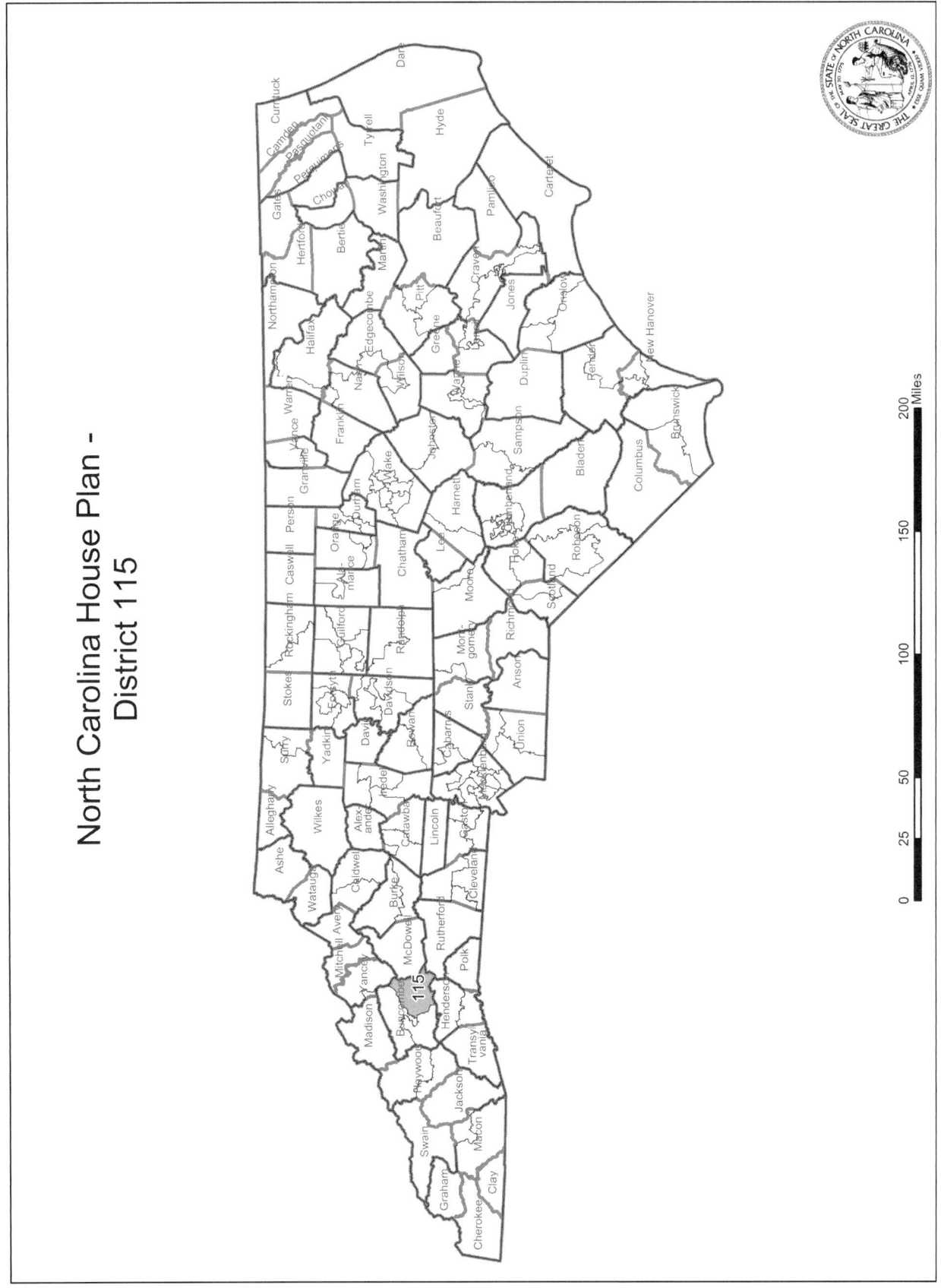

North Carolina House Plan - District 115

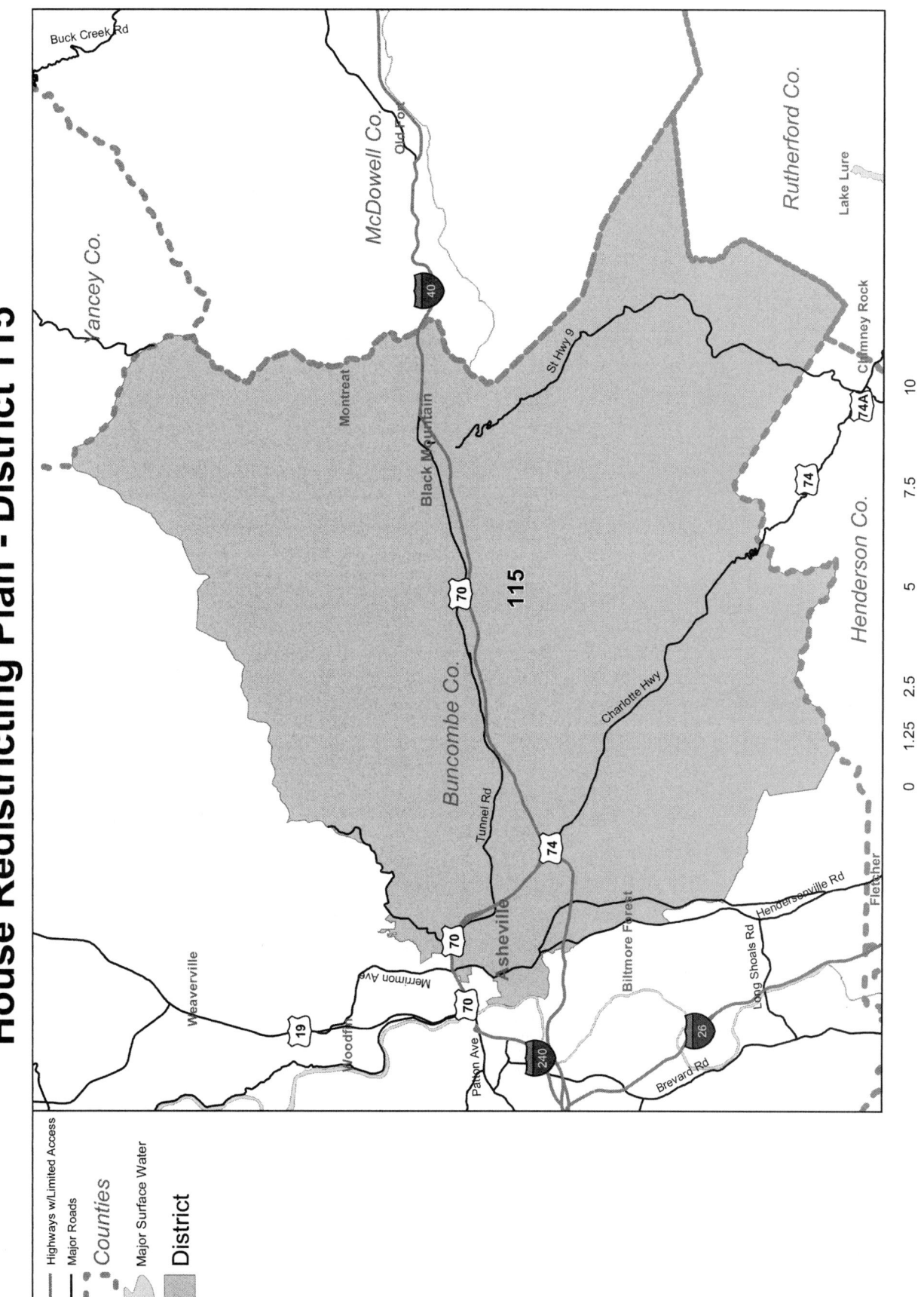

Table DP-1. Profile of General Demographic Characteristics: 2000

Geographic area: Buncombe County, North Carolina

[For information on confidentiality protection, nonsampling error, and definitions, see text]

Subject	Number	Percent	Subject	Number	Percent
Total population	206,330	100.0	**HISPANIC OR LATINO AND RACE**		
SEX AND AGE			Total population	206,330	100.0
			Hispanic or Latino (of any race)	5,730	2.8
Male	99,034	48.0	Mexican	3,541	1.7
Female	107,296	52.0	Puerto Rican	457	0.2
			Cuban	167	0.1
Under 5 years	11,646	5.6	Other Hispanic or Latino	1,565	0.8
5 to 9 years	12,706	6.2	Not Hispanic or Latino	200,600	97.2
10 to 14 years	13,052	6.3	White alone	180,721	87.6
15 to 19 years	12,782	6.2			
20 to 24 years	12,698	6.2	**RELATIONSHIP**		
25 to 34 years	28,083	13.6	Total population	206,330	100.0
35 to 44 years	32,423	15.7	In households	199,565	96.7
45 to 54 years	30,644	14.9	Householder	85,776	41.6
55 to 59 years	11,272	5.5	Spouse	43,280	21.0
60 to 64 years	9,248	4.5	Child	51,771	25.1
65 to 74 years	16,397	7.9	Own child under 18 years	40,489	19.6
75 to 84 years	11,361	5.5	Other relatives	8,476	4.1
85 years and over	4,018	1.9	Under 18 years	3,244	1.6
Median age (years)	38.9	(X)	Nonrelatives	10,262	5.0
			Unmarried partner	4,135	2.0
18 years and over	161,201	78.1	In group quarters	6,765	3.3
Male	75,855	36.8	Institutionalized population	3,444	1.7
Female	85,346	41.4	Noninstitutionalized population	3,321	1.6
21 years and over	153,566	74.4			
62 years and over	37,158	18.0	**HOUSEHOLD BY TYPE**		
65 years and over	31,776	15.4	Total households	85,776	100.0
Male	12,716	6.2	Family households (families)	55,661	64.9
Female	19,060	9.2	With own children under 18 years	23,611	27.5
			Married-couple family	43,280	50.5
RACE			With own children under 18 years	16,783	19.6
One race	203,801	98.8	Female householder, no husband present	9,227	10.8
White	183,761	89.1	With own children under 18 years	5,213	6.1
Black or African American	15,425	7.5	Nonfamily households	30,115	35.1
American Indian and Alaska Native	803	0.4	Householder living alone	24,783	28.9
Asian	1,368	0.7	Householder 65 years and over	9,063	10.6
Asian Indian	288	0.1			
Chinese	228	0.1	Households with individuals under 18 years	25,936	30.2
Filipino	211	0.1	Households with individuals 65 years and over	22,019	25.7
Japanese	121	0.1			
Korean	198	0.1	Average household size	2.33	(X)
Vietnamese	105	0.1	Average family size	2.86	(X)
Other Asian [1]	217	0.1			
Native Hawaiian and Other Pacific Islander	79	-	**HOUSING OCCUPANCY**		
Native Hawaiian	14	-	Total housing units	93,973	100.0
Guamanian or Chamorro	25	-	Occupied housing units	85,776	91.3
Samoan	15	-	Vacant housing units	8,197	8.7
Other Pacific Islander [2]	25	-	For seasonal, recreational, or occasional use	2,042	2.2
Some other race	2,365	1.1			
Two or more races	2,529	1.2	Homeowner vacancy rate (percent)	1.8	(X)
			Rental vacancy rate (percent)	8.5	(X)
Race alone or in combination with one or more other races: [3]			**HOUSING TENURE**		
White	186,063	90.2	Occupied housing units	85,776	100.0
Black or African American	16,228	7.9	Owner-occupied housing units	60,295	70.3
American Indian and Alaska Native	1,801	0.9	Renter-occupied housing units	25,481	29.7
Asian	1,757	0.9			
Native Hawaiian and Other Pacific Islander	178	0.1	Average household size of owner-occupied units	2.41	(X)
Some other race	3,019	1.5	Average household size of renter-occupied units	2.13	(X)

- Represents zero or rounds to zero. (X) Not applicable.

[1] Other Asian alone, or two or more Asian categories.

[2] Other Pacific Islander alone, or two or more Native Hawaiian and Other Pacific Islander categories.

[3] In combination with one or more of the other races listed. The six numbers may add to more than the total population and the six percentages may add to more than 100 percent because individuals may report more than one race.

Source: U.S. Census Bureau, Census 2000.

Table DP-2. Profile of Selected Social Characteristics: 2000

Geographic area: Buncombe County, North Carolina

[Data based on a sample. For information on confidentiality protection, sampling error, nonsampling error, and definitions, see text]

Subject	Number	Percent	Subject	Number	Percent
SCHOOL ENROLLMENT			**NATIVITY AND PLACE OF BIRTH**		
Population 3 years and over enrolled in school	47,002	100.0	Total population	206,330	100.0
Nursery school, preschool	2,897	6.2	Native	198,366	96.1
Kindergarten	2,540	5.4	Born in United States	196,694	95.3
Elementary school (grades 1-8)	21,135	45.0	State of residence	124,942	60.6
High school (grades 9-12)	9,653	20.5	Different state	71,752	34.8
College or graduate school	10,777	22.9	Born outside United States	1,672	0.8
			Foreign born	7,964	3.9
EDUCATIONAL ATTAINMENT			Entered 1990 to March 2000	4,384	2.1
Population 25 years and over	143,649	100.0	Naturalized citizen	2,672	1.3
Less than 9th grade	8,727	6.1	Not a citizen	5,292	2.6
9th to 12th grade, no diploma	17,267	12.0			
High school graduate (includes equivalency)	40,630	28.3	**REGION OF BIRTH OF FOREIGN BORN**		
Some college, no degree	30,522	21.2	Total (excluding born at sea)	7,964	100.0
Associate degree	10,216	7.1	Europe	2,698	33.9
Bachelor's degree	23,450	16.3	Asia	1,397	17.5
Graduate or professional degree	12,837	8.9	Africa	181	2.3
			Oceania	31	0.4
Percent high school graduate or higher	81.9	(X)	Latin America	3,327	41.8
Percent bachelor's degree or higher	25.3	(X)	Northern America	330	4.1
			LANGUAGE SPOKEN AT HOME		
MARITAL STATUS			Population 5 years and over	194,791	100.0
Population 15 years and over	168,979	100.0	English only	183,265	94.1
Never married	38,867	23.0	Language other than English	11,526	5.9
Now married, except separated	94,734	56.1	Speak English less than very well	5,122	2.6
Separated	4,347	2.6	Spanish	6,441	3.3
Widowed	13,253	7.8	Speak English less than very well	3,363	1.7
Female	11,019	6.5	Other Indo-European languages	3,493	1.8
Divorced	17,778	10.5	Speak English less than very well	1,233	0.6
Female	10,370	6.1	Asian and Pacific Island languages	1,253	0.6
			Speak English less than very well	424	0.2
GRANDPARENTS AS CAREGIVERS					
Grandparent living in household with one or more own grandchildren under 18 years	3,340	100.0	**ANCESTRY (single or multiple)**		
			Total population	206,330	100.0
Grandparent responsible for grandchildren	1,665	49.9	Total ancestries reported	185,877	90.1
			Arab	200	0.1
VETERAN STATUS			Czech[1]	383	0.2
Civilian population 18 years and over	161,148	100.0	Danish	382	0.2
Civilian veterans	24,124	15.0	Dutch	4,300	2.1
			English	27,037	13.1
DISABILITY STATUS OF THE CIVILIAN NONINSTITUTIONALIZED POPULATION			French (except Basque)[1]	4,319	2.1
			French Canadian[1]	920	0.4
Population 5 to 20 years	40,623	100.0	German	22,973	11.1
With a disability	3,224	7.9	Greek	696	0.3
			Hungarian	547	0.3
Population 21 to 64 years	120,651	100.0	Irish[1]	22,568	10.9
With a disability	24,145	20.0	Italian	4,770	2.3
Percent employed	55.9	(X)	Lithuanian	301	0.1
No disability	96,506	80.0	Norwegian	1,224	0.6
Percent employed	80.3	(X)	Polish	2,572	1.2
			Portuguese	226	0.1
Population 65 years and over	30,141	100.0	Russian	1,055	0.5
With a disability	12,514	41.5	Scotch-Irish	11,699	5.7
			Scottish	7,699	3.7
RESIDENCE IN 1995			Slovak	204	0.1
Population 5 years and over	194,791	100.0	Subsaharan African	761	0.4
Same house in 1995	103,312	53.0	Swedish	1,531	0.7
Different house in the U.S. in 1995	88,205	45.3	Swiss	609	0.3
Same county	48,358	24.8	Ukrainian	746	0.4
Different county	39,847	20.5	United States or American	29,505	14.3
Same state	15,011	7.7	Welsh	1,732	0.8
Different state	24,836	12.8	West Indian (excluding Hispanic groups)	250	0.1
Elsewhere in 1995	3,274	1.7	Other ancestries	36,668	17.8

-Represents zero or rounds to zero.   (X) Not applicable.

[1]The data represent a combination of two ancestries shown separately in Summary File 3. Czech includes Czechoslovakian. French includes Alsatian. French Canadian includes Acadian/Cajun. Irish includes Celtic.

Source: U.S. Bureau of the Census, Census 2000.

Table DP-3. Profile of Selected Economic Characteristics: 2000

Geographic area: Buncombe County, North Carolina
[Data based on a sample. For information on confidentiality protection, sampling error, nonsampling error, and definitions, see text]

Subject	Number	Percent	Subject	Number	Percent
EMPLOYMENT STATUS			**INCOME IN 1999**		
Population 16 years and over	166,200	100.0	Households	85,743	100.0
In labor force	106,066	63.8	Less than $10,000	8,771	10.2
Civilian labor force	105,965	63.8	$10,000 to $14,999	6,260	7.3
Employed	100,924	60.7	$15,000 to $24,999	13,108	15.3
Unemployed	5,041	3.0	$25,000 to $34,999	12,605	14.7
Percent of civilian labor force	4.8	(X)	$35,000 to $49,999	15,708	18.3
Armed Forces	101	0.1	$50,000 to $74,999	16,144	18.8
Not in labor force	60,134	36.2	$75,000 to $99,999	6,456	7.5
			$100,000 to $149,999	4,262	5.0
Females 16 years and over	88,000	100.0	$150,000 to $199,999	1,089	1.3
In labor force	50,455	57.3	$200,000 or more	1,340	1.6
Civilian labor force	50,441	57.3	Median household income (dollars)	36,666	(X)
Employed	48,092	54.7			
Own children under 6 years	13,426	100.0	With earnings	67,275	78.5
All parents in family in labor force	8,203	61.1	Mean earnings (dollars)[1]	46,143	(X)
			With Social Security income	25,425	29.7
COMMUTING TO WORK			Mean Social Security income (dollars)[1]	10,935	(X)
Workers 16 years and over	99,133	100.0	With Supplemental Security Income	3,716	4.3
Car, truck, or van - - drove alone	78,890	79.6	Mean Supplemental Security Income (dollars)[1]	5,797	(X)
Car, truck, or van - - carpooled	12,888	13.0	With public assistance income	2,404	2.8
Public transportation (including taxicab)	813	0.8	Mean public assistance income (dollars)[1]	2,872	(X)
Walked	1,971	2.0	With retirement income	16,399	19.1
Other means	840	0.8	Mean retirement income (dollars)[1]	17,737	(X)
Worked at home	3,731	3.8			
Mean travel time to work (minutes)[1]	21.1	(X)	Families	55,955	100.0
			Less than $10,000	2,940	5.3
Employed civilian population 16 years and over	100,924	100.0	$10,000 to $14,999	2,611	4.7
			$15,000 to $24,999	6,813	12.2
OCCUPATION			$25,000 to $34,999	7,797	13.9
Management, professional, and related occupations	32,336	32.0	$35,000 to $49,999	11,329	20.2
Service occupations	15,696	15.6	$50,000 to $74,999	13,322	23.8
Sales and office occupations	25,767	25.5	$75,000 to $99,999	5,389	9.6
Farming, fishing, and forestry occupations	321	0.3	$100,000 to $149,999	3,730	6.7
Construction, extraction, and maintenance occupations	10,052	10.0	$150,000 to $199,999	882	1.6
			$200,000 or more	1,142	2.0
Production, transportation, and material moving occupations	16,752	16.6	Median family income (dollars)	45,011	(X)
			Per capita income (dollars)[1]	20,384	(X)
INDUSTRY			**Median earnings (dollars):**		
Agriculture, forestry, fishing and hunting, and mining	937	0.9	Male full-time, year-round workers	30,705	(X)
Construction	7,928	7.9	Female full-time, year-round workers	23,870	(X)

Subject	Number	Percent	Subject	Number below poverty level	Percent below poverty level
Manufacturing	16,671	16.5			
Wholesale trade	3,894	3.9			
Retail trade	12,781	12.7			
Transportation and warehousing, and utilities	3,706	3.7			
Information	2,115	2.1	**POVERTY STATUS IN 1999**		
Finance, insurance, real estate, and rental and leasing	4,607	4.6	Families	4,338	7.8
			With related children under 18 years	3,282	12.7
Professional, scientific, management, administrative, and waste management services	7,269	7.2	With related children under 5 years	1,489	15.5
Educational, health and social services	22,930	22.7	**Families with female householder, no husband present**	2,319	25.8
Arts, entertainment, recreation, accommodation and food services	9,621	9.5	With related children under 18 years	2,063	35.2
Other services (except public administration)	5,223	5.2	With related children under 5 years	939	48.5
Public administration	3,242	3.2			
CLASS OF WORKER			Individuals	22,920	11.4
Private wage and salary workers	78,979	78.3	18 years and over	15,938	10.2
Government workers	13,590	13.5	65 years and over	2,960	9.8
Self-employed workers in own not incorporated business	8,118	8.0	Related children under 18 years	6,653	15.3
			Related children 5 to 17 years	4,618	14.3
Unpaid family workers	237	0.2	Unrelated individuals 15 years and over	9,256	23.0

-Represents zero or rounds to zero.   (X) Not applicable.
[1] If the denominator of a mean value or per capita value is less than 30, then that value is calculated using a rounded aggregate in the numerator. See text.
Source: U.S. Bureau of the Census, Census 2000.

Table DP-4. Profile of Selected Housing Characteristics: 2000

Geographic area: Buncombe County, North Carolina

[Data based on a sample. For information on confidentiality protection, sampling error, nonsampling error, and definitions, see text]

Subject	Number	Percent	Subject	Number	Percent
Total housing units	93,973	100.0	**OCCUPANTS PER ROOM**		
UNITS IN STRUCTURE			Occupied housing units	85,776	100.0
1-unit, detached	58,706	62.5	1.00 or less	84,015	97.9
1-unit, attached	2,519	2.7	1.01 to 1.50	1,333	1.6
2 units	2,172	2.3	1.51 or more	428	0.5
3 or 4 units	3,385	3.6			
5 to 9 units	4,404	4.7	Specified owner-occupied units	42,816	100.0
10 to 19 units	1,501	1.6	**VALUE**		
20 or more units	3,147	3.3	Less than $50,000	2,362	5.5
Mobile home	18,054	19.2	$50,000 to $99,999	14,246	33.3
Boat, RV, van, etc	85	0.1	$100,000 to $149,999	11,952	27.9
			$150,000 to $199,999	7,189	16.8
YEAR STRUCTURE BUILT			$200,000 to $299,999	4,458	10.4
1999 to March 2000	2,948	3.1	$300,000 to $499,999	1,806	4.2
1995 to 1998	9,331	9.9	$500,000 to $999,999	655	1.5
1990 to 1994	8,586	9.1	$1,000,000 or more	148	0.3
1980 to 1989	16,067	17.1	Median (dollars)	119,600	(X)
1970 to 1979	15,490	16.5			
1960 to 1969	12,470	13.3	**MORTGAGE STATUS AND SELECTED**		
1940 to 1959	16,296	17.3	**MONTHLY OWNER COSTS**		
1939 or earlier	12,785	13.6	With a mortgage	26,711	62.4
			Less than $300	113	0.3
ROOMS			$300 to $499	1,810	4.2
1 room	855	0.9	$500 to $699	4,510	10.5
2 rooms	2,650	2.8	$700 to $999	8,256	19.3
3 rooms	6,462	6.9	$1,000 to $1,499	7,873	18.4
4 rooms	19,373	20.6	$1,500 to $1,999	2,386	5.6
5 rooms	24,179	25.7	$2,000 or more	1,763	4.1
6 rooms	18,006	19.2	Median (dollars)	948	(X)
7 rooms	10,646	11.3	Not mortgaged	16,105	37.6
8 rooms	6,008	6.4	Median (dollars)	260	(X)
9 or more rooms	5,794	6.2			
Median (rooms)	5.2	(X)	**SELECTED MONTHLY OWNER COSTS**		
			AS A PERCENTAGE OF HOUSEHOLD		
Occupied housing units	85,776	100.0	**INCOME IN 1999**		
YEAR HOUSEHOLDER MOVED INTO UNIT			Less than 15.0 percent	16,882	39.4
1999 to March 2000	17,264	20.1	15.0 to 19.9 percent	7,263	17.0
1995 to 1998	24,832	28.9	20.0 to 24.9 percent	5,640	13.2
1990 to 1994	13,560	15.8	25.0 to 29.9 percent	3,703	8.6
1980 to 1989	13,022	15.2	30.0 to 34.9 percent	2,458	5.7
1970 to 1979	7,918	9.2	35.0 percent or more	6,571	15.3
1969 or earlier	9,180	10.7	Not computed	299	0.7
VEHICLES AVAILABLE			Specified renter-occupied units	25,115	100.0
None	6,608	7.7	**GROSS RENT**		
1	29,083	33.9	Less than $200	1,567	6.2
2	33,842	39.5	$200 to $299	1,169	4.7
3 or more	16,243	18.9	$300 to $499	6,250	24.9
			$500 to $749	9,548	38.0
HOUSE HEATING FUEL			$750 to $999	3,150	12.5
Utility gas	16,638	19.4	$1,000 to $1,499	1,003	4.0
Bottled, tank, or LP gas	6,041	7.0	$1,500 or more	318	1.3
Electricity	32,493	37.9	No cash rent	2,110	8.4
Fuel oil, kerosene, etc	27,106	31.6	Median (dollars)	551	(X)
Coal or coke	40	-			
Wood	2,765	3.2	**GROSS RENT AS A PERCENTAGE OF**		
Solar energy	119	0.1	**HOUSEHOLD INCOME IN 1999**		
Other fuel	351	0.4	Less than 15.0 percent	4,227	16.8
No fuel used	223	0.3	15.0 to 19.9 percent	3,525	14.0
			20.0 to 24.9 percent	3,180	12.7
SELECTED CHARACTERISTICS			25.0 to 29.9 percent	2,817	11.2
Lacking complete plumbing facilities	272	0.3	30.0 to 34.9 percent	1,516	6.0
Lacking complete kitchen facilities	294	0.3	35.0 percent or more	7,275	29.0
No telephone service	1,869	2.2	Not computed	2,575	10.3

-Represents zero or rounds to zero.   (X) Not applicable.

Source: U.S. Bureau of the Census, Census 2000.

TABLE 6.2 North Carolina's 115th State House District Voting History, 1994–2000.

	1994		1996		1998		2000	
Registered voters	44,980		45,771		46,924		47,181	
Voter turnout	21,696		25,632		26,398		29,526	
Turnout percentage	48.2%		56.0%		56.3%		62.5%	
Election Results	Votes	Percent	Votes	Percent	Votes	Percent	Votes	Percent
President								
Republican			11,192	47.9%			15,213	54.5%
Democrat			12,182	52.1%			12,719	45.5%
			23,374				27,932	
U.S. Senate								
Republican			11,538	49.2%	11,581	47.4%		
Democrat			11,926	50.8%	12,827	52.6%		
			23,464		24,408			
U.S. House								
Republican	11,442	58.5%	11,427	55.6%	12,094	52.8%	14,239	51.6%
Democrat	8,118	41.5%	9,133	44.4%	10,811	47.2%	13,343	48.4%
	19,560		20,560		22,905		27,582	
Governor								
Republican			11,017	47.2%			13,254	47.8%
Democrat			12,312	52.8%			14,464	52.2%
			23,329				27,718	
Attorney General								
Republican			9,729	43.8%			12,869	49.1%
Democrat			12,464	56.2%			13,319	50.9%
			22,193				26,188	
Secretary of State								
Republican			10,451	46.9%			12,346	46.4%
Democrat			11,826	53.1%			14,245	53.6%
			22,277				26,591	
State Senate	Election results for NC State Senate are not provided for prior to the 2000 election cycle due to the multi-member district system that was in place.							
Republican							13,748	51.0%
Democrat							13,210	49.0%
							26,958	
State House	Election results for NC State House are not provided for prior to the 2000 election cycle due to the multi-member district system that was in place.							
Republican							14,066	52.3%
Democrat							12,830	47.7%
							26,896	
District Attorney								
Republican	6,398	40.9%			7,339	38.5%		
Democrat	9,233	59.1%			11,707	61.5%		
	15,623				19,046			
Commissioner of Agriculture								
Republican			9,633	45.4%			12,875	48.0%
Democrat			11,578	54.6%			13,926	52.0%
			21,211				26,801	

The number of registered voters in this district for this election is: 47,529.

7

Lessons Learned

We had several objectives in mind in writing this book, the first of which was to increase readers' knowledge about campaigns and elections, and politics in general, by using real-world state legislative campaigns to illustrate concepts and ideas that are not commonly discussed in the context of U.S. election campaigns. An important feature of this first objective was to increase the reader's awareness and knowledge of the many factors that occur simultaneously in a campaign context and that can influence a state legislative campaign. With this, we hope the critical nature of the campaign plan's development became clear as a way to navigate through the difficulties that are part of the larger picture of a campaign. Part of this overall picture are fixed factors that a campaign cannot control but must take into account, as well as other elements that are more fluid to which the campaign must react. The many fixed factors can include higher-level races that are also on the ballot, national or statewide issues that might impact the race, the nature and number of opponents who are also running, election and campaign finance laws, and the nature of the voting district. More fluid elements, in addition to those that occur outside of the campaign, include how reporters and journalists cover the campaign, actions taken by the opponent's campaign, and how one's own campaign reacts to different campaign events.

A second, but more practical, objective was for readers to begin to develop specific campaign-related skills. The activities and tasks included in the simulation, such as conducting candidate research, developing a campaign message, strategizing how best to spread that message with paid and earned media, and planning how to get the most out of volunteers, help accomplish this goal and allow the reader to begin to see the many subtleties involved in campaigning. In the process of learning those campaign-related skills, we believe that readers will begin to understand and use the tools associated with the "science" element of political science. Sound research, writing, and communication skills are central to the mechanics of state legislative campaigns, and to politics in general.

Another objective we had in mind was for readers to recognize that they can acquire a number of important skills during a campaign—skills that will serve them in many different situations and contexts. Associated more with the "art" of campaigning are skills related to making judgments regarding information about citizens and their community in the district analysis, crafting a campaign message, determining the most effective way to communicate that message, and developing a strategy that will lead to victory on Election Day. To accomplish these tasks, campaigners need to have strong critical thinking and analytic skills. Moreover, there are situations that often come up in campaigns when the best or "right" thing to do is not always readily apparent. Many times these present themselves in the form of crises and ethical dilemmas. Rather than give a formulaic response, we hope readers are now aware, either in those artful aspects of the typical campaign or in the unexpected challenges of a campaign, that there is more than one way to approach many campaign scenarios.

Skills learned in campaigns can be applied to other, more general settings. Some of these skills include working as a positive and contributing member of a team, enhancing one's organizational skills, and developing an increased ability to respond effectively to challenges and crises. Being able to make sound judgment calls (often in a stressful environment and under severe time constraints) is an important aspect of the art of campaigns, politics in general, as well as many other situations. The exercises that deal with both crisis management and ethics are intended to help develop decision-making skills that will be useful within the context of a political campaign, but also useful in many other areas of one's life (for example, at work, for general leadership purposes, working effectively in small group situations, handling stressful situations, decision-making skills, and dealing with conflict).

Finally, we hoped to bring political campaigns to life for the reader. If successful, we believe that readers can become meaningful participants in a political campaign, and more informed voters and citizens, even if they never become active in a political campaign. For example, understanding how campaigns develop their message can make voters and citizens more aware of how campaigns use paid media advertising techniques to "sell" their candidates. Understanding the role of the campaign message, and campaigns' attempts to control their message, can also help voters evaluate candidates in earned media situations (in debates or interviews, for instance). Many times, these actions by candidates and the other campaigners who are part of their campaign are viewed as devious and duplicitous. We believe this is not necessarily the case, and hope that readers are now more aware of what these processes are designed to accomplish and why they are undertaken.

CAMPAIGNS AND FINGERPRINTS

We selected legislative campaigns in three different states that we believe can serve as useful examples of competitive political campaigns in general. Whether participation in the simulation has included just one legislative district, or all three races contained in this text, we believe that the experience will allow the reader to draw some important conclusions about politics, political campaigns, and the democratic process. However, caution must be taken not to think that all campaigns will be conducted in the same manner. Rather, they are like fingerprints. Everyone has fingerprints, and to some extent they look the same, but upon further examination each has its own distinguishing characteristics. In campaigns, there are also certain activities that all campaigns engage in and may appear to be consistent from campaign to campaign, but there are also aspects of campaigns that, when the details are examined, are clearly very different and individualized to the specific campaign in which they were employed.

Examples of those elements that are consistent from campaign to campaign include research, a campaign theme and message, and paid media advertising. However, how campaigns use this research, the message that is developed, and how that message is communicated to potential voters will differ in every campaign around the United States. Observers may not see these differences because they are removed from the day-to-day workings of campaigns. One way to see how individual campaigns differ, however, is to examine their campaign plans, which illustrate how different decisions have been made.

Another constant across campaigns is the importance of a campaign plan, which is at the heart of the simulation included in this book. As we described at the outset of the book, the experience of former Michigan State Senator John Kelly illustrated that the failure to plan adequately prior to the start of the campaign is likely to lead to failure on Election Day. Moreover, once a political campaign begins, an intensity of activity (and sometimes sustained chaos!) emerges such that a well-crafted campaign plan can help organize and manage the chaos over a period of several months. Although one's plan can change in response to unexpected events during a campaign, the plan also can inform the campaign team about whether changing the plan in a time of crisis or upheaval will produce greater benefits compared to sticking with the original plan.

We believe the cases presented in this book and the simulation activities surrounding them take the reader through the decisions and activities involved in developing and executing a campaign plan. However, the three different state legislative races are also unique in many ways. Consequently, they provide instructive lessons by helping to illustrate and identify not only the important features of a political campaign itself, but the possible influences that the campaign context can have on a campaign.

The Campaign Context

The context of a state legislative political campaign will be different in every campaign due to factors such as the state's economy, its political culture, and its history. Different states also promulgate their own election laws, campaign finance regulations, party registration requirements, and election dates. Other differences in the context emerge as well, including the nature of the voting district (such as voter turnout, party identification, and geography), the nature of the opponent (for example, incumbent, challenger, or open seat), the competitiveness of the election, the influence of national or statewide issues, and other influences. As Shea and Burton (2001) point out, a political campaign's context is composed of those "things that, for the most part, cannot be changed" (25). Although this is true, it also is important that a campaign team recognize and understand the potential impact of those factors on their campaign.

Variation Across States Although there are parts of the campaign context that are fixed within a legislative district, an axiom of state politics and policy is that generally, a fair amount of variation exists across states. In other words, there are things that cannot be changed in the context of a single campaign, but from race to race and state to state, the factors that are fixed are not fixed in the same manner, nor are the same elements necessarily fixed across different races.

One scholar of state politics and policy has noted, "States and communities are not alike in social and economic conditions, in politics and government, or in their public policies" (Dye 2000, 2). This variation has been apparent in the three case studies we selected. For this reason, although we believe there are many lessons that can be learned in preparation for a given campaign and election, there is no single blueprint or formula that can be applied to state legislative campaigns—or for a political campaign at any level. As illustrated in the simulation exercises, there is not necessarily just one way to achieve a campaign's objectives. Rather, every campaign is going to be different. Moreover, at several points throughout the book, we have suggested that there might be more than one "right" way to conduct an exercise or complete a campaign task. This is because each campaign has a different set of factors that are at work. No two campaigns are exactly alike, as there may be different issues (local, statewide, and/or national), different candidates, different laws, and a different potential voter pool in different states. Moreover, even within a single campaign, there is more than one way to achieve victory on Election Day.

It should be apparent from the exercises that regional differences exist too, which is one of the reasons why we selected our three states—a Midwestern state (Michigan), a Southeastern state (North Carolina), and a Southern state (Texas). As an example of regional differences across these three states, consider the industries that have traditionally led their diverging economies—automobiles in Michigan, tobacco and textiles in North Carolina, and oil in Texas. Also, the political culture of the different areas can have an impact on the races contested therein. For example, in Texas, many Democrats are more conservative than their fellow partisans in other parts of the United States; therefore being a Democrat in Texas likely is very different than being a Democrat in Michigan (or some other region of the United States).

In addition, other political differences often emerge across states. For instance, we have noted that the length of political campaigns is different in our three states—approximately three months in Michigan, and from six to eight months in Texas and North Carolina. Additionally, campaign finance laws are different in the three cases—varying contribution limits in Michigan and North Carolina, and no limits in Texas. Voter registration requirements also vary in the three states we selected, as party registration is required in North Carolina, but not in Michigan or Texas. Each of these differences across the three individual races, states, and regions can impact how a campaigner would prosecute a campaign in a particular state.

Competitive and "Safe" Districts Redistricting decisions have tended to favor the party with a majority in the state legislature; at the very least, they have created a trade-off situation in which both Democrats and Republicans cede majority status to each other in some districts in order to bolster their own majority status elsewhere. These redistricting principles create very few competitive districts—defined as a district in which the winner garnered less than 55 percent of the vote in the last election—in federal and state legislative elections.

The closeness of the U.S. presidential race in 2004, and more so in 2000, suggests that there is relative parity between the two major parties. As we pointed out in Chapter 1, after the 2004 elections, Republicans held only one more state legislative seat (out of 7,382) than Democrats, with Independents holding 14 seats and 1 undecided (NCSL 2005). But that overall appearance of competitiveness belies the increases in safe districts that the redistricting process has created for most state legislative districts. One observer of state elections noted: "Looking at the country district by district, . . . the reality is that true competition exists in only a tiny fraction of places. Even where political strength is closely balanced in the aggregate, the vast majority of individual districts are lopsidedly drawn in favor of one party or the other, engendering no real contest at the polls" (Greenblatt 2004, 23).[1] For our purposes, and for the study of campaigns generally, this means that when there is a competitive race being contested, it will garner a significant amount of attention from qualified candidates interested in running, both major political parties, campaign contributors, and maybe even journalists.

Readers also should review the geography of the three legislative districts selected for this simulation, and consider the nature of the districts that tend to be competitive. For example, it should not be a surprise that districts located exclusively or primarily in large cities are likely to be safe Democratic districts. Likewise, districts that are exclusively or primarily rural in nature are likely to be safe Republican districts. One commonality shared by districts in the city or in the country is their homogeneity. In other words, districts that are homogenous—those with large majorities of people with similar characteristics—tend to be safe districts (for either party), whereas heterogeneous districts—where the residents have different backgrounds and characteristics—tend to be competitive districts. Redistricters, who have created many of the safe districts across the country, often begin the process of creating a safe district by identifying areas that exhibit a great deal of homogeneity. Our three competitive districts are either suburban (Michigan) or some combination of urban, suburban, and rural areas (North Carolina and Texas), which is a major factor in explaining their competitiveness.

Low-Information Elections In an era of candidate-centered politics in high-information races (Menefee-Libey, 2000), most voters do not pay much attention to political campaigns in low-information races such as those for state legislature. On Election Day, voters participating in these races tend to use shortcuts (also called cognitive heuristics), such as party identification or name recognition, to make their vote choice—or sometimes they simply do not vote at all for those offices. In fact, one study of state politics observed that for state legislative elections, "Voters generally base their election decisions on three factors, listed in decreasing order of importance: political party identification, candidate appeal, and issues" (Burns et al. 2004, 61).

One factor that we have been careful to point out is that state legislative campaigns are often low-information races because the media do not usually cover them in great detail. When there is little or no coverage, even from local newspapers in the communities within the district, voters have even less information on which to base their choice of candidate. This makes the campaigns' efforts to communicate their messages even more important. It can also mean that voters will tend to rely even more often on those heuristics we noted earlier.

Increased Role of Money in Elections There is no question that increasing amounts of money have become more common in state legislative elections. Compared to 10 years ago, recent election cycles have seen a dramatic increase in the amount of money spent on state legislative campaigns. As part of this, many candidates have hired professional pollsters and media consultants to help in their campaigns. This is especially crucial in targeted legislative campaigns, where a shift of two or three seats could mean that a new majority party takes power.

It also is true that much more interest and money is generated in competitive campaigns, such as the three we are using in this book's simulations. However, we also believe it is true that most state legislative campaigns can still be considered low-information races, in which the state party organizations are not very active, and relatively small amounts of money are raised. Even though some recent state legislative campaigns have begun to look more like congressional or statewide campaigns, many candidates for state legislature still self-recruit into the race and self-finance substantial parts of their campaigns.

The Campaign

Although some of the lessons learned from this book are related to the context surrounding the campaign, many are also related to the campaigns themselves. In addition to the campaign plan, readers should not ignore the importance of campaign fundamentals, campaign ethics, and the need to respond effectively to crises that inevitably arise in a campaign.

The Campaign Plan Anyone involved in a political campaign understands the chaos that can surround it during the campaign season. Without a campaign plan, a campaign team is not organized, campaign activities are not coordinated, and volunteers are not recruited or used effectively. In addition, the campaign is likely to be reactive and disorganized rather than proactive; it may run out of money well before Election Day and not wisely spend the money it was able to raise, and the campaign organization will likely not know anything useful about the voters with whom it is trying to make a connection. A campaign plan allows even lower-level campaigns to create and implement an organizational framework within which all of their activities can most effectively be accomplished. As we have stressed previously, the campaign plan also helps the candidate be consistent in presenting the campaign message. This helps keep the campaign on track and in control of what information should be communicated to voters. As we have described earlier in this book, it is important that campaigns "stay on message," and in doing so, the campaign plan can help the campaign team even use something negative, such as an opponent's attack ad, as an opportunity to restate their campaign message. Even when unforeseen events occur, the plan allows the campaign to determine if it is even worth it to alter the plan or not.

Campaign Fundamentals The trend of increasingly large sums of money being spent on campaigns in the United States has not escaped lower-level races. With this, candidates in competitive lower-level races are also looking to media consultants and other political professionals more often for help in conducting their campaigns. As a result, some political campaigns sometimes ignore important fundamentals of politics that they would be wise to heed because they can be effective tactics.

In the 1800s, without TV and modern marketing or fund-raising techniques, political campaigns were conducted in a much more personal and face-to-face manner: Candidates (or their representatives) walked door to door to meet potential voters; candidates made personal appearances in front of audiences to answer questions and to debate the issues with their opponents; and successful campaign organizations recruited many volunteers who served as one connection between a candidate and potential voters.

In many respects, the majority of modern-day lower-level political campaigns resemble those conducted in the 1800s. In these races, there usually is no TV advertising (because airtime is too expensive), not a lot of money is raised and spent, and candidates must appeal to voters via a door-to-door strategy or through other personal contacts. Therefore, volunteers can be a key ingredient in a winning campaign formula. All these are significant reminders of the similarities between today's down-ballot races and old-style campaigns. These fundamental techniques worked for candidates in the 1800s, and they can still work today with the right plan of attack and strategy.

Winning Ethically One obvious definition of a "good" or "successful" campaign is one in which the candidate and her team win the election. After all, no one likes to lose. Moreover, candidates run for office presumably because they want to pursue policies that are different from those espoused by their opponent, and to see the opponent's priorities being promoted is disappointing. We believe, however, that winning should not be the only measure of a good campaign. In other words, campaigns do not have to subscribe to legendary Green Bay Packers coach Vince Lombardi's famous saying: "Winning isn't everything; it's the only thing." If winning is the only thing, campaigners might be willing to do anything to win an election. Such a perspective can lead candidates, their campaign managers, and volunteers into unethical—or even illegal—behaviors.

A lesser-known saying by Coach Lombardi, however, is fitting for campaigns: "The price of success is hard work, dedication to the job at hand, and the determination that whether we win or lose, we have applied the best of ourselves to the task at hand." As we argue in earlier chapters, we believe that many campaigns will likely face choices during the campaign that qualify as ethical dilemmas. Of course, sometimes the law will guide one's decision making, but in many cases, how a campaigner responds to one of those ethical dilemmas depends on factors, indicators, and judgments that are not constant across every individual. In other words, what is and is not considered to be ethical is very subjective; this is why we call these situations dilemmas.

The ethics exercises that we have presented in this book provide a way to increase awareness among future campaigners who may face similar situations throughout their careers in campaigns. In our own campaign classes, we discuss "dirty tricks," but mostly in the context of preparing for what an opponent's campaign might try to do to one's own campaign. But it has often amazed us how quickly some campaign teams have decided to conduct their campaign using some of these techniques. In this campaign simulation or in a real-life campaign, win or lose, one judgment campaigners can use to evaluate their performance is whether or not they can look themselves in the mirror the day after Election Day.

Although often viewed in negative terms, political campaigns also can bring out the best in people. Campaign team members work together toward a common goal, as they support their candidate by helping craft a message and developing an inspiring vision of the future. Campaigns also offer the opportunity for deliberation, discussion, and the practice of democracy. By offering a choice of who our representatives will be, they allow us the chance to help determine the direction public policy will likely take, and to participate in choosing what we want our world to become.

NOTE

1. In safe districts, the general election outcome is almost always certain, although the competition among the majority party candidates in the primary election can be intense. The principles of general election campaigning outlined in this book are very similar to those that would be used in primary campaigns. For example, a message still needs to be crafted from research based on the district and its residents, as well as research on the candidates, and that message still needs to be communicated to potential voters. The electoral research, however, would differ because the electorate in a primary will be very different from that in a general election (Shea and Burton 2001).

Bibliography

Agranoff, Robert. 1972. *The New Style in Election Campaigns.* Boston: Holbrook Press.

Aldrich, John A. 1995. *Why Parties? The Origin and Transformation of Political Parties in America.* Chicago: University of Chicago Press.

Barber, Denise. 2003. "Life Before BCRA: Soft Money at the State Level in the 2000 and 2002 Election Cycles." The Institute on Money in State Politics, December 17. <http://www.followthemoney.org/press/Reports/200312171.pdf> (Accessed August 16, 2004).

Beaudry, Ann and Bob Schaeffer. 1986. *Winning State and Local Elections.* New York: Free Press.

Bell, Lauren Cohen. 2005. *The U.S. Congress: A Simulation for Students.* Belmont, CA: Thomson/Wadsworth.

Benson, Paul, David Clinkscale, and Anthony Giardino. 2004. *Lone Star Politics,* 3rd Ed. Belmont, CA: Thomson/Wadsworth.

Bike, William. 1998. *Winning Political Campaigns: A Comprehensive Guide to Electoral Success.* Juneau, AK: The Denali Press.

Brown, Lyle C., Robert S. Trotter, Jr., Joyce A. Langenegger, and Sonia R. Garcia. 2001. *Practicing Texas Politics,* 11th Ed. New York: Houghton Mifflin Company.

Browne, William P., and Kenneth VerBurg. 1995. *Michigan Politics and Government: Facing Change in a Complex State.* Lincoln: University of Nebraska Press.

Burns, James MacGregor, J. W. Peltason, Thomes E. Cronin, David B. Magleby, David M. O'Brien, and Paul C. Light. 2004. *State and Local Politics: Government by the People,* 11th Ed. Upper Saddle River, NJ: Prentice Hall.

Campbell, James E. 2000. *American Campaign: U.S. Presidential Campaigns and the National Vote.* College Station: Texas A&M University Press.

———. 1993. *The Presidential Pulse of Congressional Elections.* Lexington: University Press of Kentucky.

Corpus Christi Caller-Times. 2002. "Send Miller, Rangel, Canales to House," October 11.

Crain, Ernest and James Perkins. 2003. *Introduction to Texas Politics,* 4th Ed. Belmont, CA: Thomson/Wadsworth.

Dolan, Julie, and Marni Ezra. 2002. *CQ's Congressional Election Simulation.* Washington, DC: CQ Press.

Dulio, David A. 2004. *For Better or Worse? How Professional Political Consultants Are Changing Elections in the United States.* Albany: State University of New York Press.

Dye, Thomas. 2000. *Politics in States and Communities,* 10th Ed. Upper Saddle River, NJ: Prentice Hall.

Farrell, David M. 1996. "Campaign Strategies and Tactics," in *Comparing Democracies: Elections and Voting in Global Perspective*, Lawrence LeDuc, Richard G. Niemi, Pippa Norris (eds.). Thousand Oaks, CA: Sage Publications.

Faucheux, Ron. 2004. "Writing Your Campaign Plan: The Seven Components of Winning an Election," *Campaigns & Elections*, April, pp. 26–29.

———. 2002. *Running for Office: The Strategies, Techniques and Messages Modern Political Candidates Need to Win Elections.* New York: M. Evans and Co., Inc.

———. 2001. "Watch those state legislative campaigns." *Campaigns & Elections*, August, p. 7.

Federal Election Commission (FEC). 2002. "Party Fundraising Reaches $1.1 Billion in 2002 Election Cycle." Federal Election Commission press release, December 18. <http://www.fec.gov/press/press2002/20021218party/20021218party.html> (Accessed August 16, 2004).

Fenno, Richard F. Jr. 1978. *Home Style: House Members in Their Districts.* Boston: Little Brown.

Fiorina, Morris P. 1978. *Congress: Keystone of the Washington Establishment.* New Haven, CT: Yale University Press.

Fleer, Jack D. 1994. *North Carolina Government and Politics.* Lincoln: University of Nebraska Press.

Garrett, Sam R. 2005. "Campaigns, Crises and Communication: Crisis Management in House and Senate Campaigns," Ph.D. diss. American University.

Goforth, D. Bruce. 2003. Personal interview with authors, February 24, Asheville, NC.

Greenberg, Stanley B. 1995. *Middle Class Dreams: The Politics and Power of the New American Majority.* New York: Random House/Times Books.

Greenblatt, Alan. 2004. "Whatever Happened to Competitive Elections?" *Governing.* October, pp. 22–27.

Guthrie, Keith. 2004. "San Patricio County." *The Handbook of Texas Online.* <http://www.tsha.utexas.edu/handbook/online/articles/view/SS/hcs4.html> (Accessed Mon Aug 9 13:27:09 US/Central 2004).

Haag, Stefan D., Gary A. Keith, and Rex C. Pebbles. 2003. *Texas Politics and Government: Ideas, Institutions, and Policies,* 3rd Ed. *Election Update.* New York: Longman.

Harper, Jennifer. 2004. "Cable Sees 'Big Story' in Political Conventions; But the Networks Will Offer Viewers Only an Hour Each Day," *The Washington Times,* July 14, A18.

———. 2000. "First Debate Lacks Color, But Not Rouge," *The Washington Times,* October 5, A10.

Herrnson, Paul S. 2004. *Congressional Elections: Campaigning at Home and in Washington,* 4th Ed. Washington, DC: CQ Press.

———. 1988. *Party Campaigning in the 1980s.* Cambridge, MA: Harvard University Press.

Hershey, Marjorie Randon. 2005. *Party Politics in America,* 11th Ed. New York: Longman.

Holbrook, Thomas M. 1996. *Do Campaigns Matter?* Thousand Oaks, CA: Sage Publications.

Jackson, John S., III and William Crotty. 2001. *The Politics of Presidential Selection,* 2nd Ed. New York: Longman.

Jacobson, Gary C. 2004. *The Politics of Congressional Elections,* 5th Ed. New York: HarperCollins.

Johnson, Dennis W. 2001. *No Place for Amateurs: How Political Consultants are Reshaping American Democracy.* London: Routledge Press.

———. 2000. "The Business of Political Consulting" in *Campaign Warriors: Political Consultants in Elections,* James A. Thurber and Candice J. Nelson (eds.), Washington, D.C.: Brookings Institution Press.

Kahn, Kim Fridkin, and Patrick J. Kenney. 1999. "Do Negative Campaign Ads Mobilize or Suppress Turnout? Clarifying the Relationship Between Negativity and Participation," *American Political Science Review,* vol. 93, no. 4, pp. 877–889.

Kayden, Xandra, and Eddie Mahe, Jr. 1985. *The Party Goes On: The Persistence of the Two-Party System in the United States.* New York: Basic Books.

Kazee, Thomas A. (ed.) 1994. *Who Runs For Congress? Ambition, Context, and Candidate Emergence.* Washington, D.C.: CQ Press.

Kelly, John F. 2004. Personal interview with authors. Detroit, Michigan, May 20.

Klemanski, John S. 1989. "Campaign Contribution Strategies by PACs and Parties to Michigan Legislative Candidates, 1984," *Michigan Academician,* vol. 21, no. 3, pp. 221–234.

Kolodny, Robin and David A. Dulio. 2003. "Political Party Adaptations in U.S. Congressional Campaigns: Why Political Parties Use Coordinated Expenditures to Hire Political Consultants," *Party Politics,* vol. 9, no. 6, pp. 729–746.

Kraemer, Richard H., Charldean Newell, and David F. Prindle. 2002. *Texas Politics,* 8th Ed. Belmont, CA: Thomson/Wadsworth.

Lamb, William. 2004. "Democratic Convention Draws Strong Ratings," *St. Louis Post-Dispatch (Missouri),* August 1, p. A5.

Luebke, Paul. 1998. *Tar Heel Politics: 2000.* Chapel Hill: University of North Carolina Press.

Magleby, David B. (ed.) 2000. *Outside Money: Soft Money and Issue Advocacy in the 1998 Congressional Elections.* Lanham, MD: Rowman and Littlefield Publishers.

Magleby, David B., and J. Quin Monson. (eds.) 2004. *The Last Hurrah? Soft Money and Issue Advocacy in the 2002 Congressional Elections.* Washington, D.C.: Brookings Institution Press.

Maisel, L. Sandy. 2002. *Parties and Elections in America, Post-Election Update,* 3rd Ed. Lanham, MD: Rowman and Littlefield Publishers.

Malbin, Michael J. (ed.) 2003. *Life After Reform: When the Bipartisan Campaign Reform Act Meets Politics.* Lanham, MD: Rowman and Littlefield Publishers.

Maxwell, William Earl, Ernest Crain, Edwin S. Davis, Elizabeth N. Flores, Joseph Ignagni, Cynthia Opheim, and Christopher B. Wlezien. 2004. *Texas Politics Today,* 11th Ed. Belmont, CA: Thomson/Wadsworth.

Mayer, William G. (ed.) 2004. *The Making of the Presidential Candidates 2004.* Lanham, MD: Rowman and Littlefield Publishers.

———. 2000. *In Pursuit of the White House 2000: How We Choose Our Presidential Nominees.* New York: Chatham House/Seven Bridges Press.

Mayhew, David M. 1974. *Congress: The Electoral Connection.* New Haven, CT: Yale University Press.

Medvic, Stephen K. 2001. *Political Consultants in U.S. Congressional Elections.* Columbus: Ohio State University Press.

Menefee-Libey, David B. 2000. *The Triumph of Campaign-Centered Politics.* New York: Chatham House.

Milbank, Dana. 2004. "Reaction Shots May Tell Tale of Debate; Bush's Scowls Compared to Gore's Sighs," *The Washington Post,* October 1, A10.

Miller, Arthur H. and Bruce E. Gronbeck. 1994. *Presidential Campaigns and American Self Images.* Boulder, CO: Westview Press.

National Conference of State Legislatures (NCSL). 2005. "2005 Partisan Composition of State Legislatures," <http://www.ncsl.org/ncsldb/elect98/partcomp.cfm?yearsel=2005> (Accessed February 28, 2005).

Northcott, Kaye. 1982. "Getting Elected," *Mother Jones,* November, p. 18.

Perlmutter, David. 1999. *The Manship School Guide to Political Communication.* Baton Rouge: Louisiana State University Press.

Polsby, Nelson W. and Aaron Wildavsky. 2003. *Presidential Elections: Strategies and Structures of American Politics,* 11th Ed. Lanham, MD: Rowman and Littlefield Publishers.

Pomper, Gerald M. (ed.) 2001. *The Election of 2000: Reports and Interpretations.* New York: Chatham House/Seven Bridges Press.

———. 1997. *The Election of 1996: Reports and Interpretations.* Chatham, NJ: Chatham House.

Powell, Jaime. 2002a. "Seaman Points to His Role in Helping to Pass Key Bills," *Corpus Christi Caller-Times,* October 7, A1.

———. 2002b. "Miller Touts Experience, Success in San Patricio," *Corpus Christi Caller-Times,* October 7, A1.

Powell, Larry, and Joseph Cowart. 2003. "Political Campaign Communication: Inside and Out." Boston: Allyn and Bacon.

Salmore, Stephen A., and Barbara G. Salmore. 1985. *Candidates, Parties, and Campaigns: Electoral Politics in America.* Washington, D.C.: CQ Press.

Shaw, Catherine. 2000. *The Campaign Manager: Running and Winning Local Elections,* 2nd Ed. Boulder, CO: Westview Press.

Shea, Dan and Michael John Burton. 2001. *Campaign Craft: The Strategies, Tactics, and Art of Political Campaign Management,* Rev. Ed. Westport, CT: Praeger Publishers.

Simpson, Dick. 1996. *Winning Elections: A Handbook of Modern Participatory Politics.* New York: Longman.

Sorauf, Frank J. 1980. "Political Parties and Political Action Committees: Two Life Cycles," *Arizona Law Review,* vol. 22, pp. 445–464.

Switalski, Michael. 2003. Personal interview with authors. Detroit, Michigan, April 7.

Thurber, James A. (ed.) 2001. *The Battle for Congress: Consultants, Candidates, and Voters.* Washington, D.C.: Brookings Institution Press.

Thurber, James A, and Candice J. Nelson (eds.) 2004. *Campaigns and Elections American Style,* 2nd Ed. Boulder, CO: Westview Press.

———. 2000. *Campaign Warriors: Political Consultants in Elections.* Washington, D.C.: Brookings Institution Press.

———. 1995. *Campaigns and Elections American Style.* Boulder, CO: Westview Press.

Troy, Gil. 1991. *See How They Ran: The Changing Role of the Presidential Candidate.* New York: Free Press.

Walden, Mike. 2003. "You Decide: What Can Be Done about Lost Textile Jobs?" North Carolina State University, North Carolina Cooperative Extension Service, August 19. <http://www.cals.ncsu.edu/agcomm/writing/newsrls/8-19-03b.htm> (Accessed August 16, 2004).

Wattenberg, Martin P. 1990. *The Decline of American Political Parties, 1952–1988.* Cambridge, MA: Harvard University Press.

Wayne, Stephen J. 2004. *The Road to the White House 2004: The Politics of Presidential Elections.* Belmont, CA: Thomson/Wadsworth.

———. 2003. *Is This Any Way to Run a Democratic Election?* 2nd Ed. Boston: Houghton Mifflin.

Index

A
Agranoff, Robert, 3, 11
America Coming Together, 11
automobile industry, 71–72

B
Barrett, John, 114, 130
Bauer, Gary, 8
Benson, Frank, 102–103
biennial legislatures, 109
Bike, William
   Winning Political Campaigns, 3
Bipartisan Campaign Reform Act (BCRA), 10
Brandenburg, Jack, 102
budgets, 19, 22–23, 52–54
   see also campaign finance; fund-raising
Bush, George W., 8, 9, 22, 24–25, 108
Bush, H.W., 107

C
campaign calendar, 19, 25–26, 64–65
campaign communication, 8–9
   see also media
campaign finance, 9–11, 19, 22–23, 52–54, 156
   legal requirements, 54, 74–75, 111–112, 137–138
campaign message, 18–19, 21, 49–51, 152, 156
campaign outcomes and external factors, 16, 151, 153–156

campaign plan, 17–26, 29–30, 153, 156
   budget, 19, 22–23, 52–54
   campaign calendar, 19, 25–26, 64–65
   campaign message, 18–19, 21, 49–51, 152, 156
   candidate and opposition profiles, 18, 20–21, 40–48
   demographic analysis, 30–34
   district analysis, 18, 19–20, 30–34
   electoral research, 18, 20, 35–40
   exercises, 31–34, 40, 43–48, 49–51, 54, 56, 62, 63–64, 65–68, 78–79, 115–116, 140–142
   fund-raising, 19, 23, 52–54
   get-out-the-vote (GOTV), 19, 25, 64
   media, earned, 19, 24–25, 62–64
   media, paid, 19, 23–24, 56–62
   volunteers, 19, 23, 54–56
campaigns, state legislative. *see* state legislative campaigns
campaign staff, 16–17, 28–29
   see also volunteers
campaign theme, 22
candidates
   decision to run for office, 15–16
   in Michigan's 10th State House District, 76–77
   in North Carolina's 115th State House District, 139–140
   profiles, 18, 20–21, 40–48

165

candidates (*continued*)
    recruitment of, 7–8
    role of, 28–29
    in Texas' 32nd State House District, 113–115
Cansler, Lanier, 140
case studies, choice of, 3, 12, 154
cattle industry, in Texas, 106
census data, 31, 32, 83–98, 116, 121–125, 146–150
Clark, Wesley, 5
Clinton, Bill, 107
competitive districts, 154–155
Corpus Christi Caller-Times, 127–132
Corzine, Jon, 10
cotton industry, in Texas, 106
Crawford, Mark, 139, 140
crisis management, 27–28, 65–67
Cuellar, Lauro, 127

D
Democratic National Committee, 7
demographic analysis, 30–34
    census data, 83–98, 121–125, 146–150
direct mail, 9, 24, 53, 56–57
district analysis, 18, 19–20, 30–34
    census data, 83–98, 121–125, 146–150

E
Easley, Mike, 135
electioneering services, role of parties in, 8
election procedure
    in Michigan, 73–74
    in North Carolina, 136–137
    in Texas, 109–111
elections, presidential. *see* presidential elections
elections, U.S. House of Representatives. *see* U.S. House of Representatives elections
elections, U.S. Senate. *see* U.S. Senate elections
electoral research, 18, 20, 35–40
    see also voting statistics
Engler, John, 73
ethics, 27–28, 67–68, 157–158
Ethics Commission, 111
Ethics Law, 1991, 111

F
Farrell, David M., 11
Faucheux, Ron, 18
    Running for Office, 3
Federal Election Campaign Act, 1971, 137

Forbes, Steve, 8
fund-raising, 19, 23, 52–54, 74–75, 111–112, 137–138

G
get-out-the-vote (GOTV), 11, 19, 25, 64
Gilliam, Mark, 128–129
Gire, Sharon, 76
Goforth, D. Bruce, 139–140
Gore, Al, 24–25
governors, election of, 4
Granholm, Jennifer, 73
Greenberg, Stanley
    Middle Class Dreams, 71
gubernatorial elections, 4

H
Hawley, Judy, 113, 114, 130
Hispanics, in Texas, 108–109
Huffington, Michael, 10
Hunt, James, 135, 140

I
interest groups, 11
    see also political action committees (PACs)

J
Judicial Campaign Fairness Act, 1995, 112

K
Kelly, John F., 1–2, 12, 23, 153
Kennedy, Edward, 5, 21
Kerry, John, 8, 9, 25
Keyes, Alan, 8
Kucinich, Dennis, 8

L
labor unions, 11
Laney, Pete, 129
Levin, Carl, 76
Lincoln, Abraham, 22
Lombardi, Vince, 157
Luna, Vilma, 127

M
Maceroni, Roger, 76
Macomb Daily, 100–103
Martin, James, 135
McCain, John, 5
McEntire, Charlie, 131

media, earned, 5–6, 19, 24–25, 62–64, 100–103, 127–132, 155–156
media, paid, 9, 19, 23–24, 56–62
media attention. *see* media, earned
message, campaign. *see* campaign message
message box, 21–22, 49–51
Michigan
    automobile industry, 71–72
    election procedure, 73–74
    political context, 72–75
    10th State House District, 3, 71–72, 75–79
        candidates, 76–77
        census data, 78, 83–98
        maps, 78, 81–82
        newspaper articles, 78, 100–103
        population of, 3
        voting history, 78, 99
    unemployment in, 72
Michigan Education Association, 72
Miller, Josephine, 112, 113, 114–115, 130–132
Morgan, Michael, 139

N
National Conference of State Legislatures, 2
negative campaigning, 20
    see also ethics
newspapers
    examples of articles, 100–103, 127–132
    role in elections, 5–6
North American Free Trade Agreement (NAFTA), 72, 107, 134
North Carolina
    election procedure, 136–137
    political context, 134–138
    textile industry, 134
    115th State House District, 133–134, 139–142
        candidates, 139–140
        census data, 141, 146–150
        maps, 141, 144–145
        population of, 3
        voting history, 141, 150
    tobacco industry, 133–134
North Carolina Candidates Fund, 138
North Carolina Political Parties Financing Fund, 138

O
oil industry, in Texas, 105–107
opposition profiles, 18, 20–21, 40–48

P
parties, political
    role of in campaigns, 7–8
Perry, Rick, 108, 112, 128
plan, campaign. *see* campaign plan
political action committees (PACs), 10–11, 52, 137–138
Porter, Gordon, 130, 131–132
Posthumus, Dick, 73
Powell, Jaime, 127–132
presidential election, 2000, 5, 8, 10, 24–25
presidential election, 2004, 5, 6, 8, 9–11, 11, 22, 25, 155
Public Act 388, 1976, 74

R
radio, role of, 56–57
redistricting, 2–3, 136, 154–155
Reno, Shaw v., 136
Republican National Committee, 7
Reynolds Metal Company, 106
Rice, Stephen, 76, 77, 100–103
Richards, Ann, 108, 112

S
safe districts, 154–155
salience, 6–7
Sanchez, Tony, 112
Seaman, Gene, 112, 113–114, 127–129
Selweski, Chad, 100–103
Sharpton, Al, 8
Shaw, Catherine
    The Campaign Manager, 3
Shaw v. Reno, 136
Shea, Dan and Burton, Michael John, 153
    Campaign Craft, 3
Simpson, Dick
    Winning Elections, 3
Smithee, John, 127
soft money, 10
speaker, shared, 2–3
Spindletop, 105
staff, campaign, 16–17, 28–29
    see also volunteers
State Board of Elections (SBOE), North Carolina, 137
state legislative campaigns, 4–12
    see also campaign plan; Michigan: 10th State House District; North Carolina: 115th State House District; Texas: 32nd State House District

state legislative election procedure, 73–74, 109–111, 136–137
state legislatures
   biennial system, 109
   and redistricting, 2–3
   see also Michigan; North Carolina; Texas
swing voters, 36, 39
Switalski, Michael, 75–77, 100–103
SWOT analysis, 21, 42–43, 48, 49

T
telemarketing. see telephone calling programs
telephone calling programs, 9, 53
television, role of, 5–6, 9, 24, 56–57
Texas
   cattle industry, 106
   cotton industry, 106
   election procedure, 109–111
   Hispanics in, 108–109
   32nd State House District, 105–107, 112–115
      candidates, 113–115
      census data, 116, 121–125
      maps, 115, 119–120
      newspaper articles, 116, 127–132
      population of, 3
      voting history, 116, 126
   oil industry, 105–107
   political context of, 107–112

Texas Campaign Reporting and Disclosure Act, 1973, 111
Texas Election Code, 109
textile industry, in North Carolina, 134
theme, campaign, 22
timing. see campaign calendar
tobacco industry, in North Carolina, 133–134
Tower, John, 107
turnout, voter, 37–38, 40

U
unemployment, in Michigan, 72
United Auto Workers (UAW), 72
U.S. Congress elections, 1994, 16
U.S. House of Representatives elections, 5–6, 8, 10
U.S. Senate elections, 5–6, 8, 10

V
volunteers, 19, 23, 54–56, 157
voting statistics, 35–40, 99, 116, 126, 150
   see also electoral research

W
Watergate, 16
Williams, Clayton, 112

Z
Zaffirini, Judith, 115, 131